NATIONAL IDENTITIES AND EUROPEAN LITERATURES
NATIONALE IDENTITÄTEN UND EUROPÄISCHE LITERATUREN

J. Manuel Barbeito | Jaime Feijóo |
Antón Figueroa | Jorge Sacido (eds.)

NATIONAL IDENTITIES AND EUROPEAN LITERATURES
NATIONALE IDENTITÄTEN UND EUROPÄISCHE LITERATUREN

PETER LANG
Bern · Berlin · Bruxelles · Frankfurt am Main · New York · Oxford · Wien

Bibliografische Information Der Deutschen Bibliothek
Die Deutsche Bibliothek verzeichnet diese Publikation in der Deutschen Nationalbibliografie;
detaillierte bibliografische Daten sind im Internet über ‹http://dnb.ddb.de› abrufbar.

British Library and Library of Congress Cataloguing-in-Publication Data: A catalogue record
for this book is available from *The British Library*, Great Britain.

Library of Congress Cataloging-in-Publication Data

National identities and European literatures = Nationale Identitäten und europäische
Literaturen / J. Manuel Barbeito ... [et al.] (eds.).
p. cm.
Includes bibliographical references.
ISBN 978-3-03911-228-9 (alk. paper)
1. European literature–20th century–History and criticism. I. Barbeito, J. Manuel, 1953-
II. Title: Nationale Identitäten und europäische Literaturen.
PN771.N38 2008
809'.933581–dc22
         2007049271

MINISTERIO
DE EDUCACIÓN
Y CIENCIA

Die Veröffentlichung dieses Bandes wurde vom spanischen Ministerium für Bildung und
Wissenschaft (Ministerio de Educación y Ciencia) unterstützt, und zwar im Rahmen des Plan
Nacional de Investigación Científica, Desarrollo e Innovación Tecnológica (Acción
Complementaria HUM2004-21037-E).

Umschlagsbild: (c) Kulturrecycling, ‚Artur & Artur'
Umschlagsgestaltung: Eva Rolli, Peter Lang Bern

ISBN 978-3-03911-228-9

© Peter Lang AG, Internationaler Verlag der Wissenschaften, Bern 2008
Hochfeldstrasse 32, Postfach 746, CH-3000 Bern 9
info@peterlang.com, www.peterlang.com, www.peterlang.net

Alle Rechte vorbehalten.
Das Werk einschliesslich aller seiner Teile ist urheberrechtlich geschützt.
Jede Verwertung ausserhalb der engen Grenzen des Urheberrechtsgesetzes ist ohne
Zustimmung des Verlages unzulässig und strafbar. Das gilt insbesondere für
Vervielfältigungen, Übersetzungen, Mikroverfilmungen und die Einspeicherung und
Verarbeitung in elektronischen Systemen.

Printed in Germany

Contents

J. MANUEL BARBEITO, JAIME FEIJÓO, ANTÓN FIGUEROA,
JORGE SACIDO
Literature and Identitary Processes: An Introduction 7

PART I
Literature, Culture, Identity

TERRY EAGLETON
Culture and Identity 33

PART II
Integrität und Anerkennung im Rahmen europäischer
und globaler Konstellationen. Fünf literarische Analysen

ANDREA ALBRECHT, HORST TURK
Identität und Integrität. Ein alteuropäisches Thema. Einleitung 43

ANDREA ALBRECHT
Ein literarischer Kampf um Integrität und Anerkennung.
Juan Goytisolos *Rückforderung des Conde don Julián* 47

KORA BAUMBACH
Supplementäre Anerkennung:
Zu Uwe Timms Roman *Morenga* 61

ZAAL ANDRONIKASHVILI
Kollektive Integrität als Integrationshindernis.
Aluda im Spiegel von Muzal 75

MATTHIAS BEILEIN
Auf diesem Markt ist Österreich. Doron Rabinovicis *Ohnehin* 93

HORST TURK
"Mooristan" und "Palimpstine". Die Integration Europas
ein Vabanquespiel säkularisierter Monotheismen? 105

PART III
Identitary Processes in European Literatures

J. MANUEL BARBEITO, JORGE SACIDO
The Ghost of the Empire
and the 'English' Postcolonial Identity 123

BRAD EPPS
"No todo se perdió en Cuba":
Spain between Europe and Africa in the Wake of 1898 147

JAIME FEIJÓO
Deutsch-deutsche Identitätsfragen nach der Wende.
Mit einer Lektüre von Christa Wolf und Wolfgang Hilbig 173

ANTÓN FIGUEROA
Discourse on National Identity: Notes from Galicia 203

DOLORES VILAVEDRA
The Galician Reader: A Future Project? 221

JON KORTAZAR
Diglossia and Basque Literature 233

JAUME SUBIRANA
National Poets and Universal Catalans.
Writers and Literature in Contemporary Catalan Identity 247

Notes on the Contributors 267

J. MANUEL BARBEITO, JAIME FEIJÓO, ANTÓN FIGUEROA,
JORGE SACIDO

Literature and Identitary Processes

The question of identity is an extremely complex problem where political, social, economic, aesthetic, ethical and psychic elements coalesce. The title of this volume, *National Identities and European Literatures*, alludes to a highly intense and relevant debate taking place today both inside and outside the European academia. Within the general context of the conflict between the defence of plurality and the attempts to establish a uniform ideology on a planetary scale in tune with the global economic powers, Europe is engaged in a project of political unification while efforts to defend communitarian identities proliferate. The identity of the nation-states is challenged, on the one hand, by the urgent need to nourish and consolidate the identity of a united Europe against America's influence and, on the other, by the peripheral nationalisms and the reluctance of immigrant communities to abandon their national or ethnic identity, which is quite often linked to a colonial past.

The role of literature in the formation or "invention" of the identity of peoples and nations has always been an important one. However, it is not until the Enlightenment and the upsurge of the Romantic Movement that the literary field[1] as a whole would become reflexively involved in these processes. The present collection of essays aims at contributing to the ongoing debate on the role that literature has played in the last two centuries and can still play in the configuration of national identity, while at the same time introducing

---

1   See Pierre Bourdieu's *Les règles de l'art: Genèse et structure du champ littéraire* (1992) for a theoretical analysis of this notion.

the reader to some of the key issues concerning the problem of identity. Some of the essays question the very notion of "identity" itself and offer alternatives to it; others study the drama of personal and collective identity as it is represented in literary works; and yet others reflect on the historical role that the literary field has played in the formation of identities, consider the ways in which literature can intervene in the public sphere, and raise questions concerning the responsibility and the social function of both literary authors and scholars.

The world of art is built with material taken from experience and it pragmatically interpellates, consolidates and contributes (to various degrees depending on the concrete historical situation) to the modification, reinforcement or destabilisation of cultural habits and traditions. Literary works, however, do not depend on themselves to exert their influence. On the one hand, the representation of the drama of identity in fiction offers no guarantee of ideological stability, so much so that conventional identity models may easily be debunked. As with the spectre in the opening scene of Shakespeare's *Hamlet*, it is difficult to *fix* fiction and place it at the service of a single ideological discourse[2] (though this does not mean that an author's position may not be subject to analysis and judgement; it is only that, as Deconstruction has shown, the text destabilises and tends even to invert the author's intention). On the other hand, the literary text, itself a point where disparate discourses intersect,[3] participates in the struggle for primacy, not only because the author may adopt a particular ideological position, but also because readers make use of it to defend their own stand. Yet, neither the relevance of what is at stake in this struggle nor its resolution depend exclusively or even largely

---

2   The soldiers guarding the battlements of Elsinore try to no avail to stop the spectre with their weapons: "It is here"/ – "It is here"/ "It is gone" (1.1.145–147).
3   In his *Criticism and Ideology* (1976), Terry Eagleton provides a theoretical clarification of the different "ideologies" concurring in a literary work, the author's included.

upon either the private activity of reading or writing, or upon the literary field as a whole.

The dialogue concerning different ways of approaching the function of the literary field in present-day society relates to the problem of both artistic and academic autonomy. Now that literature, like so many other fields of specialisation, has achieved the autonomy Kant once claimed for philosophy, it becomes pertinent to raise the following questions: Are writers autonomous, or are they always involved in a dynamic that is beyond their control? Should literary authors and scholars limit their activity to just representing, reflecting, and analysing social reality, or should they also assume ethico-political responsibilities? To what extent do they participate in the formation of social, ethic and aesthetic values, or is their function merely to explain their formation? Do they have a choice, or are they always involved in politics since, as Eagleton put it in *Literary Theory: An Introduction* (1983), this was already there from the very beginning? And, finally, are books such as this one of any value outside of the academic field?

The profound transformation that the means and modes of communication have undergone (so much so that the very survival of the book is feared to be jeopardised) goes hand in hand with those changes taking place in the cultural, social and political fields that affect the role of "letters". Anxiety about the book's survival does not have to do with technical problems alone, for it also arises from the fear that the world of letters may be losing ground within the field of communication, which is currently dominated by images and the news.

Bearing all this in mind, one can understand Eagleton's ironic uneasiness in Part I of this volume concerning the future of the literary institution. His irony and restlessness have the same root cause: critics and writers are paid for doing something useless and, on top of this, they are further compensated by being able to read and write fiction or about fiction. The literary institution's lack of capability to influence socio-political reality nowadays is thus acknowledged. Culture (with a capital "C") has lost its privileged leading role awarded by the critical tradition of "bourgeois cultural idealism," and, except for nationalist contexts, the literary field has little influence in terms of communitarian identity. But, if the uselessness of literary vocation works against its foundational possibilities in a utilitarian context, the fact that it is also an enjoyable activity introduces a utopian aspect with certain political potential as it is out of step with commodified culture (Estévez and Sacido 1999).

In a utilitarian context and within a public sphere that is dominated by images and the news, Shakespeare, for instance, becomes an icon and is no longer a site of debate – that sort of *agora* that is the defining feature of a classic (Barbeito 2006) – in which issues of public interest are at stake. In the film *Love Actually* (2004) we can find a comical example of this cultural levelling when the British prime minister defends English identity before the arrogant president of the United States by saying that his is the nation of Shakespeare... and of Beckham. Even in some nationalist contexts literature may be losing the foundational role it once had. As Jaume Subirana argues in his essay in Part III, literary aura is no longer the only or even the most important mythicising agent for Catalan nationalism: today the image of any public figure, literary or not, can fuel Catalan national pride as long as that image takes on an international status thus allowing recognition to extend beyond national borders and to reach global dimensions.

As an icon, European Culture and its canonical figures and works do still retain a significant amount of socio-economic relevance and entail common practices of veneration and exploitation. Stratford-upon-Avon is a good example of an economic dynamics that is typically postmodern (in contrast, Rosalía de Castro's house in Galicia has been preserved more for sentimental reasons than for profit, lacking the organisation and management that characterises contemporary tourism).[4] However, this aspect and the practices associated

---

[4] Tourism to myths of place began in the middle of the nineteenth century. Lash and Urry (1994) analyse this phenomenon of cultural tourism as part of the

with it belong (as Eagleton would have it) to "culture" with a small "c" (p. 38); that is, in the anthropological sense of the common practices and customs of a particular society. Shakespeare's texts do open the ground for political debate as poststructuralist approaches of all persuasions (Marxist, feminist, or postcolonial) have shown. The question then is not whether academia is free of political interests, but what sort of relevance it has in a public sphere where economic and political interests have priority over the rational and objective analysis of facts.

Autonomy and heteronomy are a sort of Scylla and Charybdis for the academic venture. Autonomy is the necessary condition for rational debate and for the constitution of a critical attitude based on scientific protocols (data processing and validation, analysis of arguments and motives, etc.), while political interests try to put the academic field at their service by tempting it with some degree of social relevance at the cost of rigour in rational debate. But the benefit of autonomy may be bought at the price of isolation. Autonomy, which allows and promotes the free debate of ideas, may also confine that debate to a secluded space that turns it into a parody of a real political *agora* insofar as little is at stake in it.

There is a lesson here for intellectuals who arrogantly pretend to be in a position to guide their fellow citizens by lecturing them from an academic podium wielding the works of the great tradition in their hands and, as Eagleton states, who think that they can "resolve political conflicts in a higher or deeper spiritual ground" (p. 39). For academia to be influential at all it must implicate itself in affairs and issues that are of any political and social relevance in a given period. Likewise, it must explore ways of reaching out to society; after all, this is precisely what the classics it praises did in their own time. Even if those ways are small in number, this is no reason to give up and fall back into a position of isolation, though one must certainly acknowledge the situation with a grain of humour and irony.

---

economic and social importance that aesthetics has acquired in the era of the so-called disorganised capitalism.

The essays composing Part II, titled "Integrität und Anerkennung im Rahmen europäischer und globaler Konstellationen" ("Integrity and Recognition in the Context of European and Global Constellations"), analyse the works of authors who criticise dominant culture and propose alternatives to it, specially (but not only) those concerned with the relationship with other cultural or national identities affected by European ethnocentrism. That literature has lost its leading position does not mean that it is a worthless tool for approaching the question of identity, as Eagleton also underlines. On the contrary, identity can be problematised in literature, for instance, when it presents intersubjective relations that question ideologically regulated social relations and, consequently, their corresponding system of social identities.

These essays also analyse the operative concepts that permit a reexamination of the problem of identity and inspect literary texts in search for challenges to the dominant discourse of social critique that constitutes for these authors the practical institutional framework of their intervention. The central categories in this part, as the title indicates, are those of integrity, recognition and acknowledgement, and hybridisation and constellation.[5] According to these critics, the notion of integrity, which is linked here to the dynamics of the struggle for recognition, makes it possible to avoid essentialism and leave behind the static idea that a sum of characteristics constitutes an atemporal identity which is presumably natural and objective.

The notions of hybridisation and constellation acquire their full meaning and effectiveness when they are linked to the recognition and acknowledgement of a denominator that is common to all individuals and cultures; namely, that we are all different in relation to ourselves.[6] The European tradition is profoundly different from itself; it could

---

5   The notion of "Constellation" suggests 1) popular non-scientific representations of cosmos, 2) social and political relevance of popular representations, and 3) diversity of the elements that are integrated in them.
6   This is a practice to which Eagleton invites us all to participate in *Holy Terror* (2005). See also his *Figures of Dissent* on Slavoj Žižek (2003).

even be argued that it is not less different from itself than it is from any other tradition. An examination of such elementary notions of our culture as body, soul, flesh, and spirit would be enough to show this (Badiou 1997). Acknowledging inner difference would allow us to avoid the relativist imperative of absolute respect for alterity that forbids judging the practices of a community from any perspective alien to its own internal norms. This position, which is basically a functionalist one, always defends anything that contributes to maintain the integrity of a community and rejects any sort of external intervention that may threaten it. But our acknowledgement of the common denominator of being different with respect to ourselves becomes, when required from the other, a sign of respect for that other. This demands a revision of the respective ideologies that always conceal difference. It would be possible then for us all to be equally responsible concerning the values that have been achieved and the tasks that have been set after such a revision. In this way, the notion of respect for difference that results from the incommensurability of discourses – from the scraps that are produced in the translation from one to the other – could become a two-fold instrument for a critique of ideology that denounces both the ideological attempt to translate existing diversity within a culture into a unitary discourse and the wide gap separating reality from a culture's ideals. One such case is the ideological opposition Western vs. Eastern culture and its presumption that each of them is coherent and uniform. Another occurs in the Western world where the ideals of freedom and equal opportunity are hardly reflected in real life, even in those societies that have presumably achieved those ideals. Still another takes place on a global scale in the gap between the ideal of universal human rights and the human exploitation that is going on.

In her essay on Juan Goytisolo's *Reivindicación del Conde don Julián*, Andrea Albrecht interprets the central conflict of the protagonist narrator as a "violation of personal integrity" (p. 48) in the light of Axel Honneth's theory of the "struggle for recognition" (*Kampf um Anerkennung*). The recognition of individual autonomy is denied to him by centralist, homophobic fascist Spain, forcing him to adopt an attitude of "dissenter" through which he tries (by way of identification with "the legendary figure of Count Julian" (p. 51)) to recover his integrity, while betraying his presumably homogenous and immaculate homeland.

This betrayal does not only entail the debunking and destruction of given identitary symbols in favour of particular interests, but also the "struggle" for the "constitution" of a new identity in the sense of the "liberal and post-national cosmopolitanism" endorsed by authors such as Habermas or Derrida. Individuals may initiate the formation of their own identity as an alternative to assimilation insofar as they engage in a struggle for recognition. However, as Albrecht states by referring to Mead and Tugendhat, individual identity cannot be achieved within an isolated space but is rather a "process of dynamic interaction between individuals and their respective collectivities" (p. 52), and, therefore, the marginal individual (like Goytisolo: a homosexual and a liberal in Francoist Spain) has to move beyond truly existing collectivities and transcend to "a superior community", which he can only do through a "universal discourse" (Tugendhat). The "cosmopolitan individual" is thus born and the structural necessity of this ideal community shown. A universalism of this kind is instrumental for abandoning an essentialist view of collective identity in favour of an "open and dynamic" conception (p. 58). Goytisolo does, indeed, assign cultural differences (and the communitarian perspective adopted by some one like Charles Taylor) a central role in the context of the universality of human rights.

A group's legitimacy depends on to what degree it acknowledges its own inner diversity and on how willing it is to be enriched through hybridisation. In *Reivindicación del Conde don Julián*, the author rejects the Francoist version of Spanish identity that concealed diversity, and, against traditionalist fundamentalism, he vindicates Spain's (and Europe's) repressed history. By underscoring the actual permanence of a *repressed* Islamic influence on Spanish (and European) culture, he calls for a new version of Spanish identity that is hybrid and multiple, which is opposed to the pure and immutable identity of "eternal" Spain.

We come across another identitary dissenter in Uwe Timm's documentary and historical novel *Morenga* (1978), which is analysed by Kora Baumbach in her essay in Part II. Confronting a native people's fight to the death for recognition and integrity, the main character (a military veterinarian) experiences how his own European identity crumbles down. The struggle for recognition in a colonial context brings to the fore the deep contradictions originating in the contrast between materialist exploitation and ideological cant. For recognition to be valid the other who recognises me must be placed at the same level as I am. This is not possible in a context of colonial exploitation in which natives become slaves. Besides, the coloniser desires to be recognised not by the native other but by the Other that presides over his own culture.[7] The voice of the colonised does not count, as denounced by Gulliver's devastating satire when he argues his decision not to take possession of the territories he visited in the Queen's name, the embodiment of the Other *qua* Symbolic Order in Lacanian terms.[8] Gulliver's syllogism should logically conclude stating his duty to take possession of those territories; instead, he incongruously adopts the point of view of the other, exactly the opposite of what colonisers do (Barbeito 2004: 99–125). The ideological justification of colonisation that Gulliver quotes in the first part of his argument and then undoes consists precisely of spreading the values of western cultures, thus creating an unbridgeable gap between actual inhuman exploitation and the spiritual benefits that the

---

7   For Lacan the subject can find justification only in relation to the Other. See Kurtz's case in Conrad's *Heart of Darkness*.
8   Here are the three steps of Gulliver's syllogism: 1) "But ... To say the Truth, I had conceived a few Scruples with relation to the distributive Justice of Princes upon those Occasions." 2) "But this Description, I confess, doth by no means affect the British Nation, who may be an Example to the whole World for their Wisdom, Care, and Justice in planting Colonies ... " 3) "But, as those Countries which I have described do not appear to have any Desire of being conquered, and enslaved, murdered or driven out by Colonies ... I did humbly conceive they were by no Means proper Objects of our Zeal, our Valour, or our Interest" (Greenberg 1961: 258–59).

natives are said to receive in turn. Gottschalk, the western protagonist of *Morenga*, experiences the contradiction stemming from this gap when he sees the ideal of universal human rights incarnated in Morenga, the native other, and his fight to the death for recognition. As a logical consequence of his attitude, Gottschalk stops justifying himself before the Other who rules over his own world thus seeking to establish an intersubjective relation with the native other. Once deprived of that possibility after the massacre of the natives occurs, Gottschalk can only survive in an identitary void.

The problem posed in *Morenga*, however, transcends the sphere of mere individual identity. Europe is moving towards the hole it has dug by its own lack of solidarity. And it will continue to do so as long as it is incapable of establishing a dignified relationship with the exploited who stand up to defend their rights and of assuming historical responsibility for the consequences of colonisation, which till now it has only assumed cynically without true practical consequences or by hiding the bloody episodes of its colonial history (as is the case of Germany in Uwe Timm's novel). Instead of trying to find justification within itself, Europe must stop ignoring its necessity to be recognised by the other whose struggle for emancipation incarnates the very same values that Europe preaches.

In his study of Giwi Margwelaschwili's *Muzal* (1991), Zaal Andronikasvili contrasts two versions of the law as the foundation of society. In the first version, the law is sacred, thus an unalterable given; in the second, the lay version, the law is the result of a process of a social debate that seeks to reach consensus, thus opening up the possibility for change. The communitarian model proposed by Taylor and the liberal model defended by Habermas are thus confronted in a way that helps to understand how literature can contribute to either the defence, or the transformation of a paradigm. *Muzal* is a postmodern rewriting of *Aluda Keltelauri* (1888), a novel in which the main character is expelled from his community for trying to establish a relationship with the foreign other in terms of personal recognition and against social norms. This was a way of giving expression to a subversive idea while at the same time transforming that idea into an ideal by forcing the reader to identify with the novel's protagonist. If, on the one hand, the respect due to the realist principle of verisimilitude blocks the possibility of the protagonist's success, the free play of the imagination transforms this limitation into a trick which at once triggers and frustrates desire, a pattern followed by many literary works such as George Eliot's *The Mill on the Floss* in which realism frustrates poetic justice and moves the reader to lamenting the death of a protagonist whose character and behaviour are unacceptable in strictly conventional terms.

Matthias Beilein analyses *Ohnehin* (2004) by Doron Rabinovici, an Austrian author born in Israel. This novel draws a multicultural panopticon of contemporary Viennese society and highlights the perplexity that the irreversible process of hybridisation provokes in the large majority of the Austrian population which is reluctant to acknowledge that reality as a part of their identity. Therefore, *Ohnehin* does not present an idyllic multicultural society, nor a social system that had fully assumed its own multicultural nature, but one in which diverse and numerous characters carry out an incessant struggle for recognition and integrity. Austrian-Jewish Ravinovici, as with some of his contemporary fellow writers like Robert Schindel or Robert Menasse, is involved in the struggle for recognition in the face of a society that chooses to disavow its own complicity with anti-Semitism by hiding behind the shield of its nature as victim and primary objective of the Nazi invasion.

According to Horst Turk, in *The Moor's Last Sigh* (1995) Salman Rushdie examines the features of European identity, a constellation of secularisation and nationalism, socialism and capitalism, that aspires to the globalisation of modernity and democracy, and opposes the Clash of Civilisations thesis (put forward by Samuel P. Huntington and spread by fundamentalisms of all sorts) through the endorsement of hybridity in a postcolonial and postmodern context. Rushdie uses the estranging effect of fiction so dear to the Russian formalists to force the European reader to reflect on his own problems. *Outside* Europe, in India, a series of truly European problems concerning identity are represented: the coexistence of Christian, Jewish and

Islamic religions engender contradictions that also affect a Europe whose culture, like Goytisolo's Spain, was born out of the intersection of these three great monotheistic religious and cultural traditions, to which Hinduism is added in India According to Turk, Rushdie's novel maintains that, despite all these contradictions, it is still possible to struggle for a utopia of reciprocal influences from which the different secular and religious components that make up European civilisation may benefit.

Though it is true that Culture's capability dreamt up by bourgeois idealism has proved illusory, literature did have a foundational role as a part of nationalist culture. The passage from Culture to culture entails the transition from an academic field, in which an ideally rational and objective knowledge establishes the relevance of cultural products, to the socio-political field, in which imagination and belief are relevant in the struggle for recognition. The essays in Part III approach that "particular form of struggle over classifications that is constituted by the struggle over the definition of 'regional' or 'ethnic' identity" (Bourdieu 1992a, 221) in the context of different European nationalities as well as the participation in it of different cultural institutions.

The formula of the nation – invented in Europe and brought to former colonies during the nineteenth century (Thiesse 1999: 14) – refers to local ways of life while at the same time a manner of relating to the global. The existence of the nation requires that its members identify themselves as part of *the people*, that its identity traits be instilled into the minds as common sense; hence the need to be daily taught and argued. It also depends on its power to gain international recognition, which requires inventing ways of obtaining access to the global where identity is tested and the nations are forced to renovate it. These dynamics determine the ways to deal with specific contingencies like immigration and which will be diverse in nature depending on the given tradition and the activity of the ghosts that haunt the socially constituted common sense.

The first three essays in Part III deal with three nation-states: Britain, Spain, and Germany. The following four deal with three nations that are part of the Spanish state – Galicia, the Basque Country, and Catalonia – and which are *historic autonomous communities* each with their own language.[9]

The opening two essays examine the discursive consequences of two historical situations with two common denominators: the end of Spanish and British colonial empires – emblematised, respectively, in the "loss" of Cuba (1898) and of India (1946) –, and the ghost that originates in the loss of an *empire*. Today, this is of primary importance since the ghost often returns to haunt a major contemporary phenomenon: immigration.

The idea of a community and of a *people* is a fundamental element in nationalist discourse, and it is invoked in times of crisis when national identity has to be reaffirmed. Taking as their starting-point George Orwell essay "The English People", written to promote the idea of the people during the Second World War (right before Britain lost India), J. Manuel Barbeito and Jorge Sacido analyse this notion in the English postcolonial and multicultural context. The ghost of the loss of the empire appears both in the way international relations are conceived – haunting cultural products that tackle the issue of the UK's relationship with the United States (a former colony that is now the world leader) – and in the views on the relations between communities within the nation haunting immigrants as well as natives from the ex-colonies. Barbeito and Sacido maintain the necessity for each group to learn how to deal with their own ghosts so that they do not interfere in intercultural and interracial relations. Apart from Orwell's text, this chapter also analyses two popular films, *Notting Hill* and *Love Actually* (two contemporary ways of dealing with the theme of the ghost that troubles the relationship between the UK and the US) and the trope of the ghost as is used in multicultural discourses that delve into interracial relations within the UK.

9   *Autonomous communities* is the translation of *comunidades autónomas*, the largest sub-state units in which Spain's territory is divided.

Like in England and other European countries, the term "empire" acquired positive connotations in Spain during the second half of the nineteenth century as it came to be associated with the strength and greatness of a nation, hence the impact produced by the loss of the last Spanish colonies and the sense of decadence felt and expressed by the '98 Generation of writers. The crisis fuelled the ongoing revision of the idea of Spain and of its position in the international arena, particularly as regards Europe (at the turn of the nineteenth and twentieth centuries Spanish intellectuals began to look north, thus reversing the European romantic artist's movement towards the south). Two main positions can be traced: one defended the necessity of a material transformation of Spain applying the scientific and technological developments that had transformed Europe (*regeneracionists* like Costa and Ramón y Cajal), while the other thought that materialist Europe still had something to learn from Spain. Among the latter were the '98 Generation and the "marroquistas". The '98 Generation found in Castille the expression of the Spanish spirit, while the "marroquistas" reacted against the conventional association of Africa with backwardness and conceived the Spanish connection with Morocco in positive terms.

Brad Epps argues that there exists a much ignored tradition that goes back to medieval romances and that continues in the work of Juan Goytisolo today. This tradition acknowledges and sympathises with the relevance for Spanish identity of Spain's historical relationships with the north of Africa and maintains that the regeneration of Spain should start from this acknowledgement. This contrasts with the representation of Black sub-Saharan Africans that, according to María Dolores F.-Fígares, "has its roots in the lost overseas Empire," which produces "a discourse of compassion" and "a discourse of superiority" (quoted in Epps, p. 166). Such a discourse is very much alive in the current reception of *pateras* and *kajukos*. Moreover, Aznar's farcical repetition of Thatcher's intervention in the Falklands (Malvinas in Spanish), i.e. his overreaction to the 'invasion' of a tiny Mediterranean isle by a few Moroccan soldiers, is a reminder that the illusion of the empire has remained present in a part of the Spanish political class even well beyond 1976 (when Spain was pressured by Morocco to abandon the Sahara, which probably haunted the Spanish former president). Even a more serious concern, because of its effect on the popular representation of immigration, is the way in which some media portray the continuous arrival of *pateras* and *kajukos* from Mahgreb and sub-Saharan Africa as a sort of invasion.

The notion of the nation remains a valid and active one in Europe. Germany's reunification is the most relevant example of this because of its political and economic importance as well as the number of people involved in the process. That it was pursued knowing the socio-economic problems that would follow demonstrates how forceful the idea is. But, as Jaime Feijóo argues, problems of all sorts also show how shortly after the integration of the GDR the "national common sense" can be disturbed by socio-economic and political circumstances. As a consequence, the new scenario caused open wounds that are difficult to suture for the discourse that had justified the reunification based on the existence of a national identity.

In this way, German identity becomes "provisional" and even precarious. On the one hand, there is an ongoing process of constructing an integrative common sense in which writers are directly involved. On the other hand, a dividing *wall* is rebuilt due to the "minorisation" of the former GDR by West Germany and the transformation of its culture into a source of exoticism. Given that they fail to achieve recognition on equal terms, the people of the East stand up and demand respect for their former identity (*Ostalgie*). Artists and writers contribute significantly to this by claiming their own symbolic capital, even to the point of questioning the unity of the German literary field.

In the so-called nations without a state, the focus of the last four essays in Part III of this volume, the role that culture plays becomes more political the less consolidated national identity is. When this is in the making, political strategies are more visible and actively present in the literary field in general and even in academia. This "epic" national function, as Jon Kortazar calls it, contributes to reinforcing the role of the literary field. Nonetheless, if writers embark on a staunch defence of an essentialist identity, they may not only give up autonomy, but also condemn traditional culture either to exoticism or to its appropriation by the militant few who are out of tune with the majority of the population. Therefore, "minor literatures" are embroiled in a contradiction between autonomy, necessary for the development of the arts and the functioning of academia, and heteronomous political action, equally indispensable for the (re)birth and subsistence of national culture.

In this context, strategies are devised that aim at renovating and promoting the identification of the population with the idea of *people*. This requires obtaining the recognition of this identity by other nations as well as preserving and reinventing common traits. A recurrent feature present in the theoretical discourses produced within these communities is precisely their concern with the survival and the future of their culture, giving rise to a series of interrogations and proposals of actions to take. The last four essays of this book explore the different strategies used by those institutions that defend Galician, Basque, and Catalan national identities and the various roles that literature and traditional culture played and continue to play in terms of local identification and exterior projection.

Antón Figueroa looks into the heteronomy of the Galician literary field derived from its participation in the political struggle and questions the total division between objective, rational discourse and its object of analysis (particularly, when the latter is identitary discourse itself). According to Figueroa, "discourses on identity may, to different degrees, turn into a discourse of identity" (p. 219). His paper examines the factors intervening in the determination of the different functions which, depending on the specific historical moment, academic discourse assumes, particularly in the case of Galicia: "scholarly discourse and, particularly, discourse engaged with identity-oriented issues always contain some element that is originally or explicitly political, or *ends up being political* given the particular 'common sense' incorporated by its addressers and addressees. This makes the scholar a political agent" (p. 210).

In the context of the conflict of identities (for instance, between Spanish identity and Galician, Basque or Catalan identity), a presumption of objectivity may hide discriminatory political attitudes when scientific discourse assumes a position of superiority to prove that minority nationalist discourse is an invention and therefore denounce its naturalist pretence by lifting the ideological veil that conceals its historical production and even the falsity of the historical data it uses. It is not a question of simply deciding whether this account provided by scientific discourse is true or not. Rather, the crucial issue is to find out to what particular interests this discourse is lending its support in a given historical context by determining whether it scrutinises identitary discourses of minority cultures to show their artificiality, without equally criticising the presumed naturalness of dominant discourses; whether it ignores that a struggle for recognition underlies any identity discourse, thus evading the analysis of those conditions under which these discourses were produced; whether it overlooks the extent to which these discourses actually made history, thereby implying that some agents (the dominant ones) are really capable of making history while others are purely imaginary; finally, whether it disregards that identity does not exist without identification, or, borrowing Anne Marie Thiesse's words, that "le sentiment national n'est spontané que lorsqui'l á été parfaitement interiorisé" (Thiesse 1999: 14).

This does not mean that academics should give up rationality and the effort to be rigorous and objective. On the contrary, rationality demands that scholars should take into account the conditions in which scientific discourse is produced and circulates. Figueroa points out how these conditions vary depending on whether one refers to emerging cultural identities or consolidated ones. In the first case, the politisation and militancy of academic discourse is stronger, whereas in the second the revision of the discourses that contributed to identity building becomes more liable. This means that the chronology of identities in conflict may be very different: As for dominant cultures, discourses can easily be explicit about and criticise the artificial and historical construction of their consolidated identity. In the case of marginal cultures, however, discourses cannot as easily afford to do the same. But the times can change so that a consolidated identity (i.e., an identity produced 500 years ago and both nationally and internationally recognised) may need to renovate identification, as is the case with present-day Spain.

The situation Dolores Vilavedra describes in her essay as regards Galician culture is so serious that it just may drive militant identity discourse into a contradictory position: it may inhabit the space of tradition presided over by an ideal *people* but be bereft of any real population. Vilavedra asks how Galician literature can extend its readership beyond the restricting bounds of militancy and objects to today's readers who resist change, unlike writers, who have already undergone the necessary process of transformation.

Currently, the function of literature should be precisely that of "seducing" the reader into reading texts in Galician even if this means giving up traditional indentitary themes for which the bulk of readers seem to show little interest. The main goal is to keep the fundamental element of identity, language, from dying of sclerosis caused by its isolation in a discourse of essences that is alien to most of the Galician population. With the arrival of democracy in Spain, it became widely accepted that literature should abandon its identitary themes and contribute to the reinforcement of the identitary function of language. Writers had to adapt to the times and get in tune with a new type of reader who felt detached from identitary discourse – even if this meant foregoing or transferring tradition to a new scenario. After all, this is what *tradere*, the root of the word *tradition*, means (which, curiously, shares the etymology with *treason*). Jon Kortazar also addresses this transformation of the function of literature as regards national identity and shows how the Basque literary system has already embarked on an attempt to transcend the boundaries of the nation to seek recognition beyond the nationalist system.

In "Diglossia and Basque Literature", Kortazar analyses the present situation of Basque language and culture. He admits that coincidences exist with Galician culture as analysed by Figueroa in his *Diglosia e texto* (1988), but Kortazar also points out that the state of a given culture does not depend exclusively on the issue of diglossia.

There are other historically variable factors which determine the state of Basque culture nowadays such as the fact that, with the restoration of the democratic system, the study of Basque has entered school curricula and people are now proud of possessing and speaking their own tongue. Moreover, in this new context, Basque literature has veered from the traditional motif of lamenting the loss of the Basque nation while managing to rise above the state of technical backwardness, typical of minority cultures, when Basque authors were able to create "an aesthetic tendency in other literary systems" thanks to the translation of their texts.

Therefore, as is true of consolidated cultures, what is important is that a writer be identified as Basque regardless of the language in which he is read, so that by achieving international recognition literature can contribute to the increase in symbolic capital of the Basque nation. There is a certain common thread between the situation Kortazar portrays and Vilavedra's proposal: the epic function – the militant writer's aspiration to contribute to the foundation of the nation – is substituted by literature's capability to create worlds that readers are attracted to. The desired increase in readership has been somewhat fulfilled in the Basque Country precisely by internationalisation.

Like the Basque Country, Catalonia also employs the strategy of internationalising their symbolic capital as a way of increasing it. Unlike in the Basque Country where writers in Basque have pre-eminence in this regard, in Catalonia writers have been removed from the frontline of identitary culture giving way to "universal Catalans". Jaume Subirana describes the transformation that identitary discourse has undergone in Catalonia, from associating both literature and collective identity to the language to dissociating the literary figure from Catalan tradition, language or nation. Formerly, writers did play a decisive role in Catalan society, so much so that they were awarded a relevant status for their service to the nation, often whether or not their work was of any literary value; now it is enough to be Catalan and internationally famous. The symbolic power of the national poet who conferred on the people their sense of identity and on the nation its legitimacy and who the community considered the spokesperson of the collective spirit, has been substituted by its function as a link, which may not have any Catalan identitary content at all, to connect whatever is Catalan to the international scenario. The poet's place now is more like that of Cacofonix, the bard in Asterix's village: he may well do as an ornamental element, but the message of his song is irrelevant, not to say unpleasant. As in the case of *Love Actually*, the equation "Shakespeare = Beckham" is a valid one in the international cultural market.

In this introductory essay, we have reflected on the relevance of the literary field regarding identity. As for individual identity, literature may lend support to ideology by promoting aspirations that fit into a conventionally fixed identity, but it may also offer a critical evaluation of it and of the ideologically determined relations among individuals and communities. It may even go as far as activating or expressing the desire for alternative identities and models of human relations. As for national identity, the function of literature may vary depending on the militancy required in a particular historical situation.

How much leadership power writers possess is often directly proportional to the degree of their political involvement and inversely proportional to the amount of artistic autonomy they have, particularly in the context of emerging nationalisms and in situations of crisis. On the one hand, militancy that defends national identity means a greater dependence of the literary field on its political function. In turn, political involvement increases leadership power. However, increased militancy and leadership do not necessarily mean a greater influence on society at large. Foundational literature runs the risk of becoming marginal when there is an unbridgeable gap separating the population of a nation from the people that this type of literature vindicates. On the other hand, as consolidation increases and, concomitantly, militancy decreases, the autonomy of the literary field is reinforced and it becomes possible to critically assess the texts of foundational militancy. It might be that, with the abandonment of militancy, literature could stop being a decisive identitary element in terms of its content. However, as long as formal and thematic innovation gains new readers, literature keeps the language alive, that distinctive fundamental element of nations such as Galicia, the Basque Country, or Catalonia. In this case, the institutionalisation of the study of language and literature may compensate for the loss of political influence in terms of message.

The role of intellectuals varies according to how close they stand to endorsing a nationalist or a cosmopolitan position. The more they transcend the local sphere, the more the function and influence of "the man of letters" will be affected by the weakness of the public sphere today. This weakness lies in the commodification of culture and in that, rather than presiding over the debates on great issues, currently reason more often than not serves the interests of the lobbies that dominate the media.

In these circumstances, intellectuals, now disaffected after being dispossessed of their superior function of moral leadership, may be tempted to shut themselves up in their realm. If they follow that path, however, they will betray those great works that they presumably respect and which have always tried to find (more or less successfully) ways to reach and influence the reader. Intellectuals should not forget that the great poet Isaiah attributed to God alone the full power of the Word: "For as the rain cometh down, and the snow from heaven, and returneth not thither, but watereth the earth, and maketh it bring forth and bud, that it may give seed to the sower, and bread to the eater: So shall my word be that goeth forth out of my mouth: it shall not return unto me void, but it shall accomplish that which I please, and it shall prosper in the thing whereto I sent it" (Isaiah 55, 10–11). As this comparison suggests, not even God's Word produces Its effect without getting muddied. The rest is magic. Barbeito and Sacido bring their text to a conclusion by stating that "there cannot be authentic recognition until we learn how to deal with our own ghosts" (p. 144); *we* intellectuals, to begin with.

WORKS CITED

Badiou, Alain (1997): *Saint Paul. La fondation de l'universalisme*. Paris: PUF.

Barbeito, J. Manuel (2006): *Las Brontë y su mundo*. Madrid: Síntesis.

Barbeito, J. Manuel (2004): *El individuo y el mundo moderno*. Oviedo: Septem.

Bourdieu, Pierre (1992): *Les règles de l'art: Genèse et structure du champ littéraire*. Paris: Éditions du Seuil.

Bourdieu, Pierre (1992a): *Language and Symbolic Power*. Cambridge, Polity.

Eagleton, Terry (1976): *Criticism and Ideology: A Study in Marxist Literary Theory*. London: Verso.

Eagleton, Terry (1983): *Literary Theory: An Introduction*. Minneapolis: University of Minnesota Press.

Eagleton, Terry (2003): *Figures of Dissent*. London: Verso.

Eagleton, Terry (2005): *Holy Terror*. Oxford: Oxford University Press.

Estévez Saá, Margarita and Jorge Sacido Romero, eds. (1999): "A Debate with Eagleton on Eagleton," *Round Table at the conference 'Terry Eagleton or Towards a Revolutionary Criticism'*. Santiago de Compostela (Forthcoming).

Figueroa, Antón (1988): *Diglosia e texto*. Vigo: Xerais.

Greenberg, R. A., ed. (1961): *Jonathan Swift. Gulliver's Travels*. New York: Norton.

Lash, Scott and John Urry (1994): *Economies of Signs and Space*. London: Sage.

Taylor, Charles (1992) "The Politics of Recognition". *Multiculturalism and "The Politics of Recognition"*. Gutmann, Amy (ed.). New Jersey: Princeton University Press, 25–73.

Thiesse, Anne-Marie (1999): *La création des identités nationales.* Paris, Seuil.

Part I

Literature, Culture, Identity

TERRY EAGLETON

Culture and Identity

Literary critics like myself live in a chronic state of dread – a dread that one day, someone in some minor government ministry idly turning a page will suddenly get wise to the fact that we draw salaries for reading poems and novels. This is as scandalous as being paid for sunbathing, eating chocolate or having sex, and it is surely only a matter of time before the state stumbles upon our guilty secret and takes appropriate action. Not only are we paid for talking about books; even more outrageously, we are paid for talking about books which concern people who never existed. In everyday life, talking about imaginary people as though they were real is known as psychosis; in universities, it is known as literary criticism.

Quantum physicists work on things that *may* not exist, or may only exist while they are working on them, or that may exist in one sense and not in another. In this sense, by the way, they are oddly similar to theologians. Some mathematicians, known as realists, hold that numbers really are in some sense actually out there, whereas others, known as constructivists or conventionalists, do not. Chemists used to think that certain substances existed which we now know do not, but it sounds pretty implausible for us literary critics to claim that we *thought* there was someone called Don Quixote but now we know better. Even wild-eyed archaeologists in search of the lost city of Atlantis *may* just be on to something – we can't rule it out.

But we literary critics cannot even reap the benefit of these doubts and ambiguities. Unfortunately, it is simply undeniable that there never was a Heathcliff or Lady Macbeth or Emma Bovary, despite the acres of scholarly analysis devoted to them. Moreover, even if there were, it would make no difference to our analyses, for literary-theoretical reasons too complicated to go into here. Before long, no doubt, some obscure civil servant will make a momentous discovery and go running to his Master with a cry of Eureka; the scandalous secret we have managed to suppress for so long will be bruited abroad; and lit critics will be thronging the employment exchanges, jeered at by mocking crowds of people who work on things like sick dogs and dental cavities that actually exist.

We need, then, some robust defence of what we are doing in studying literature; and one way of lending it importance is to claim that it plays a vital role in the process of identity. Before we come to consider this, however, let us examine another defence of the study of literature – the claim that it contributes to the deepening and enriching of the creative imagination.

Like almost everyone, this argument blandly assumes that the imagination is indeed, unequivocally, a creative force. Indeed, the very word 'imaginative' is one of those words at the very sound of which everyone is expected to rise and cheer. (Other such words are community, world peace, Nelson Mandela and Homer Simpson). This is strange, since the imagination, like the unconscious, can be a thoroughly unpleasant place. Mustn't there be something amiss about a civilisation which places such supreme value on a faculty which deals with non-existent things? What does this say about the nature of the existent? What Romantics affirm as 'vision' is unnervingly close to what psychoanalysis calls fantasy, which is far from pure and edifying. As usual, the high and the low, sublimity and monstrosity, border alarmingly on one another, as Jonathan Swift knew well.

It is misleading, however, to call the imagination a place, as I just did, because, like the unconscious, it is much more of a non-place. For Romanticism, the imagination is not bound to any particular time or place; on the contrary, it is nothing but the infinitely plastic, protean, diffused, decentred power by which one can enter and inhabit any time or place whatsoever. The imagination is absolutely nothing in itself; it is quite displaced and disembodied, utterly without substance or identity of its own. This is one reason why it is odd to summon literary studies, which deal with the imagination, to the cause of identity; for in one sense such studies are all about non-identity. The imagination is not a principle, entity or fixed essence; it is nothing *but* the power to enter empathetically into any place, object or identity whatsoever, while ultimately transcending them all.

Like the Almighty, for whom it is among other things a secular substitute, the creative imagination is therefore both all and nothing. Like Ariel, it makes up in range and plurality for what it lacks in Caliban-like rootedness and tenacity. It is immune to scrutiny itself – which is to say that as an absolute it is technically speaking transcendental, unable to curve back on itself – at the same time that, while being universal itself, it is able to penetrate, appropriate, and occupy from the inside any merely particular place, culture or style of selfhood. It is, indeed, able to understand any specific culture better than that culture can understand itself. There are several names for this universal, all-powerful, all-knowing force which can occupy all other cultures while transcending them all. If one such name is God, or the imagination, another is imperialism.

There is another charge which can be brought against the concept of the imagination. In the eighteenth century, English empiricist philosophers imagined that men and women were solitary beings, each locked within the prison-house of his or her sense data. This raised a problem about how we could then come to communicate on any very deep level. If your experience is private to you, and mine is to me, then how could I ever come to share your experience in any significant way? How could we be certain of having a world in common? The stakes here were high, since if sharing our experience proved to be impossible, then the whole basis of human solidarity, and with it human society itself, seemed to be under threat.

The question, then, was how I could come to place myself on the inside of your experience, and the answer was: by virtue of a mysterious, elusive force known as empathy, or the imagination. Later on, this would become one rationale for literature, which lifts us out of our own narrow circle of experience and enables us vicariously to enjoy the experiences of others. The idea of the imagination, then, sprang from a radically false epistemology. It was a way of compensating for a kind of possessive individualism of the senses, which allowed each of us access only to our immediate experience, and which turned the human body into a kind of enclosure which locked out all other such bodies. If empiricism had not laboured under such illusions, it might not have needed the mysterious supplement or corrective known as the empathetic imagination. The imagination in the sense of empathy was an answer to a misposed question.

In any case, the idea that to understand another is to put oneself in their shoes, come somehow to occupy their subjectivity from the inside, is surely a Romantic myth. I do not need to experience your sorrow to understand that you are sad. How can I understand you by 'becoming' you? For one thing, this would leave nobody there to do the understanding (as Keats sees in his *Ode to a Nightingale*); and for another thing, it assumes that you are perfectly transparent to yourself, which is by no means the case. Nor does imaginative empathy necessarily go hand in hand with moral virtue, as a tradition of English writers from William Wordsworth to George Eliot seems to suppose. On this theory, lack of compassion is basically the result of imaginative obtuseness. If only I could feel what you are feeling, I would surely be moved to come to your help. But why should we assume this? The sadist tries hard to feel what his victim is feeling, but this does not stop him from torturing him. Quite the contrary. I can be perfectly aware of how you feel, without feeling in the least obliged to sympathise morally with your situation.

There are, then, a number of problems with the concept of the imagination. To possess what you desire not in reality, but in imagination, can be a way of compensating for an inadequate social reality, and thus of confirming it. If men and women are too impoverished or hard-worked to travel to the Far-East, then let them read Joseph Conrad instead. In this sense, literature becomes the opium of the people. It is second only to that most powerful opium of all: sport. Without the abolition of sport, radical social change is highly unlikely.

Another way of justifying what we do is to appeal to the idea of fiction. In one sense, as I have pointed out, the fact that we deal in a discourse of the non-existent is precisely our embarrassment. But it can always be turned to our benefit. There is a utopian impulse in fiction, which constantly seeks to compare how things are with the way they might be. The English novelist Henry Fielding remarks in *Tom Jones* that there is a pious doctrine which holds that the just will get their reward in this life – a doctrine, Fielding adds, which has only one defect, namely that it is not true. There is, however, a place in this world where the good do indeed get their reward, and the villains get their punishment, and it is known as the novel. In this sense, the novel is a utopian counterpoint to the injustices of actual history. Yet the novel knows very well that allowing virtue to have its reward is grotesquely unreal. This is why it is a supremely ironic genre – why, as in *Tom Jones*, it ends by appropriately distributing rewards and penalties, but all the while in the wry awareness that it would never happen like this in everyday life. There is a tension here between the unregenerate content, and the artificial, symmetrical form. In everyday life, the villain would not be worsted; he would probably become prime minister. If the novel's utopian function is to be authentic, then, the form must be ironically conscious of its own unreality. Something of the same may be said of the conclusions of some Shakespearian comedies.

In the modern period, literature regains a certain relevance to the world by playing a part in the constitution of national, ethnic and regional identities. This is curious, since literature since the Enlightenment has usually been considered as universal in status. Yet the local and the universal are not necessarily such antagonists. The French, for example, manage superbly to be local and universal at the same time. The French language and its literature belong like any other language and literature to a particular time and place; yet they have also often enough presented themselves as the very paradigm of language, writing, reason or civility as such – just as the French Revolution is at once a universal affair (a matter of human rights which should be available to French and non-French citizens alike) yet also a universal which is instantiated in a specific time and place. In the Romantic period, the term we give to this remarkable interweaving of the universal and the particular is the symbol.

But there is another sense in which the universal and the local are not at odds, namely that nothing is more international than nationalism. Just as there is nothing more common in the advanced capitalist world than selfish individualism, so ironically, the movement to affirm or reclaim one's unique national identity is global in scope. Within this movement, literature has played a vital role – far more vital, in fact, than it has played in metropolitan societies which have already lived through their national revolutions. In fact, one sociologist has described nationalism as the invention of literary men. In crossing from the universal to the local, ethnic or regional, literature in the modern period is able to reclaim a social function and political centrality of which it was deprived by modernity in general. And the reason for this is not hard to find. For nationalism is perhaps the most profoundly *cultural* of all modern political currents – which may be one reason why it is also far and away the most successful form of radical politics of the modern age. People may not be deeply stirred by trade agreements or constitutional affairs, but they will very often fight to the death when it comes to their identity. Indeed, one definition of culture would be: that for which men and women are prepared to kill, or to die. It is, of course, not Balzac or Beethoven you are prepared to die for, but a language, a history, a religious faith, a way of life. Not Culture, in other words, culture. Cultural politics are the kind of politics which are most subtly bound up with the roots of selfhood. This is why they are so powerful. The most important piece of literature in the world at present is the Koran.

For more traditional forms of political conflict, like, say, the industrial class-struggle, it is quite often material survival, rather than cultural identity, which is centrally at stake. In this sense, there is something rather privileged about even the most desperate forms of cultural politics. Culture – in the broad, anthropological sense of identity, value, sign, meaning, homeland, language, custom, religion, heritage and the like – is the very language of nationalist, ethnic or gender politics, the very terms in which those conflicts are articulated. It is not simply an agreeable bonus or the property of an elite. Nor is it an attempt, as with some classical modern conceptions of culture, to *resolve* political conflicts on a higher or deeper spiritual ground. In fact, it is exactly the opposite of this bourgeois cultural idealism, which runs all the way from Goethe and Schiller to Arnold, I. A. Richards and Northrop Frye.

One reason, then, why culture has been such a prevalent topic in our own time is because the forms of politics which have dominated the Western agenda for the last few decades have been for the most part cultural politics. With the so-called war on terror, this may now have to change. Once again, sheer material survival is back at the top of the agenda, along with struggles over global resources, the forced migration and dispossession of peoples, and the conflict between political states. None of this is especially 'cultural', despite the so-called clash of civilisations and the doctrines of both US neo-conservatives and radical Islam. Radical Islam, I would suggest, has ultimately more to do with neo-colonialism, slums, unemployment, festering political despair and military occupation than it has to do with 'culture'. Neo-conservatism has more to do with power and possession than it has with questions of religion or nationality. In this sense, both sides are waging a kind of phantom war. The same is true of the role of the conflict in Northern Ireland, which is certainly not a religious struggle.

There is, one might suggest, a 'good' and a 'bad' form of identity politics. With a 'bad' identity politics, you imagine that you know exactly who you are. It is just that someone out there – the state, colonialism, capitalism, patriarchy – is preventing you from being what you are. Yet how, if you are really oppressed, can you know who you truly are? A 'good' form of identity politics is one in which you claim the right, enjoyed already by certain others, to determine what you would wish to become. And this is not something that can be pre-drafted. The irony of identity politics, however, is that in order to create the conditions in which you can discover what you want to be, you must already have a fairly strong identity in the first place. The danger is then that this existing identity will prevent you from being open to future possibilities. Yet if you do not already have an affirmative enough sense of selfhood, it is unlikely that you will be able to defeat the power which is preventing you from exploring what you might like to be.

In this sense, a national, ethnic or regional identity is rather like social class. In order to get rid of it, you must first have it. Marx believed in a classless society, but only by taking the divisions of class seriously, not just by some liberal wishful thinking, could we arrive at one. Similarly, if women are to be as free and equal as anyone else, they must first be conscious of their gender rather than simply trying to set it aside. Those who have power do not need to worry about who they are; it is only those whom they exploit and dispossess who carry the burden of their own identity on their backs, as a daily problem. The aim of the dispossessed, then, should be to get to the point where they can be as careless of the question of identity as their rulers. It is just that, to do this, you need a sense of identity in the first place.

In the modern word, literature is in my view likely to play less and less of a part in this process – though language is of course another question. It is true that, say, Pablo Neruda signifies something to the common people of Latin America that T. S. Eliot could not possibly mean to the common people of England. Where cultural identity is at stake, literature takes on an importance of which it has otherwise been robbed. It is politics, in other words, which determines whether literature is to be significant or insignificant in any particular time and place. Yet the transition from modernity to postmodernity has been among other things a transition from literature to culture; and literature is now for the most part important only as a metonym of culture. What is vital nowadays to the problem of identity is not *Culture* (in the sense of the fine arts and a notion of universal civility) but *culture*. It is not texts but national languages, not authors but religious faiths, not the aesthetic but questions of tradition and belonging, which have come to the fore, for both good or ill. This is another reason why literary criticism, in the more classical sense of the term, has less and less a part to play in the public sphere, and why therefore we should live in dread of that government clerk.

Part II

Integrität und Anerkennung im Rahmen Europäischer und Globaler Konstellationen. Fünf Literarische Analysen

ANDREA ALBRECHT, HORST TURK

Identität und Integrität. Ein alteuropäisches Thema. Einleitung

In seinem Essay *Mörderische Identitäten* aus dem Jahr 1998 prangerte Amin Maalouf die identitätspolitischen Mechanismen unserer Gesellschaft an, die ihm – einem Araber christlichen Glaubens, der sich sowohl dem Libanon als auch Frankreich zugehörig fühlt – immer wieder Aussagen zu seiner personalen Identität abverlangten. Die hinter diesem Appell zur "Identitätsprüfung" (Maalouf 2000: 19) stehende Auffassung treibe die Menschen in eine "parteiische, sektiererische, intolerante, herrische, manchmal selbstmörderische Haltung". Das "Wort Identität sei" daher ein gefährlicher, "ein 'falscher Freund'" (Maalouf 2000: 31). Etwa zur gleichen Zeit diagnostizierte der Historiker Lutz Niethammer aus kulturwissenschaftlicher Perspektive die irritierende, "unheimliche[] Hochkonjunktur" des "Plastikworts" (Niethammer 2000: 9ff.) Identität und beklagte ganz im Sinne Maaloufs das "semantische Gefahrenpotential" dieses "neuen Modeworts" (Wehler 2003: 147ff.): Da Identitätskonzepte, sobald sie auf Kollektive übertragen würden, unkontrollierbare politische Folgen für die identifizierten Individuen und Kollektive zeitigen könnten, plädierte er für einen generellen Begriffsverzicht (Niethammer 2000: 627ff.), ohne allerdings überzeugende begriffliche Alternativen anzubieten.

Der "Hochkonjunktur" haben weder Maaloufs Protest noch Niethammers engagierter Appell Einhalt gebieten können. Die Passepartout-Vokabel der Identität erfreut sich auch weiterhin größter Beliebtheit, in letzter Zeit besonders ausgeprägt im Zusammenhang politisch-kultureller Gemeinschaftsbildung wie der europäischen Integration. Doch gerade im Blick auf den europäischen Prozess kann man, wie Adolf Muschg dies unlängst getan hat, mit guten Gründen fragen, ob "Identität nicht das falsche Wort" (Muschg 2003) ist. Die Frage nach der europäischen Identität ist, wie Jacques Derrida in seinem Europa-Essay *Das andere Kap* festgestellt hat, ein überkommenes, "verbrauchte[s]" (Derrida 1992: 19) Thema, ein Thema des "alten Europa", das nach dem Ende des Kalten Krieges nicht mehr wisse, "was oder wer" überhaupt noch Europa heißen soll (Derrida 1992: 9ff.), sich aber gleichwohl auf sich selbst besinnen müsse (Derrida 1992: 27).

Angesichts dieser Erschöpfung und der anhaltenden Zweifel an der Praxis europäischer Identitätspolitik hat sich nicht nur Derrida, sondern haben sich auch die literarischen Phantasien längst an die Dekonstruktion kollektiver Identitätsvorstellungen gemacht: so der eingangs zitierte Amin Maalouf, so aber auch die Autoren, die in den folgenden Beiträgen diskutiert werden. Die Kritik an essentialistischen Konzepten kollektiver Identität erfolgt dabei nicht in nur destruktiver Absicht, sie soll vielmehr der Konstruktion eines hybriden Zusammenhalts dienen, der europäischen und globalen Konstellationen gleichermaßen Rechnung trägt und damit selbst in einer "Konstellation der Grenzüberschreitungen" (Habermas 1998: 7) steht. Ein dieser Konstruktion entsprechendes sozialphilosophisches Denkmodell, das eine Alternative zu den auf Identität setzenden Vorstellungen zu sein verspricht,[1] wird in der sozialwissenschaftlichen, moral- und rechtsphilosophischen Theoriebildung der letzten Jahre unter den Stichworten "Anerkennung" und "Integrität" verhandelt. Integrität bezeichnet dabei den begründeten Anspruch auf die Unverletzlichkeit einer Person oder eines Kollektivs – so die implizite, auf Personen zugeschnittene, später aber auch auf Kollektive übertragene Definition von Axel Honneth.[2] Integritätsvorstellungen resultieren aus Anerken-

---

1 Vgl. dazu auch Andrea Albrecht (2004): "Politik der Differenz oder Politik des Universalismus. Fragen nach der europäischen Integrität". *Trans. Internet-Zeitschrift für Kulturwissenschaften* 15. URL: <http://www.inst.at/trans /15Nr/01_1/albrecht15.htm>.
2 Axel Honneth (1994): *Kampf um Anerkennung*. Frankfurt am Main: Suhrkamp;

nungskämpfen zwischen Individuen, zwischen Individuen und Kollektiven sowie zwischen Kollektiven, in denen die Standards begründeter Integritätsansprüche zur Disposition gestellt und ausgehandelt werden. Zu Kontroversen kommt es hier insbesondere im Hinblick auf die Anerkennung der Unverletzlichkeit minoritärer kollektiver Identitäten, die in einem multikulturellen oder hybriden Zusammenhang stehen und innerhalb dieses Zusammenhangs um die Respektierung ihres jeweiligen Differenzanspruchs kämpfen. Auch Europa befindet sich in einem solchen Anerkennungskampf, wenn es die innereuropäischen Grenzen durch Integrationsstrategien und die außereuropäischen Grenzen durch die Übertragung europäischer Integritätsstandards zu transzendieren sucht.

Welche normativen Vorstellungen verbergen sich aber hinter den formulierten europäischen Integritätsansprüchen? Wie verhalten sich kollektive zu personalen Integritätsansprüchen? Auf welche Integritätsstandards rekurrieren die Anerkennungskämpfe innerhalb und außerhalb der europäischen Gesellschaft? In welchem Verhältnis zueinander stehen schließlich Identitäts- und Integritätskonzepte?

Die folgenden Beiträge, die erstmals auf dem Kolloquium *Literatur und Identitätsbildung in Europa* in Santiago de Compostela 2004 diskutiert wurden und inzwischen teils in einer ausführlicheren, teils in einer anders akzentuierten Fassung in einem Sonderband der *Monatshefte für deutschsprachige Literatur und Kultur*[3] im Sommer 2005 erschienen sind, nähern sich der Beantwortung dieser Fragen anhand des *literarisch* entfalteten Repertoires aktueller und historischer Anerkennungskonflikte und daraus resultierender personaler und kollektiver Integritätsansprüche. Sie verstehen sich insofern als

---

Axel Honneth, "Integrität und Mißachtung". *Merkur* 44.501 (1990) 1043–1054; Nancy Fraser, Axel Honneth (2003): *Umverteilung oder Anerkennung? Eine politisch-philosophische Kontroverse.* Frankfurt am Main: Suhrkamp.

3   *Integrität. Europäische Konstellationen im Medium der Literatur.* Special Issue der *Monatshefte für deutschsprachige Literatur und Kultur.* Hgg. Hans Adler u.a., 97.2, Summer 2005.

Beiträge zur aktuellen Debatte um europäische Identität und Integrität, als sie eine Brücke zwischen Literatur und Theorie zu schlagen und auf diese Weise eine wechselseitige Stimulierung der narrativ und diskursiv entfalteten Positionen anzuregen suchen.

ZITIERTE LITERATUR

Derrida, Jacques (1992): *Das andere Kap. Die vertagte Demokratie. Zwei Essays zu Europa.* Übers. v. Alexander García Düttmann. Frankfurt am Main: Suhrkamp.

Habermas, Jürgen (1998): *Die postnationale Konstellation. Politische Essays.* Frankfurt am Main: Suhrkamp.

Maalouf, Amin (2000): *Mörderische Identitäten.* Übers. v. Christian Hansen. Frankfurt am Main: Suhrkamp.

Muschg, Adolf (2003): "Berlin als Frontstadt der Kultur. Ein Gespräch mit Adolf Muschg". *Neue Zürcher Zeitung* 12./13. Juli 2003.

Niethammer, Lutz (2000): *Kollektive Identität. Heimliche Quellen einer unheimlichen Hochkonjunktur.* Reinbek bei Hamburg: Rowohlt.

Wehler, Hans-Ulrich (2003): "Identität: Unheimliche Hochkonjunktur eines 'Plastikworts'". *Konflikte zu Beginn des 21. Jahrhunderts. Essays.* München: Beck.

ANDREA ALBRECHT

Ein literarischer Kampf um Integrität und Anerkennung. Juan Goytisolos *Rückforderung des Conde don Julián*

I   Juan Goytisolos "gekränkter Conde". Axel Honneth

Juan Goytisolos Roman *Rückforderung des Conde don Julián* bildet den Bewusstseinsstrom eines durch Tanger wandernden Sprechers ab, der die Zerstörung des franquistischen Spaniens imaginiert. Gerahmt von leitmotivisch wiederkehrenden Wirklichkeitspartikeln bildet die Figur des Conde don Julián das organisierende Zentrum der Narration. Julián, nach der spanischen Geschichtsschreibung jener "Verräter", der im Jahr 711 aufgrund interner Querelen die islamische Invasion ermöglichte, wird von der Erzählstimme in den Rang eines Rächers an dem Regime erhoben, das im Zuge der Reconquista die jüdischen und arabischen Wurzeln seiner Kultur verdrängt und an deren Stelle eine kastilisch-katholische Reinheitsideologie etabliert habe. Sie zerstörte nach der Überzeugung Goytisolos die kulturelle Blüte Spaniens, die auf der mittelalterlichen Koexistenz von katholischen, islamischen und jüdischen Einflüssen beruht und den kulturellen Aufschwung Europas maßgeblich geprägt habe.[1] Gegen homogenisierende Reinheitsideologien setzt Goytisolo in seinem Roman ein hybridisiertes spanisches Selbstverständnis, das die Perspektive auf eine ebenfalls

---

1   Vgl. Nicolás Rivero Salavert (1983): *Geschichte und Gesellschaft Spaniens im Werk Juan Goytisolos*. Bamberg: Diss. Masch.; Michael Ugarte (1982): *Trilogy of Treason. An Intertextual Study of Juan Goytisolo*. Columbia u.a.: Univ. of Missouri Press, 73–78.

hybride, europäische Kollektivbestimmung für die Gegenwart eröffnet. Der Ich-Erzähler konstatiert:

> das Vaterland ist aller Laster Anfang: das rascheste und wirksamste Mittel, sich davon zu kurieren, besteht darin, es zu verkaufen und zu verraten: [...] sich zu befreien von dem, was uns identifiziert, uns definiert: uns ohne unseren Willen zum Sprachrohr von irgend etwas macht: uns ein Etikett aufklebt, eine Maske aufsetzt: welches Vaterland?: alle: die der Vergangenheit, der Gegenwart, der Zukunft: die großen und die kleinen, die mächtigen und die armseligen [...] (Goytisolo 1986: 126).

Die Passage präsentiert uns ein Individuum in der Rolle des Erzählers, das beobachtet, dass die Mitglieder seines vaterländischen Kollektivs wie auch die Mitglieder aller anderen vaterländischen Kollektive "ohne" ihren "Willen" auf eine homogene Nationalidentität festgelegt werden. Auf diese Weise werde jedes Individuum zum Zwecke der Stabilisierung politischer, religiöser, ökonomischer oder kultureller Ideologeme des Kollektivs seiner individuellen Stimme beraubt. Ergebnis dieser Operation sind in Goytisolos Textausschnitt etikettierte und maskierte, also problematische Existenzen, deren Selbstbilder nicht zu den willkürlichen Identifikationen des Kollektivs passen: "die Maske drückt uns: die Rolle, die wir spielen, ist falsch" (Goytisolo 1986: 129).[2]

Die kollektiven Identifizierungen, die als Eingriff in die Souveränität der Individuen erfahren werden, lassen sich – in der Terminologie Axel Honneths – als Verletzungen personaler Integrität beschreiben. Die Integrität einer Person wird nach Honneths analytischem Problemaufriss durch die intersubjektive Anerkennung erstens der physischen, zweitens der sozialen, rechtlich kodierten Unversehrtheit sowie drittens der sittlichen, kulturell kodierten Würde der Person bestimmt. Den drei Integritätsbestimmungen entsprechen drei systematisch unterscheidbare "Interaktionssphären", in denen sich Anerkennungsverhältnisse aushandeln lassen: "auf dem Weg emotionaler Bindungen, der Zuerkennung von Rechten oder der gemeinsamen",

---

2   Vgl. dazu auch Rivero Salavert 1983: 409f.

solidarischen "Orientierung an Werten" (Honneth 1994: 152). Honneth kann so drei Formen der Integritätsverletzung unterscheiden: die Missachtung der leiblichen Integrität durch körperliche Gewalt, die Missachtung des normativen Selbstverständnisses einer Person durch den strukturellen Ausschluss aus dem Rechtsverband einer Gemeinschaft und schließlich die "Herabwürdigung von individuellen oder kollektiven Lebensweisen" (Honneth 1990: 1045ff.; 1994: 212ff.). Intersubjektive Anerkennungsverhältnisse hingegen können nach Honneths Gesellschaftstheorie die Bedingungen der Möglichkeit für personale Integrität herstellen. Personale *Integrität* ist somit als ein relationales Konzept bestimmt, dass zum Konzept personaler *Identität* in einem Abhängigkeitsverhältnis steht: Integrität bezeichnet den begründet erhobenen Anspruch auf Unverletztheit und intersubjektive Anerkennung der Person inklusive ihres "Wissen[s] um" die "eigene, unverwechselbare Identität" (Honneth 1994: 42).

Welche Integritätsverletzung diagnostiziert Goytisolo? Da sein Protagonist autobiographische Parallelen[3] zu seinem Autor aufweist, bietet es sich an, diese zur Kommentierung der Textstelle heranzuziehen: Als Spanier katalanisch-baskischer Herkunft unter kastilischer Hegemonie, als kosmopolitisch gesinnter, linker Intellektueller unter einer rechtsgerichteten Diktatur, als arabophiler Homo- und Bisexueller in einer homophoben Gesellschaft, erfährt er das franquistische Spanien als ein Land der Identifikations- und Rollenangebote, die ihm untersagen, seine spezifischen Neigungen und Interessen zu entfalten. Er genießt als Individuum weder die körperliche noch die rechtliche noch die solidarische, wertschätzende Anerkennung durch das Kollektiv, sondern sieht seine homosexuell-körperlichen Bedürfnisse durch die rigide Sexualmoral der Spanier, seine grundrechtlichen Ansprüche durch die Franco-Diktatur und seine Ansprüche auf die Anerkennung seiner individualistisch-kosmopolitischen Lebensweise

---

3 Vgl. die autobiographischen Texte: Juan Goytisolo (1985): *Jagdverbot. Eine spanische Jugend*. Übers. v. Eugen Helmlé. München, Wien: Hanser; Juan Goytisolo (1995): *Die Häutung der Schlange. Ein Leben im Exil*. Übers. v. Eugen Helmlé. München, Wien: Hanser.

durch die spanisch-nationalistische Mentalität und Kultur missachtet und verletzt. Eine Integration in die spanische Gemeinschaft ließe sich nur assimilatorisch, unter Preisgabe seiner individuellen Besonderheit vollziehen. Also wendet sich Goytisolo mit seiner Kritik kategorisch gegen das Kollektiv und zieht sich auf die Dissidenz, auf die Außenseiterposition eines "moralische[n], soziale[n], ideologische[n] und sexuelle[n] Exil[s]" zurück (Goytisolo 1984: 244f.).

II Der Verrat des Dissidenten. *Restitutio in integrum*

In Goytisolos Leben ist dieser dissidente Zufluchtsort das freiwillige Exil in Paris und Marrakesch, in der *Rückforderung* Tanger, genauer: ein "maurische[s] Café: wo du sicher bist vor den Deinen in der afrikanischen Wahlheimat" (Goytisolo 1986: 119). Der Ich-Erzähler versucht, die personale Integrität durch eine selbstbestimmte Exklusion aus dem sozialen Verband zu erwirken, und zwar mittels einer im Roman inszenierten Wiederherstellung der Integrität durch den intellektuellen "Verrat" des Vaterlandes:

> um des einfachen, aber ausreichenden Vergnügens des Verrates willen: [...] allgemeiner Ausverkauf, alles verschleudern: Geschichte, Glauben, Sprache: Kindheit, Landschaften, Familie: die Identität ablehnen, wieder bei Null beginnen (Goytisolo 1986: 126f.).

Es geht, beschreibt man die Operation in der juristisch-verfahrensrechtlich kodierten Terminologie der römischen Rechtssprache, um eine Wiedereinsetzung seiner selbst in einen noch unversehrten Stand, um eine individuelle *restitutio in integrum*.[4] Dabei hat ein Stand der

---

4   Im juristischen Rahmen kann dies auf eine Wiederherstellung, Abgeltung oder Vergeltung hinauslaufen, dient aber in der Regel dem Ziel, einen unrechtmäßigen Zustand der Verletzung auf den der Verletzung vorausgehenden Zustand zurückzuführen. Vgl. dazu "Restitutio". *Paulys Realencyclopädie der*

Unversehrtheit, ein *Nullzustand* eigentlich nie vorgelegen, vielmehr war das Individuum von Geburt an den Bestimmungen der "Rabenmutter" (Goytisolo 1986: 15) Spanien ausgeliefert. Von einer *restitutio in integrum* kann daher nur im übertragenen Sinn gesprochen werden: Es handelt sich um die Imagination eines Zustandes, mit Hilfe dessen eine Distanz zum abgelehnten, aktuellen Zustand hergestellt und ein zukünftiger, unversehrter und insofern idealer Zustand entworfen werden kann. Das Individuum nutzt die im Zuge der Destruktion gewonnene Freiheit zu einer neuen, selbstbestimmt provozierten, nun ausdrücklich exkludierenden Identifizierung: Es kommt, dem dissidenten Selbstbild Goytisolos entsprechend, zur Stigmatisierung als Verräter. Zur Identifikations- und Projektionsfigur dieses Verrats avanciert im Laufe des Romans die legendäre Figur des Conde don Julián. Der Ich-Erzähler macht ihn zum zweiten Mal zum Vernichter der "geheuchelte[n] Ordnung" (Goytisolo 1986: 49) der spanischen Herrschaft, lässt ihn in einem literarisch fingierten, ekstatischen Gewaltexzess "plündern", "zerstören" und "vergewaltigen" (Goytisolo 1986: 148) und auf diese Weise die untragbar gewordenen kollektiven Depravationen offenlegen. Aus der Perspektive des spanischen Kollektivs bringt sich der Autor mit dieser polemischen Attacke um jeden Anspruch auf Anerkennung. Aus der Perspektive Goytisolos aber stellt sich der temporäre Integritätsverlust in der bewusst herbeigeführten Ekstase der rauschhaften Zerstörungsphantasie als ein transitorischer Moment dar. Das ästhetische Verfahren zielt auf eine Katharsis, eine zur Befreiung und Reinigung von franquistisch-römisch-katholischen Werten und Normen eingesetzte, literarisch und rhetorisch vermittelte Affektabfuhr, die die für eine Restitution notwendige Desintegration provoziert. Welche Ressourcen stehen aber für eine Restitution bereit, wenn die imaginierten Taten Julián moralisch, rechtlich, politisch und konfessionell disqualifizieren? Auf welche Weise lässt sich der im Rahmen der Fiktion performierte Destruktionsgestus ins Konstruktive wenden?

---

classischen Altertumswissenschaft. Hgg. Wilhelm Kroll, Kurt Witte, Bd. 2/1. Stuttgart: Druckenmüller, 1962.

III Selbstbestimmung.
Mead, Tugendhat, Habermas und Derrida

Da Goytisolo gegen die franquistisch-spanische Ordnung insgesamt anschreibt, kann sich die dissidente Restitution seiner personalen Integrität nur aus einem Impuls jenseits dieser herrschenden Ordnung vollziehen. Versteht man mit dem symbolischen Interaktionismus George Herbert Meads und Ernst Tugendhats den Prozess der personalen Identitätsbildung als dynamischen Interaktionsprozess zwischen Individuen und zugehörigen Kollektiven, kann das Individuum seine Identität nur durch die "Antwort" auf die "Einstellung, die die anderen zu ihm einnehmen", bestimmen. Kämpft es jedoch um seine Anerkennung, dann bestimmt es sein Selbst offensiv, d.h. es wählt selbst, "wer" es "sein will".[5] Dieser Akt der freien Selbstbestimmung kann nicht als *creatio ex nihilo* vorgestellt werden. Auch der von Goytisolo kathartisch hergestellte Nullzustand muss demnach seine propositionale Bestimmung in einem interaktionistischen Rahmen erhalten, also auf "eine umfassendere Gemeinschaft" (Tugendhat 1993: 281) moralischer, politischer, religiöser oder kultureller Gestalt Bezug nehmen. Lässt sich diese Bezugnahme nicht durch einen Grenzübertritt in ein anderes Kollektiv bewerkstelligen, lässt sich der von Mead und Tugendhat postulierte "universale Diskurs" nur jenseits real bestehender Kollektive imaginieren (Tugendhat 1993: 281f.). Damit allerdings Verletzungen der etablierten Ordnung als legitime "moralische[] Provokation[en]" interpretiert und ihnen eine "katalytische Funktion" für die Fortentwicklung der Gesellschaft in Richtung auf die imaginierte höhere Gemeinschaft zuerkannt werden kann, muss nach Honneth das Individuum mit seiner "Gegenwehr" nicht nur für partikuläre Interessen streiten, sondern die Gesellschaft mit

---

5   George Herbert Mead (1968): *Geist, Identität und Gesellschaft.* Hg. Charles W. Morris. Übers. v. Ulf Pacher. Frankfurt am Main: Suhrkamp, in der Rekonstruktion von Tugendhat (1993), 279f.

umfassenderen normativen Erwartungen konfrontieren (Honneth 1994: 39, 90f.). In der *Rückforderung* scheinen diese konstruktiven normativen Aspekte nur in vagen An- und Vorausdeutungen auf: So wird Julián als "Neuschöpfer der Welt" tituliert (Goytisolo 1986: 139); zur Überwindung der antidemokratischen (ebd. 131), nationalistischen (ebd. 142) und antieuropäischen (ebd. 67) Haltung Spaniens will er eine "Metamorphose" (ebd. 134) des spanischen Selbstverständnisses einleiten, die "kurieren" (ebd. 126), "befreien" (ebd. 129) und "Vorzeichen eines besseren, freieren Lebens" (ebd. 17) sein soll. Expliziter entfaltet wird Goytisolos positive Zielvorstellung in seinen politischen Äußerungen. So spricht er in den *Dissidenten* von einem "neuen, freien und unabhängigen Diskurs" (Goytisolo 1984: 244), einem "freien Ideenaustausch", der den "ideologische[n] Monolithismus", die "kulturellen Blockaden" und die "Insichversunkenheit" der Nationalkulturen destruieren und die kulturelle "Permeabilität für fremde Ideen und Strömungen" (ebd. 248f.) verbessern soll. Diese Bestimmungen erinnern an liberale postnationale Weltbürgervorstellungen, wie sie seit den späten 1980er Jahren von Jürgen Habermas, aber auch von Jacques Derrida,[6] Ulrich Beck[7] u.a. vertreten werden. Im Zentrum dieser Vorstellungen steht das kosmopolitische Individuum, dessen personale Integrität – definiert über universell gültige, auf das Individuum bezogene Grundrechte – vor willkürlichen Übergriffen der Kollektive geschützt werden soll. Habermas plädiert in diesem Zusammenhang für die Vorstellung einer "Assoziation freier und gleicher Weltbürger", die "über die Köpfe der kollektiven Völkerrechtssubjekte hinweg auf die Stellung der individuellen Rechtssubjekte" durchgreifen und auf diese Weise zugunsten individueller Autonomie die Grenzen nationaler Kollektive transzendieren soll (Habermas

---

6   Jacques Derrida (1997): *Cosmopolites de tous les pays, encore un effort!*. Paris: Éditions Galilée.
7   Vgl. dazu Andrea Albrecht (2003): "Kosmopolitismus in der Wende". *Engagierte Literatur in Wendezeiten*. Hgg. Willi Huntemann u.a. Würzburg: Königshausen & Neumann, 301–318.

1996: 210f.). Die von Goytisolo immer wieder beschworene nomadisch-autonome Außenseiterexistenz des Dissidenten führt über diese rechtsliberalen Forderungen noch hinaus. So wie Derridas Kosmopolitismusvorstellung auf die Konstituierung einer moralisch und politisch engagierten, nationale Grenzen übergreifenden Gemein-schaft der Intellektuellen zielt, die sich global für die Anerkennung diskriminierter Individuen einsetzt, nutzt auch Goytisolo seine intellektuelle Sonderrolle für die Inszenierung eines weiter gefassten Anerkennungskampfes. "Meine Leidenschaft", heißt es in den *Dissidenten*, "gehört dem nationalen Kampf der arabischen Völker" (Goytisolo 1984: 258). Die Solidarisierung mit dem vermeintlichen Feind dient nicht nur der Brüskierung Spaniens, sondern richtet sich grundsätzlich gegen alle Identitätsbildungsverfahren, die im Zeichen eines "homogenen, makellosen" (Goytisolo 1995: 11) Vaterlandes kulturelle Differenzen zu unterdrücken oder auszuschließen suchen. Goytisolos Engagement richtet sich dabei gegen islamistische Bestrebungen (Goytisolo 1994: 102) ebenso wie gegen den globalisierenden "*American way of life*" (Goytisolo 1984: 263) oder Bestrebungen der "europäische[n] Gesellschaft", ihre multiple kulturelle Herkunft aus dem "griechisch-lateinischen, hebräischen und arabischen" Kulturkreis zu leugnen (Goytisolo 1995: 15).

IV Missachtungen kollektiver Integrität

Es ist wenig überraschend, dass Goytisolos Standpunkt des dissident-nomadischen Weltbürgers für Kollektive, die wie die franquistische spanische Gesellschaft auf Abschottung und eine homogene kollektive Identitätsbildung bedacht waren, eine Provokation darstellen musste. Goytisolos Intention reicht jedoch weiter. Indem sein Roman in der imaginierten Schändung der Heiligen Grotte gipfelt (Goytisolo 1986: 156–162), rührt er an das zentrale Symbol für die auf jungfräuliche Reinheit bedachte Integrität Spaniens und inszeniert auf diese Weise eine metaphorische Vergewaltigung und Entwürdigung des nationalen Kollektivs. So wie die Integrität des Individuums nach Honneth vom Kollektiv oder einem anderen Individuum durch einen Vergewaltigungs-, Entrechtungs- oder Entwürdigungsakt missachtet werden kann, wird in Goytisolos literarischer Phantasie ein Kollektiv von einem seiner Mitglieder *vergewaltigt*, d.h. in seiner Integrität massiv verletzt. Durch die Schändung der Symbole provoziert der Autor eine Reaktion der missachteten Gemeinschaft – ein Vorgang, zu dessen Beschreibung man in Analogie zur Vorstellung personaler Integrität eine Vorstellung kollektiver Integrität benötigt.

Die spanische Rezeptionsgeschichte Goytisolos zeigt, dass Spanien seine Texte in der Tat temporär als Missachtung und Verletzung interpretierte und den Autor entsprechend negativ sanktionierte.[8] Der Fall Goytisolo gibt damit Anlass zu einer grundsätzlicher gestellten Frage: Unter welchen Bedingungen lässt sich von einem Konzept kollektiver Integrität analog zum Konzept personaler Integrität sprechen? Inwiefern und von wem kann die Integrität eines Kollektivs verletzt werden? Welchen Anspruch auf Anerkennung ihrer Unverletzlichkeit können Gruppen erheben und auf welche (völker)rechtlichen und kulturellen Integritätsstandards können sie sich dabei berufen? Drei Fälle der Integritätsverletzung eines Kollektivs lassen sich unterscheiden: *Erstens* kann die Integrität eines Kollektivs durch ein anderes, nicht zugehöriges Kollektiv missachtet und verletzt werden. In der rechtlichen Kodifikation begründet das moderne Völkerrecht[9] einen legitimen Anspruch auf die territoriale und politische Unverletzlichkeit eines Staates gegenüber einem anderen. In Goytisolos Roman wird eine Verletzung dieser Art zum Agens der Handlung,

---

8   Erst in den späten 1970er Jahren, also nach Francos Tod, reüssierte Goytisolo auch in Spanien zu einem anerkannten Autor. Vgl. Randolph D. Pope 1995: 34ff.

9   Zur völkerrechtlichen Integrität vgl. Brigitte Daum (1999): *Grenzverletzungen und Völkerrecht: eine Untersuchung der Rechtsfolgen von Grenzverletzungen in der Staatenpraxis und Folgerungen für das Projekt der International Law Commission zur Kodifizierung des Rechts der Staatenverantwortlichkeit*. Frankfurt am Main u.a.: Peter Lang.

wenn die Verletzung der spanischen Integrität durch die Invasion arabischer Krieger ausgemalt wird. Der Kampf um Anerkennung eskaliert, wenn auch nur in der Fiktion, zu einer wieder eröffneten Konfrontation zweier wechselseitig voneinander abgegrenzter kultureller Kollektive: der Mauren und der Spanier.

Die Besonderheit von Goytisolos literarischer Fiktion liegt allerdings darin begründet, dass die Initiierung der Integritätsverletzung aus dem Kollektiv selbst hervorgeht. Als dissidentes Mitglied der spanischen Gesellschaft schließt er eine Allianz mit dem Feind Spaniens. Integritätsverletzungen eines Kollektivs können demnach *zweitens* durch zugehörige Mitglieder des Kollektivs erfolgen. Goytisolo versucht das überkommene homogene Selbstbild des franquistischen Spaniens durch ein hybrides zu ersetzen und auf diese Weise auch die imaginierte Konfrontation von Arabern und Spaniern nicht als Kulturkampf, sondern als kulturelle Ausdifferenzierung und Erweiterung zu akzentuieren. *Drittens* können kollektive Integritätsansprüche mit Integritätsansprüchen zugehöriger Teilkollektive kollidieren, etwa wenn Mehrheits- und Minderheitsinteressen einer Gruppe nicht vereinbar sind. Goytisolos Parteinahme für die marginalisierte arabisch-maurische Kultur Spaniens und die muslimische Kultur Europas, aber auch sein Kampf um die Anerkennung homosexueller Lebensweisen innerhalb einer mehrheitlich heterosexuell ausgerichteten Gesellschaft (Pope 1995: 103f.) fußen auf dem Integritätsanspruch einer im Prinzip zugehörigen, aber diskriminierten Minderheit. Wie nimmt sich unter diesen Voraussetzungen seine literarische Strategie des Anerkennungskampfes aus?

V Goytisolos Europavision. Strategien kultureller Hybridisierung.

Das franquistische Spanien hat nach der Analyse Goytisolos seine kollektive Identität durch die Behauptung einer dichotomischen Grenze zwischen arabisch-muslimischer und spanisch-katholischer Identität zu wahren gesucht, eine Grenzziehung, die sich heute im Umgang Europas mit seinen arabisch-muslimischen Minderheiten, aber auch im Umgang Europas mit der Türkei als potenziellem Mitglied der Gemeinschaft fortschreibe. Auf diese identitätspolitische Ausgrenzung reagiert Goytisolo mit einer dekonstruktiven, literarischen Kohärenzbildung: In der *Rückforderung* wird die spanische Nation, "die sich narzißtisch über sich selbst neigt" (Goytisolo 1986: 185), auf ihre im Zuge der Reconquista verdrängte, hybride Struktur hin transparent gemacht.[10] So werden die spanischen National-Mythen von Goytisolo ironisiert und umgeschrieben, und Schlüsselbegriffe der spanischen Sprache, darunter der Stierkampfruf Olé, werden auf ihre arabischen Wurzeln zurückgeführt: "das Olé!: das schöne, uralte wa-l-lah!" (Goytisolo 1986: 186).[11]

Während dieser Nachweis sprachlicher Hybridität Kohärenzen zwischen der arabisch-muslimischen und der spanisch-katholischen Welt offenbart, spielt Goytisolo an anderer Stelle in subvertierender Absicht mit der Auflösung vermeintlich unauflöslicher Identitätskomponenten: Wenn er in Gestalt des Sprachpuristen Señor Gramático die arabischen Lexeme der spanischen Sprache (und damit die arabischem Einfluss unterliegenden Speisen) zurückfordert und auf diese Weise eine karge Nationalsprache (und eine noch kärgere Speisekarte) entstehen lässt (Goytisolo 1986: 183ff.), so dient dieses ironisch-satirische Trennungsverfahren, wie das Kohärenzbildungsverfahren, der Freilegung von Überlagerungen, die die kollektive spanische Identität wie die kollektive europäische Identität durchziehen und den Anspruch auf Homogenität und Reinheit konter-

---

10 Vgl. dazu Rainer Vollath (2001): *Herkunftswelt und Heterotopien. Dekonstruktion und Konstruktion literarischer Räume im Werk Juan Goytisolos*. Frankfurt am Main u.a.: Peter Lang, 75–110.
11 Vgl. zur Funktion des "olé" Horst Turk (1992): "Übersetzung ohne Kommentar. Kulturelle Schlüsselbegriffe und kontroverser Kulturbegriff am Beispiel von Goytisolos *Reivindicación del Conde don Julián*". *Die literarische Übersetzung als Medium der Fremderfahrung*. Hg. Fred Lönker. Berlin: Schmidt, 3–40, hier: 26ff.

karieren. Goytisolo veranlasst seine Leser, in der palimpsestuösen literarischen Imagination Konfrontationen und Infragestellungen vermeintlich festgeschriebener Identitäten herbeizuführen. Die kulturelle Identität eines Kollektivs erscheint aus dieser Perspektive nicht mehr als essentialistisches, sondern als ein offenes und dynamisches Konstrukt, das im nach innen wie nach außen geführten "Kampf um Anerkennung" seine personalen wie seine kollektiven Integritätsansprüche verhandelt, sie zu stabilisieren oder zu destabilisieren sucht. Dabei kommt bei aller menschenrechtlichen Universalität gerade den kulturellen Differenzen ein besonderer Wert zu: "Kultur wird geschmiedet und gefestigt durch den Kontakt, die Vermischung verschiedener Gruppen von Menschen" (Goytisolo 1995: 12) und die "Verbindungen mit anderen Kulturen" (Goytisolo 1995: 14), heißt es in Goytisolos Essay *Der Wald der Literatur*. Auch das europäische Kollektiv hat sich als eine hybride Konstruktion zu begreifen, die sich nach Goytisolo insbesondere zur arabischen Welt ins Verhältnis zu setzen hat. Erst in der Anerkennung der kulturellen Zusammengehörigkeiten wie in der Anerkennung der unaufhebbaren kulturellen Inkongruenzen wird Europa seiner Aufgabe als "Sammelpunkt aller kulturellen Strömungen des Westens und des Ostens" (Goytisolo 1995: 12) gerecht werden können. Anders, so ist zu vermuten, wird sich die Devise der europäischen Verfassung: "In Vielfalt geeint" in ihr Gegenteil verkehren.

ZITIERTE LITERATUR

Goytisolo, Juan (1984): *Dissidenten*. Übers. v. Joachim A. Frank. Frankfurt am Main: Suhrkamp.

Goytisolo, Juan (1986): *Rückforderung des Conde don Julián*. Übers. v. Joachim A. Frank. Frankfurt am Main: Suhrkamp.

Goytisolo, Juan (1994): *Ein algerisches Tagebuch.* Übers. v. Thomas Brovot. Frankfurt am Main: Suhrkamp.

Goytisolo, Juan (1995): "Der Wald der Literatur. Wider den kulturellen Ethnozentrismus". *Exilforschung. Ein internationales Jahrbuch.* Bd. 13: Kulturtransfer im Exil, 11–15.

Habermas, Jürgen (1996): Die *Einbeziehung des Anderen. Studien zur politischen Theorie.* Frankfurt am Main: Suhrkamp.

Honneth, Axel (1990): "Integrität und Mißachtung". *Merkur* 44.501, 1043–1054.

Honneth, Axel (1994): *Kampf um Anerkennung. Zur moralischen Grammatik sozialer Konflikte.* Frankfurt am Main: Suhrkamp.

Pope, Randolph D. (1995): *Understanding Juan Goytisolo.* Columbia: Columbia Univ. Press.

Rivero Salavert, Nicolás (1983): *Geschichte und Gesellschaft Spaniens im Werk Juan Goytisolos.* Bamberg: Diss. Masch.

Tugendhat, Ernst (1993): *Selbstbewußtsein und Selbstbestimmung. Sprachanalytische Interpretationen.* 5. Aufl. Frankfurt am Main: Suhrkamp.

Vollath, Rainer (2001): *Herkunftswelt und Heterotopien. Dekonstruktion und Konstruktion literarischer Räume im Werk Juan Goytisolos.* Frankfurt am Main u.a.: Peter Lang.

KORA BAUMBACH

Supplementäre Anerkennung:
Zu Uwe Timms Roman *Morenga*

Im Zentrum von Uwe Timms Roman *Morenga* (1978) steht eine Episode, die sich als eine symbolische Manifestation wechselseitiger Anerkennung (Honneth 1994: 177f.) interpretieren lässt: Nach einem auf Nama geführten "Gespräch" zwischen Gottschalk, dem in Gefangenschaft geratenen Oberveterinär der deutschen Schutztruppe, und Morenga, dem Anführer der aufständischen Nama, kommt es zu einem Handschlag der beiden Männer, obwohl Morenga vor dem Gespräch diese Geste des Tierarztes noch ignoriert hatte. "Aufgefallen sei ihm nichts Wichtiges", gibt ein Mitgefangener zu Protokoll,

> wenn man einmal davon absähe, daß der Oberveterinär, als er zu Morenga geführt wurde, diesem die Hand hingestreckt habe, die dieser einfach übersehen habe [...]. Zum Abschied habe Morenga dem Veterinär die Hand gereicht (Timm 2000: 397f.).

Timm präsentiert diese Episode aus unterschiedlichen Figurenperspektiven: Die Beschreibung durch den Mitgefangenen wird durch einen von Gottschalk verfassten und von einem Militär mit empörten Randglossen versehenen "Bericht an das Kommando der Kaiserlichen Schutztruppe" (Timm 2000: 392ff.) und durch eine private Rechtfertigung Gottschalks gegenüber Pater Meisel ergänzt (Timm 2000: 418ff.). Für den Leser wirft das exzeptionelle Ereignis und seine Darstellung sowohl innerhalb des Romangeschehens als auch im Kontext der politischen Wirkungsabsicht des Romans Fragen zur personalen und kollektiven Integrität auf: Was führt zu der Geste wechselseitiger Anerkennung, und warum bleibt sie folgenlos? Auf welchen Integritätsstandards basiert die Verständigung und welche

Bedeutung kommt ihr im Hinblick auf die von Timm eingeforderte Aufarbeitung der deutschen Kolonialgeschichte zu? Seinem dokumentarisch-aufklärerischen Erzählinteresse entsprechend,[1] richtet der Autor den Fokus auf das Missverhältnis zwischen europäisch-abendländischer Moral und kolonialistischer Ideologie und Praxis und fragt insbesondere nach dem Verhältnis von individueller Verantwortung und Mittäterschaft. *Morenga* ist in dieser Hinsicht, dies ist die These der folgenden Ausführungen, als eine *supplementary question*[2] zu werten, die ihr Provokationspotential im geschichts- und gesellschaftskritischen bundesrepublikanischen Diskurs der 1970er Jahre entfaltet.

I Irritationen und Verunsicherungen. Gottschalks "Verkafferung"

Der aus militärischer Perspektive verdächtige Handschlag bildet für den Protagonisten Gottschalk den positiven Abschluss eines Desillusionierungsprozesses, der ihn sukzessive von seiner Truppe entfernt und dem "Feind" (Timm 2000: 29), den Nama, näher gebracht hat. Umso erstaunlicher ist es, dass er nicht ernsthaft an Desertion denkt.[3] Im Anschluss an die Begegnung mit Morenga fasst er nur den "Entschluß", sein "Abschiedsgesuch" (Timm 2000: 420) einzureichen, um kurz darauf Afrika zu verlassen. In welche Situation hat Uwe Timm seinen Protagonisten konkret gebracht, und wie hat er ihn für diese Situation ausgestattet? Welche moralische oder auch politische Verbindlichkeit hat für ihn die Loyalität gegenüber der Schutz-

---

1 Vgl. z.B. Göttsche 2003: 266, Hermand 1995: 52, oder Streese 1991: 67.
2 *Supplementary question* im Sinne von Bhabha 2000: 230ff. und Derrida 1974: 250. Vgl. dazu die Ausführungen am Ende dieses Artikels.
3 Gottschalk hat die "fixe Idee [...], abzuhauen", vgl. Timm 2000: 419. Vgl. auch 265: "Er dachte, man müsse zu denen überlaufen [...]".

truppe? Als Veterinär hat er bis zu einem gewissen Grad eine Sonderstellung, den daraus resultierenden Spielraum nutzt Gottschalk allerdings nur privat. Er ist durch seine charakterlichen und habituellen Dispositionen eher als "mittlerer Held"[4] konzipiert und auch in seiner akademischen Ausbildung von nur durchschnittlicher Statur. Seine mimetische Lernfähigkeit (Timm 2000: 23f.) hält ihn in der Abhängigkeit von Autoritäten und lässt ihn als einen noch ungefestigten Charakter erscheinen, bei dem der Akzent primär auf dem sinnlichen alltagsästhetischen Erfahren und Erleben liegt. Er ist ein sensibler "Träumer" (Timm 2000: 22, 159, 334 passim), der sich ohne patriotische, heroische oder kolonialistische Ambition in der naiven Erwartung zur Schutztruppe gemeldet hat, in Afrika als einer neuen Heimat eine biedermeierliche Idylle aufbauen zu können (Timm 2000: 21f.). Timm geht es um die Entlarvung dieser Erwartungshaltung, die sich in bedenklicher Nähe zur Kolonialpropaganda und zu den Kolonialromanen der Zeit bewegt.[5] Der Erzähler wirbt allerdings zugleich durch eine breite biographische Motivierung um Verständnis für die Dispositionen seines Protagonisten (Timm 2000: 23–27). Zwar ist Gottschalk in seiner Mentalität und Identität nicht eben gut auf die Konfrontation mit der Realität des Kolonialismus vorbereitet, er verfügt aber – und das lässt ihn zu einer partiellen Identifikationsfigur werden – über eine Sensibilität und Offenheit, die es ihm ermöglicht, einen moralischen Erkenntnisprozess zu vollziehen.

So folgen seiner ersten Empörung über das Vorgehen der Schutztruppe, die für ihre vorgebliche Zivilisationsarbeit überflüssige Opfer auf Seiten der indigenen Bevölkerung programmatisch in Kauf nimmt, zaghafte Versuche, über konkrete Eingaben (Timm 2000: 28f.) deren Verhalten zu korrigieren und zu humanisieren. Allerdings muss Gottschalk zur Kenntnis nehmen, dass diese Versuche teils aufgrund seiner marginalen Position innerhalb der militärischen Hierarchie, teils

---

4 Göttsche 2003: 268. Vgl. auch Streese 1991: 89, Hermand 1995: 58f., oder Horn 1995: 106.
5 Vgl. dazu Fiedler s.a., sowie Streese 1991: 82, 84.

aufgrund der praktizierten wilhelminischen Ideologie keine Aussicht auf Erfolg haben.

Auf einer zweiten Stufe strebt er daher eine Verbesserung der Lage im begrenzten Rahmen seiner Profession als Veterinär an, indem er beginnt, Konzepte der "gegenseitige[n] Hilfe" (Timm 2000: 172),[6] beispielsweise die Einrichtung einer tierärztliche Fakultät, zu entwerfen (Timm 2000: 171). Doch auch diesen Versuch lässt der Erzähler ins Leere laufen: Ein solcher Plan kann unter den gegebenen politisch-militärischen Umständen nicht gelingen und wäre auch insofern problematisch, als er mit dem asymmetrischen Konzept der Kulturmission konvergiert (Agossavi 2003: 46f.). Die kulturmissionarische Problematik wird an Gottschalks Äußerung deutlich, wenn er die Intellektualität auf Seiten der Europäer und die Gefühlsstärke auf Seiten der Nama verortet und damit ein evolutionistisches Denkmuster über die Gesellschaftsentwicklung[7] bestätigt.

Temporär bemüht er sich trotz der polarisierten Lage auf einer dritten Stufe um eine Alternative, indem er sich erotisch durch eine Liebesbeziehung[8] zu dem Namamädchen Katharina und kulturell durch das Erlernen der Sprache dem fremden Kollektiv zuwendet, was aus der Sicht des Militärs Anzeichen für eine beginnende 'Verkafferung' aufweist. Aus der anerkennungstheoretischen Sicht Axel Honneths hingegen konstituiert die Liebe eine Interaktionssphäre, in der sich das Subjekt seiner personalen Integrität bewusst

---

6 Auch wenn Kropotkin sich mit der gegenseitigen Hilfe zwischen Angehörigen derselben Gruppe und nicht mit der Hilfe zwischen Menschen verschiedener Zugehörigkeiten beschäftigt, lässt Gottschalk sich von dem Kropotkin'schen Ausblick in dessen Schlusswort anregen: In der Übertragung des Prinzips der gegenseitigen Hilfe auf die gesamte Menschheit liege "die beste Bürgschaft für eine noch stolzere Entwicklung des Menschengeschlechts" (Kropotkin 1910: 275).
7 Vgl. Raum, 1998: 247–272. So schreibt Sabine Wilke, dieser Plan baue "auch in dieser harmlosen Form auf einem Hierarchiemodell" und auf der "Höherwertigkeit der Kultur, die vermittelt werden soll", auf (Wilke 2001: 349).
8 Zu den Liebesbeziehungen bzw. der "erotische[n] Spannung" zwischen Europäern und Afrikanern vgl. Fabian 2001: 114–123.

werden und sich durch die Erfahrung des Liebens und "Geliebtwerdens" der "intersubjektive[n] Anerkennung" (Honneth 1994: 64) vergewissern kann.[9] Bei Gottschalk stellt sich jedoch anlässlich eines Besuchs bei Katharinas Familie das "[b]eklemmende" Gefühl "einer unüberwindbaren Ferne" (Timm 2000: 332) ein, das ihn die Beziehung abrupt abrechen lässt. Anders als im Honneth'schen Konzept entwickelt sich auf Gottschalks Seite kein "Vertrauen", dass "das Andere", Katharina, "für" ihn sei (Honneth 1994: 63). Gottschalk überblendet seine Liebeserfahrung immer wieder auf geradezu zwanghafte Weise mit den obszönen Äußerungen seiner Kameraden (Timm 2000: 25, 253f.). Sein romantisches Liebeskonzept[10] scheitert, die Liebe erweist sich unter den asymmetrischen militärischen und gesellschaftlichen Bedingungen als kein geeigneter Rahmen für die Wahrnehmung von Wechselseitigkeit.

Stattdessen gewinnt an dieser Stelle der Aspekt kultureller Differenz an Bedeutung. Aus Sicht des Militärs ist die Distanz zwischen Europäern und Afrikanern zur Stabilisierung des Feindbildes[11] nötig und uneingeschränkt zu wahren. In den Augen der Truppe stellt sich Gottschalks "[S]ympathisiere[n]" (Timm 2000: 369) mit den Eingeborenen daher als ein schleichender Prozess der Identitätspreisgabe und Desintegration dar (Timm 2000: 170). Für den Leser kündigt sich hingegen verdeckt bereits das erste Nebenthema

---

9 Eine alternative Einschätzung der Liebesbeziehung lässt sich mit Fabian treffen, dessen Kolonialismusstudien zufolge Beziehungen zu einer Eingeborenen zwar auch "auf die Befriedigung sexueller Bedürfnisse" abgestellt waren, aber vor allem als soziale Beziehungen "unentbehrlich waren" (Fabian 2001: 118). Timm differenziert jedoch deutlich zwischen den üblichen Beziehungen des Militärs und Gottschalks romantischer Beziehung zu Katharina.

10 Niklas Luhmann, *Liebe als Passion. Zur Codierung von Intimität*. 5. Aufl. Frankfurt am Main: Suhrkamp, 1999.

11 Michael Jeismann, *Das Vaterland der Feinde. Studien zum nationalen Feindbegriff und Selbstverständnis in Deutschland und Frankreich 1792–1918*. Stuttgart: Klett-Cotta, 1992.

zur Desertion, die Versuchung des *going native*, an.[12] Gottschalk vernachlässigt sein Äußeres, beugt sich nur mit zunehmendem Widerwillen der militärischen Disziplin und wagt einmal sogar den offenen Widerspruch, was ihm den Ruf der "Renitenz" (Timm 2000: 271) einträgt. Er gerät schließlich in eine "Identitätskrise", die Timm im Rückgriff auf das topische Metaphernarsenal als "Riß" zwischen Denken und Handeln, zwischen Person und Rolle schildert:

> Zwischen dem, was er tat, und dem, was er dachte, war ein Riß. Zuweilen hatte er das Gefühl, als sei der, der da ritt, die Sporen gab, Befehle erteilte, Treiber kontrollierte, ein anderer als der, der alles betrachtete und überdachte. Was ihn beruhigte, was die beiden Teile seines Selbst verband, war der Gedanke, daß ihm momentan nichts anderes zu tun übrigblieb als dieses: seine Pflicht. Aber dann dachte er wieder daran, daß er mithalf, den Kreislauf von Gewalt und Terror fortzusetzen (Timm 2000: 273).

Dies ist die unentscheidbare, dilemmatische Situation, in der Timm es zur eingangs zitierten Begegnung zwischen Gottschalk und Morenga kommen lässt. Im Hinblick auf Gottschalks instabile psychische Lage und im Rahmen der Auseinandersetzung mit der deutschen Kolonialgeschichte bildet die Episode den narrativen Höhepunkt des Romans. Und auch im Hinblick auf die zur Verhandlung stehenden Integritätsstandards erweist sich die Episode als Schlüsselstelle.

---

12 Das Konzept des *going native* bezeichnet eine Grenzüberschreitung und den Übertritt des Forschers in die Kultur der Indigenen und wird deshalb in der Ethnologie seit den Anfängen der Feldforschung im 19. Jahrhundert als Verlust der Wissenschaftlichkeit und somit als Gefahr aufgefasst, da es "the apparent loss of validity, integrity, criticality, necessary distance, formality, and, ultimately, reputation" bedeutet (Fuller 1999: 226). Die Grenzübertretung wird deshalb als "wissenschaftliches Tabu" aufgefasst, "dessen Überschreitung eine 'übernatürliche' Bestrafung nach sich zieht, den Ausschluss ex cathedra aus der scientific community" (Lindner 1988: 101). Vgl. dazu auch Kora Baumbach, "Literarisches *going native*: Zu Uwe Timms Roman *Morenga*". *„(Un-)erfüllte Wirklichkeit". Neue Studien zu Uwe Timms Werk.* Hgg. Frank Finlay, Ingo Cornils, Königshausen und Neumann, 2006.

II Das "Gespräch". Identifikation durch den Gegner

Moralphilosophisch liegt die Pointe der Timm'schen Konstruktion darin, dass Gottschalk erst nach der Identifikation *durch* den anderen (Morenga) zu einer Identifikation *mit* den anderen (den Nama) geführt wird. Die durch Morenga erzeugte Fremdidentifikation kehrt die Asymmetrie zwischen dem Europäer und dem Afrikaner um, lässt sie dadurch für den Europäer aber erst recht unaufhebbar werden. So ist es nicht Gottschalk, der gemäß seiner moralischen Einsichten handelt, sondern Morenga. In Gottschalks Bericht über sein Gespräch mit dem Anführer der Nama heißt es:

> Auf meine Frage, ob er glaube, gegen das mächtige Deutsche Reich gewinnen zu können, sagte er nur: Nein. [...] Morenga betonte aber auch, daß er bis zum letzten Mann weiterkämpfen werde. Und auf meine Frage, warum, gab er die verwunderliche Antwort: Damit *ihr* und *wir* Menschen bleiben können. (Randbemerkung: Eingeborenenlogik!) (Timm 2000: 394f.).

Auf Seiten der Nama geht es, in der Terminologie Honneths, um einen "Kampf auf Leben und Tod," dem deswegen ein "ausgezeichneter Stellenwert" zukommt, weil er "diejenige Erfahrungsstufe im individuellen Bildungsprozeß" markiere, "durch die die Subjekte sich endgültig als mit 'Rechten' ausgestattete Personen zu begreifen" lernten (Honneth 1994: 79f.). Die Bereitschaft, im Kampf um Anerkennung sein Leben einzusetzen, drücke aus, dass "das Ganze" der Person auf dem Spiel stehe (Honneth 1994: 41). Nach Honneth führt die damit manifestierte "Vorwegnahme der Endlichkeit des Anderen" den Beteiligten "jene existentielle Gemeinsamkeit" vor Augen, "auf deren Basis sich beide Subjekte reziprok als verletzbare und bedrohte Wesen zu betrachten lernen" (Honneth 1994: 81).

Tatsächlich begegnet Gottschalk in Morenga kein Opfer, sondern ein selbstbewusster Kämpfer, der nicht nur *behauptet*, für seine Integrität bis "zum letzten Mann" weiterzukämpfen, sondern dies in der Folge auch *tut*. Obwohl die Aufständischen aus der Perspektive des deutschen Militärs rechtlose Rebellen sind, respektiert Gottschalk in Morenga den Krieger und versucht, diesem Respekt in ritualisierter Form Ausdruck zu geben: Er reicht dem Nama zur Begrüßung die Hand, was dem militärischen Ehrenkodex entspricht, aus der Perspektive der preußischen Truppe in diesem Fall aber unangemessen ist. Denn zwischen regulären und irregulären Einheiten darf es keine wie auch immer manifestierte Anerkennung geben. Wenn Morenga Gottschalks Begrüßungsgeste ignoriert, sich also so verhält, als gehöre er einer regulären und Gottschalk einer irregulären Einheit an, muss diese Umkehr der Vorzeichen dem preußischen Militär als eine "unglaubliche Unverschämtheit" (Timm 2000: 397) erscheinen.

Die eigentliche Provokation im "Gespräch" geht jedoch von der "verwunderlichen" Begründung aus, in der der moralphilosophische Aspekt der Begegnung deutlich wird, denn es stellt sich die Frage, wieso Morenga der Auffassung sein kann, durch die Fortsetzung des Kampfes im Namen des Menschseins – die fremde und die eigene Bezugsgruppe einschließend – zu handeln. Er imaginiert offensichtlich aus der Position des militärisch Unterlegenen eine alternative oder zukünftige Gemeinschaft, die die real "vorgefundene Gemeinschaft überstimmt" (Mead 1973: 210), um den gegebenen Rahmen des normierenden Systems zu überschreiten, da "die rigiden Normen seiner sozialen Umwelt" (Honneth 1994: 133)[13] unter den Bedingungen des Kolonialismus dies erforderlich werden lassen. Damit erweist er sich als der moralisch Überlegene.

Der Satz, den der Militär mit der "Randbemerkung: Eingeborenenlogik!" versieht und somit empört zurückweist, leitet bei Gottschalk die entscheidende Wende ein: Er erkennt nicht nur die Asymmetrie, sondern erkennt sie auch an, indem er im Anschluss an das Zusammentreffen sein Entlassungsgesuch einreicht und so sein Handeln erstmals konsequent an seinen moralischen Normen orientiert. Er hat einsehen müssen, dass sich der bis dahin als selbstverständlich angenommene Superioritätsanspruch der Weißen nicht nur in rechtlicher, sondern auch in moralischer Hinsicht

---

13 Vgl. dazu Mead 1973: 243. Vgl. zur Mead'schen Theorie der Selbstbehauptung auch den Beitrag von Andrea Albrecht in diesem Band.

umgekehrt hat. Während Gottschalk schon vor dem Zusammentreffen mit Morenga klar war, dass die Nama um ihr Überleben als Menschen kämpfen, hat ihn Morengas Begründung darüber belehrt, dass im Völkermord an den Nama auch das Überleben der Deutschen als (zivilisierte) Menschen auf dem Spiel steht.

Eine den Frontwechsel einschließende Solidarisierung gelingt Gottschalk jedoch nicht, obwohl sie nach der Einsicht in die moralische Überlegenheit der Nama und nach der mit dem Handschlag vollzogenen Anerkennung eigentlich nahe gelegen hätte. Gottschalk aber kehrt zur Truppe zurück und rechtfertigt sein Verhalten später gegenüber Pater Meisel durch eine Erfahrung, die er während des Festes nach seiner Gefangennahme gemacht habe:

> Gegen Abend habe das große Fest begonnen. [...] Er, Gottschalk, habe zunächst nur den Takt mitgeklatscht. Dann aber habe er sich dazu hinreißen lassen mitzutanzen. Einen Moment habe er versucht, die Bewegungen Morengas nachzuahmen [...]. Aber es wollte ihm nicht gelingen. [...] Und noch während er versuchte zu tanzen, und trotz seines dunen Kopfes, war ihm klar, daß er nicht würde bleiben können. Diese Menschen waren ihm nah und doch zugleich so unendlich fern (Timm 2000: 419f.).

Am Ende verhindert die sinnliche und körperliche Dimension des Kulturkontakts Gottschalks Überwechseln ins Nama-Kollektiv. Die ideelle und reflexive Solidarisierung mit den Aufständischen fällt ihm nach dem Gespräch mit Morenga nicht schwer, der physische Frontwechsel unter den fremdkulturellen Bedingungen aber gelingt nicht. Die "moralische Grammatik sozialer Konflikte" (Honneth) folgt unter den Bedingungen der literarischen Fiktion nicht allein idealen normativen Standards. Timm jedenfalls scheint hier einem Realismus interkultureller Begegnung verpflichtet zu sein, der idealisierende Lösungen ausschließt. Seine Figuren sind vielmehr mit unwägbaren, reflexiv nicht auflösbaren Faktoren wie auch mit habitualisierten Mustern kultureller Vorprägung konfrontiert, die sich nicht umstandslos verflüssigen lassen.

So bleibt Gottschalk am Ende nur der melancholisch-resignative Rückzug in die Utopie: Timm lässt seinen Protagonisten seinem

Integritätsproblem in einem Fesselballon entschweben (Timm 2000: 442ff.). Dieser surreale Abgang trägt allerdings auch dem Umstand Rechnung, dass es im Rahmen der deutschen Kolonialgeschichte zu keiner progressiven Erweiterung der sozialen Integritätsstandards gekommen ist. Uwe Timms Roman ist aus dieser Perspektive als die fiktionale Umsetzung einer *supplementary question* zu lesen.

III Supplementary Questions

In Homi K. Bhabhas politischer Deutung des Derrida'schen Konzepts des Supplements[14] wird dieses zu einer von der Ordnung legitimierten "Strategie der Einmischung" (Bhabha 2000: 231) aufgewertet: *Supplementary questions* können demnach, obwohl und weil sie Teil der Ordnung sind, die Ordnung selbst zur Disposition stellen. Im Hinblick auf die Verhandlung von Integritätsstandards können *supplementary questions* dann einen Effekt haben, wenn Integritätsverletzungen aus einer marginalen Position heraus auf der Basis noch nicht etablierter Standards oder in Ausweitung auf noch nicht anerkannte Felder anzuprangern sind, die Verhandlung jedoch nur auf dem Boden bereits anerkannter Standards und im Rahmen der herrschenden Ordnung eröffnet werden kann.

Timm lässt in der literarischen Fiktion Morenga dieser Strategie folgen, wenn der Nama-Führer erstens den militärischen Ehrenkodex für sich reklamiert und damit gegen eben diesen Ehrenkodex verstößt

---

14 Die Doppelbedeutung von lt. *supplere* (ergänzen und ersetzen) aktualisierend, verbindet Derrida im Konzept *supplementärer* Rede zwei Tendenzen: Ein Supplement ist nicht selbstständig, sondern bezeichnet zum einen etwas Hinzugefügtes, Ergänzendes, zum anderen bildet das Supplement einen Ersatz, es "gesellt sich nur bei, um zu ersetzen. Es kommt hinzu oder setzt sich unmerklich *an-(die)-Stelle-von*; wenn es auffüllt, dann so, wie man eine Leere auffüllt" (Derrida 1974: 250).

und zweitens moralische Standards in Anspruch nimmt, die die Europäer zwar als universale Standards ausgeben, den "Kaffern" (Timm 2000: 74) aber rassistisch vorenthalten. Diese supplementäre "Einmischung" wird durch den militärischen Kommentator, selbst wiederum supplementär, negativ sanktioniert. Beide im Text ausgebrachten Supplementierungen verfolgen die "Strategie" der ergänzenden Ersetzung des Vorhergehenden, einmal aus der Position des moralisch Über- und politisch Unterlegenen: Morenga, einmal aus der Position des moralisch Unter- und politisch Überlegenen: dem Militär. Der Erfolg oder Misserfolg der Supplementierungen bemisst sich nach Bhabha danach, ob die legitimierende Ordnung korrodiert, modifiziert oder im Anwendungsbereich erweitert werden kann. Da sich Timm mit seinem Roman an die historischen Fakten hält, kann der Effekt nicht im Rahmen der Diegese erzielt werden. Die supplementäre Rede Morengas richtet sich vielmehr an den Leser, der weiß, dass der subversive Impuls im Rahmen der deutschen Kolonialgeschichte ausgeblieben ist. Diesem Leser wird vorgeführt, dass er sich seiner moralischen Gleichstellung nicht durch eine einseitige Solidarisierung mit den Opfern versichern kann, sondern er auf die Anerkennung durch die Opfer angewiesen ist. Damit zielt Timms Roman auf die Aufdeckung von Schuldverkettungen (Durzak 1995: 322), die durch das Selbstbild des Deutschen als des vermeintlich besseren Kolonisators im deutschen Kolonialismus- und Imperialismusdiskurs verdrängt wurden und – sieht man von der im Jahr 2004 ergangenen offiziellen Entschuldigung für den Völkermord an den Nama ab[15] – bis heute fortdauern.

15. Die Entschuldigung von deutscher Seite erfolgte durch die Ministerin Wieczorek-Zeul (vgl. Susanne Bittorf, "Wieczorek-Zeul entschuldigt sich bei Herero für Gräueltaten", *Süddeutsche Zeitung* 16.8.2004). Die mangelnde Auseinandersetzung mit der deutschen Kolonialvergangenheit ist im Zuge des hundertsten Jahrestages des Nama- und Herero-Aufstandes in der deutschen Presse einhellig bemängelt worden (vgl. z.B. Bartholomäus Grill, "Aufräumen, aufhängen, niederknallen!" *Die Zeit* 5.8.2004; Jürgen Zimmerer, "Keine Geiseln der Geschichte", *die tageszeitung* 10./11.1.2004; Jochen Bölsche, "Die Peitsche des Bändigers", *Spiegel* 12.1.2004, 102–109, oder auch Steffen Richter, "In der

Zitierte Literatur

Agossavi, Simplice (2003): *Fremdhermeneutik in der zeitgenössischen deutschen Literatur: An Beispielen von Uwe Timm, Gerhard Polt, Urs Widmer, Sibylle Knauss, Wolfgang Lange und Hans Christoph Buch*. Sankt Ingbert: Röhrig.

Bhabha, Homi K. (2000): *Die Verortung der Kultur*. Übers. v. Michael Schiffmann, Jürgen Freudl. Tübingen: Stauffenburg.

Derrida, Jacques (1974): *Grammatologie*. Übers. v. Hans-Jörg Rheinberger. Frankfurt am Main: Suhrkamp.

Durzak, Manfred (1995): "Die Position des Autors. Ein Werkstattgespräch mit Uwe Timm". *Die Archäologie der Wünsche: Studien zum Werk von Uwe Timm*. Hgg. Manfred Durzak, Hartmut Steinecke. Köln: Kiepenheuer und Witsch, 311–344.

Fabian, Johannes (2001): *Im Tropenfieber. Wissenschaft und Wahn in der Erforschung Zentralafrikas*. Übers. v. Martin Pfeiffer. München: Beck.

Fiedler, Matthias (s.a.): *Zwischen Abenteuer, Wissenschaft und Kolonialismus*. Phil. Diss. unveröffentlicht.

Fuller, Duncan (1999): "Part of the action, or 'going native'? Learning to cope with the 'politics of integration'". *Area* 31.3, 221–227.

Göttsche, Dirk (2003): "Der neue historische Afrika-Roman: Kolonialismus aus postkolonialer Sicht". *German Life and Letters* 56.3, 261–280.

Hermand, Jost (1995): "Afrika den Afrikanern! Timms 'Morenga'". *Die Archäologie der Wünsche: Studien zum Werk von Uwe Timm*. Hgg.

Wüste, wo das 20. Jahrhundert begann", *Frankfurter Allgemeine Zeitung* 3.2.2004).

Manfred Durzak, Hartmut Steinecke. Köln: Kiepenheuer und Witsch, 47–63.

Honneth, Axel (1994): *Kampf um Anerkennung. Zur moralischen Grammatik sozialer Konflikte*. Frankfurt am Main: Suhrkamp.

Horn, Peter (1995): "Über die Schwierigkeit, einen Standpunkt einzunehmen. Zu Uwe Timms 'Morenga'". *Die Archäologie der Wünsche: Studien zum Werk von Uwe Timm*. Hgg. Manfred Durzak, Hartmut Steinecke. Köln: Kiepenheuer und Witsch, 93–118.

Jeismann, Michael (1992): *Das Vaterland der Feinde. Studien zum nationalen Feindbegriff und Selbstverständnis in Deutschland und Frankreich 1792–1918*. Stuttgart: Klett-Cotta.

Kropotkin, Peter (1910): *Gegenseitige Hilfe in der Tier- und Menschenwelt*. Hg. und übers. v. Gustav Landauer. Leipzig: Verlag von Theod. Thomas.

Lindner, Rolf (1988): "Wer wird Ethnograph? Biographische Aspekte der Feldforschung". *Kulturkontakt – Kulturkonflikt. Zur Erfahrung des Fremden*. Hgg. Ina-Maria Greverus, Konrad Köstlin, Heinz Schilling, Bd. 1. Frankfurt am Main: Institut für Kulturanthropologie und Europäische Ethnologie, 99–107.

Luhmann, Niklas (1999): *Liebe als Passion. Zur Codierung von Intimität*. 5. Aufl. Frankfurt am Main: Suhrkamp.

Mead, George Herbert (1973): *Geist, Identität und Gesellschaft aus der Sicht des Sozialbehaviorismus*. Hg. Charles W. Morris. Übers. v. Ulf Pacher. Frankfurt am Main: Suhrkamp.

Raum, Johannes W. (1998): *Evolutionismus. Ethnologie. Einführung und Überblick*. Hg. Hans Fischer. 4. Aufl. Berlin, Hamburg: Reimer.

Streese, Konstanze (1991): *"Cric?"–"Crac?" Vier literarische Versuche, mit dem Kolonialismus umzugehen*. Bern: Lang.

Timm, Uwe (2000): *Morenga*. München: Deutscher Taschenbuchverlag.

Wilke, Sabine (2001): "'Hätte er bleiben wollen, er hätte anders denken und fühlen lernen müssen': Afrika geschildert aus der Sicht der Weißen in Uwe Timms 'Morenga'". *Monatshefte für deutschsprachige Literatur und Kultur* 93.3, 335–354.

ZAAL ANDRONIKASHVILI

Kollektive Integrität als Integrationshindernis. Aluda im Spiegel von Muzal

Die Integritätstheorie Axel Honneths (Honneth 2003) geht von einem Modell aus, das auf moderne Demokratien zugeschnitten ist (Taylor 2004: 20). Daher mögen die Texte, die ich zur Illustration des dilemmatischen Verhältnisses zwischen Integrität und Integration ausgewählt habe, auf den ersten Blick befremdlich erscheinen. Wascha-Pschawelas *Aluda Keltelauri* (1888), ein kanonischer Text der georgischen Literatur, handelt von einem Konflikt zwischen christlichen und moslemischen Stämmen des Kaukasus, und auch die postmoderne Bearbeitung des Sujets im deutschsprachigen Roman *Muzal* (1991) von Giwi Margwelaschwili, die unter anderem als eine Parabel der Dissidenzbewegung in der UdSSR gelesen werden kann, hält sich politisch im Rahmen eines vor- und außerstaatlichen Kommunitarismus. Nun wird aber in der politischen Philosophie des Kommunitarismus ebenfalls auf vormoderne bzw. nichtstaatliche Gemeinschaftsformen zurückgegriffen (Walzer 1993), die ihre Integrität behaupten – mit dem erklärten Ziel, das erforderliche Maß an Gemeinschaftlichkeit in den heutigen Gesellschaften auszuleuchten. Deswegen glaube ich nicht anachronistisch zu verfahren, wenn ich im Folgenden die sozialen und nicht die politischen Aspekte der kollektiven Integrität in den Vordergrund stelle. Am Beispiel von *Aluda Ketelauri* möchte ich das exklusionistische Integritätsmodell eines Kollektivs illustrieren, das in der Bearbeitung von Giwi Margwelaschwili in ein inklusionistisches "Anerkennungsmodell" umgewandelt wird. Die postmoderne Transformation verlagert zugleich den Akzent von einer statischen Ordnung, für die Integrität im Sinn der Unverletzlichkeit beansprucht wird, auf die Integration als Prozess.

I Kollektive Integrität

Unter welchen Bedingungen kann ein Kollektiv als integer im Sinne eines begründeten Anspruchs auf seine Unverletzlichkeit bezeichnet werden? Innerhalb der Liberalismus/Kommunitarismus-Debatte wird diese Frage aus zwei ontologisch gegensätzlichen, entweder atomistischen oder holistischen Positionen vorgenommen (Taylor 1993: 116): Der Kommunitarismus stellt die Sicherung kollektiver Identitäten (Taylor 1997), der Liberalismus das Recht auf gleiche individuelle Freiheit (Habermas 1997; Taylor 1993: 116) bzw. die Sicherung personaler Integrität in rechtlicher Hinsicht in den Vordergrund. Bei der Definition des Kollektivs greift der holistische Ansatz auf den Begriff der Gemeinschaft zurück (Zahlmann 1992: 10). Für die Begründung des Anspruches auf Unverletzlichkeit hat dies den Wert, dass aus kommunitaristischer Perspektive die soziale Integration von Gesellschaften nur dann "angemessen" vor sich geht, "wenn deren Mitglieder statt nur über Rechtsbeziehungen auch durch gemeinsame Wertorientierungen aufeinander bezogen sind" (Honneth 1992: 20). Aus dieser Position kann die liberale (individualistische) Gesellschaft als "das genaue Gegenteil von Gemeinschaft" (Walzer 1993: 161) erscheinen, als eine Gemeinschaft von "Fremden" (Rorty 1988: 96). Dagegen sind die Subjekte aus holistischer Sicht in "konstitutive Gemeinschaften" eingebettet (Sandel 1982: 172), so dass "die Identität jedes Einzelnen mit der des Kollektivs untrennbar verbunden oder gar in ihr aufgehoben ist" (Forst 1993: 184). Unter dieser Voraussetzung könne das Kollektiv als ein "wider subject", als ein "Ganzes" verstanden werden, das die Form "konstitutiver Gemeinschaften" wie "family or tribe or city or class or nation or people" annimmt (Sandel 1982: 172; Forst 1993: 184) und als solches einen Anspruch auf seine Unverletzlichkeit erhebt. Der "Einzelne" hat sich dem Ganzen, d.h. dem Kollektiv und seinen identitätsbildenden Lebensformen und Traditionen ein- und gegebenenfalls unterzuordnen (McIntyre 1993: 87). "Partikulare Loyalitäten" (Rössler 1992: 80) dieser Art strukturieren die Welt dichotomisch in den Kategorien eigen/fremd und können in Konflikt mit der Moralität des unparteiischen Urteils aus universalistischer Perspektive geraten. Im Konfliktfall wird das "Überleben" der "besonderen Gemeinschaft" zum obersten Ziel erklärt; die Gemeinschaft fordert von ihren Mitgliedern die rückhaltlose Verteidigung ihrer Interessen, was die Bereitschaft einschließt, "für seine Gemeinschaft in den Krieg zu ziehen", auch wenn es sich etwa um einen völkerrechtswidrigen Angriffskrieg handelt (MacIntyre 1993: 88).

Im konsequent atomistisch-liberalistischen Modell beschränkt sich die Gewährleistungsfunktion des Rechts auf die Gewährleistung personaler Integrität. Dies hat neben den aus kommunitaristischer Sicht bereits angedeuteten Nachteilen auch beträchtliche Vorteile, auf die ich hier nicht weiter eingehen kann, die aber die Frage nahe legen, ob sich das kommunitaristische Interesse nicht auch auf der Basis von Gesetz und Recht – sei's auch im weiteren Sinn – statt auf der Basis von Ganzheitsvorstellungen wahrnehmen lässt. Die moderat kommunitaristische Position von Charles Taylor geht vom Gesetz und von den "Institutionen" mit ihren "Verfahren" statt von der Ganzheit des Kollektivs aus. Das Gesetz wird demnach als "Identifikationspol" und "Inbegriff der zentralen Institutionen und Verfahren des politischen Systems" interpretiert, die jedoch ihrerseits "als Gemeingut betrachtet und gepflegt" werden, weil alle Beteiligten in ihnen Quelle und Schutz ihrer Würde sehen (Taylor 2004: 19). Dieser Positionsnahme scheint nichts mehr hinzuzusetzen zu sein. Wenn ich mir gleichwohl im Folgenden erlaube, Taylors Basisannahme in einer kommunitaristisch verschärften Form zu benutzen, erfolgt dies in der heuristischen Absicht, einen theoretischen Rahmen für den Stellenwert traditionaler Gesellschaften sowie für die sich mit ihnen befassende Textinterpretation zu gewinnen. Das "Gesetz" soll dabei differenzieller ausgelegt werden: Es ist als Identifikationspol der Gesellschaft im Sinn der "Zivilgesellschaft" (Taylor 2004a: 83) sowie als Identifikationspol der gegenseitigen Anerkennung von Subjekten, Personen oder Individuen aufzufassen. Letztere sind mit bestimmten Rechten ausgestattet, jedoch nicht durch "höhere" Instanzen des politischen Systems resp. des Staates (Hegel 1969), sondern durch konkurrierende

Instanzen der Religion, der Sitte, der Tradition. Vor allem verstehe ich das Modell nicht evolutionistisch – als eine Stufe, die zur staatlichen Organisation führt –, sondern als ein Modell nichtstaatlicher Organisation (Taylor 2004a: 74, 76, 84), die zeitlich vor dem Staat, parallel zum Staat und im Staat zur Vergesellschaftung führt. Das "Gesetz" ist nach diesem Modell so zu verstehen, dass die "wechselseitigen Verpflichtungen" (Honneth 2003: 86) nicht notwendigerweise als solche artikuliert sein müssen. Man denke dabei an Formen wie Sitten, Bräuche, Konventionen und Traditionen, die das gesellschaftliche Leben organisieren und von allen Mitgliedern dieser Gesellschaft als ein organisierender Mechanismus anerkannt werden.[1]

In traditionalen Gesellschaften wird den Mitgliedern der Gesellschaft ihr "Platz" zugewiesen. Wird dieser "Platz" akzeptiert, dann ist die Integrität der Gemeinschaft nicht verletzt, auch wenn nicht "alle" (Taylor 2004: 21) an den gesellschaftlichen Prozessen im Sinne Taylors partizipieren (Taylor 2004: 14). Die Partizipationsform ist eine andere: durch die Erfüllung der Pflichten und Wahrnehmung von Rechten gemäß dem jeweiligen Platz in der Gesellschaft. Wenn in traditionalen Gesellschaften das Bewusstsein des Identifikationspols verblasst und eigens durch traditionspflegende Maßnahmen gestützt werden muss, dann hängt die überkommene Integrität der Gemeinschaft auch im nichtemanzipatorischen Sinn von der Bereitschaft und Initiative, wenn nicht aller, so doch maßgeblicher Mitglieder der Bevölkerung ab, diesen Zustand aufrechtzuerhalten. Letzteres gilt auch für moderne demokratische Gesellschaften, solange die "Institutionen und Verfahren des politischen Systems" als "Gemeingut betrachtet und gepflegt werden müssen". Die Frage wie ein "Selbst sich gegen traditionellgemeinschaftliche Selbstverständnisse wenden [kann], wenn seine Identität mit diesen auf so untrennbare Weise verbunden ist" (Forst 1993: 186), eröffnet das Spektrum eines in

---

1   Die Möglichkeit der Auslegung der Idee des Vorrangs gemeinsamer Werte gegenüber individuellen Rechten (etwa bei Sandel und MacIntyre), "so dass gemeinschaftskonstituierende Wertbindungen *an die Stelle* von Rechtsbeziehungen treten", findet sich bei Rössler 1992: 78.

dieser Konstruktion enthaltenen Konfliktpotentials, das auch in den modernen rechtsstaatlichen und demokratischen Zuständen virulent ist, sich nicht in der evolutionären Juridifikation, Etatisierung und Ökonomisierung auflöst und dem in der nachfolgenden Textanalyse – historisch und aktuell perspektiviert – meine Aufmerksamkeit gilt.

II Interne und externe Verletzung der kollektiven Integrität

Wascha-Pschawelas Gedicht *Aluda Ketelauri*[2] setzt mit der Verletzung der Integrität einer chewsurischen Gemeinde ein. Die Kunde vom Raubüberfall des benachbarten muslimischen Stammes der Kisten erreicht das Dorf Schatili. Aluda Ketelauri, der seinen persönlichen Anteil an der von den Kisten geraubten Pferdeherde hat, entscheidet, die Räuber zu bestrafen. Die Integrität des Kollektivs ist aber nicht nur durch den Besitzverlust verletzt. In seiner Analyse des hegelschen Systems der Sittlichkeit betont Axel Honneth, durch das Verbrechen der Beraubung werde ein Subjekt zunächst zwar nur in seinem Recht auf das ihm zustehende Eigentum beschnitten, dadurch aber zugleich so angegriffen, dass es als "Person" im Ganzen verletzt sei (Honneth 2003: 39, 74ff.). Die Aufgabe von Aluda besteht demnach darin, die von außen verletzte Integrität seines Kollektivs auf materieller und auf symbolischer Ebene wiederherzustellen. Er muss die Pferdeherde zurückführen und die Räuber bestrafen – ihnen das Leben nehmen und als Symbol seines Sieges die abgeschnittene rechte Hand des Gegners seinem Kollektiv vorweisen. In einem dramatischen Duell tötet Aluda den Kisten Muzal und seinen Bruder. Dem

---

2 Wascha-Pschawela, "Aluda Ketelauri". *Gesammelte Werke in zehn Bänden*. Hg. Giorgi Leonidze. Bd. 3 (Tbilissi: Sabchota Sakartvelo, 1964) 58–74. [In georgischer Sprache.] Übersetzung der zitierten Stellen von Zaal Andronikashvili.

toten Bruder Muzals schneidet er regelkonform die rechte Hand ab. Aber beeindruckt vom Mut und der Kampfes- und Lebenslust Muzals verzichtet er hier auf die konventionelle Geste, was eine Verschiebung des symbolischen Werts impliziert: Aus einem Symbol des Triumphs über den Feind in wiederhergestellter Ehre und Integrität des Kollektivs wird ein Symbol der Anerkennung des (ehemaligen) Feindes in Respektierung seiner Ehre und körperlichen Unverletzlichkeit. Zugleich aber wird Aludas Stellung innerhalb des Kollektivs nachhaltig erschüttert.

Zieht man zur Interpretation dieser Handlung Hegels rechtsphilosophischen Ausführungen zum Kampf auf Leben und Tod heran, wird deutlich, dass das beleidigte Subjekt, indem es im Kampf sein Leben aufs Spiel setzt, seinen moralischen Horizont erweitern kann (Hegel 1969: 211). Weil beide Subjekte im Kampf auf Leben und Tod jeweils "das Andre als reines Selbst gesehen" hätten, besitzen sie nach Honneth's Hegelinterpretation anschließend ein "Wissen des Willens", in das ihr Gegenüber prinzipiell als eine mit Rechten ausgestattete Person einbezogen sei (Honneth 2003: 80ff.). Der Schluss, zu dem Aluda kommt ("Töte einen Anderen, wirst du auch getötet, die Familie wird dem Mörder das Blut heimzahlen"; Wascha-Pschawela 1964: 64) enthält jedoch noch ein weiteres: Aluda rekurriert (wie Hegel) auf seine Familie. Sie agiert als ein "rächender Agent" in den Konflikten, die innerhalb des eigenen Kollektivs ausgetragen werden. Die Tötung eines Mitglieds des eigenen Kollektivs mit anderer Familienzugehörigkeit trägt aber nicht zum Ruhm bei, sondern ist eine Sünde (Wascha-Pschawela 1964: 64). Indem Aluda an Muzal in den Kategorien des Mitglieds eines eigenen Kollektivs denkt, sieht er ihn nicht mehr als einen *Anderen* an, was zur Folge hat, dass er seine Tat in der Kategorie der Sünde überdenkt. Dieser gedankliche Schritt erweitert die Grenzen des *Gleichen* und sprengt damit die des *Eigenen*, wie sie dem chewsurischen Kollektiv gezogen worden waren. Aluda erkennt Muzal als Seinesgleichen zunächst in der "imaginierten Gemeinschaft" der "Heroen" an (Mead 1972: 199),³ um ihm in einem weiteren Schritt auch die gleichen Rechte einzuräumen und ihn schließlich sogar wie einen Christen zu behandeln. Dieser Anerkennungsprozess manifestiert sich im Verlauf der Handlung anlässlich eines religiösen Fests, bei dem sich Aluda entscheidet, für den toten Muzal einen Stier zu opfern. Die Bedeutung dieser Opferhandlung versteht auch der Oberpriester: "Du machst den Ungläubigen zum Gläubigen". Ohne auf Aludas Motive einzugehen, begründet der Oberpriester seine Weigerung, das Opfer zu vollbringen, traditionell: "Die Väter haben das nicht geboten [...] Besinne dich, Du bist ein Christ, und wirst damit zum Ungläubigen" (Wascha-Pschawela 1964: 69f.). Seine Argumentation enthält zwei wichtige Punkte: Erstens verwandelt er das Argument Aludas in sein Gegenteil: Wenn Aluda durch sein Opfer den Feind zum Freund macht und damit die Grenzen des Kollektivs inkludierend erweitert, dann verfährt der Oberpriester Berdia dagegen exkludierend, indem er behauptet, durch das Opfer für den Ungläubigen schließe Aluda sich selbst aus dem chewsurischen Kollektiv aus und werde somit zum Fremden oder Feind. Zweitens rekurriert der Priester auf das durch die Tradition gewährleistete heilige Gesetz des chewsurischen Kollektivs im Sinn der religiösen Basisunterscheidung: "Wie kann ich für den Hund beten, aus dem Hundestamm, lieber falle mir der Himmel auf die Erde, die Erde soll mich verschlingen oder ich soll im Meer untergehen und den Meeressand essen" (Wascha-Pschawela 1964: 70). Die eschatologischen Metaphern bringen die Folgen der Übertretung des Gesetzes zum Ausdruck: Wird das Gesetz gebrochen, verliert es nicht nur seine soziale und lokale Geltung, sondern es geht die Welt (wie sie Berdia versteht) unter. In seiner Gegenargumentation begründet Aluda sein Recht, das Opfer zu vollbringen, lokal durch seine Zugehörigkeit zum chewsurischen Kollektiv: "Verweigere mein Opfer nicht, [...] wir sind eins Berdia, die

---

3 Der Weg Aludas unterscheidet sich aber von Meads Konzept insofern, als Aluda keine "Verwurzelung" in einer anderen, sei es auch in einer imaginierten Gemeinschaft anstrebt. Sein Weg ist der eines Einzelgängers, der ihn zur Entwurzelung führt.

Bewohner eines Berges" (Wascha-Pschawela 1964: 70). Auf die erneute Weigerung des Oberpriesters, das Opfer für den Kisten zu vollbringen, folgt der Schritt Aludas, der den Bruch mit seinem Kollektiv endgültig besiegelt: Er opfert selbst für Muzal und verstößt damit doppelt gegen das "Gesetz". Er usurpiert die Zuständigkeit des Oberpriesters und er opfert für den "Ungläubigen". Um die Tat Aludas zu interpretieren, kann man erneut auf Hegel zurückgreifen. In der Jenaer Realphilosophie heißt es:

> Seine [des Verbrechers – Z.A.] innere Rechtfertigung ist, der Zwang, das Entgegenstellen seines einzelnen Willens zur Macht, zum Gelten, zum Anerkanntsein. Er will etwas sein (wie Herostrat), nicht gerade berühmt, sondern dass er seinen Willen zum Trotz dem allgemeinen Willen ausgeführt hat (Hegel 1969: 224).

In seiner anerkennungstheoretischen Interpretation vertritt Honneth die Meinung, durch das Mittel der provozierenden Handlung versuche ein Subjekt entweder den einzelnen Anderen oder die vereinigten Vielen dazu zu bewegen, das durch die sozialen Verkehrsformen jeweils noch nicht Anerkannte der eigenen Erwartungshaltungen zu respektieren (Honneth 2003: 89). Durch seine Tat versucht Aluda zweierlei zum Ausdruck zu bringen: einerseits seinen Willen zur Durchsetzung seiner Vorstellungen in der Auslegung des Gesetzes oder Rechts, andererseits seinen Anspruch auf die Partizipation an den zentralen Aktivitäten des Kollektivs. Folgt man Honneth, dann sind zwei "Lernschritte" in Anschlag zu bringen, mit denen die "vereinigten Rechtssubjekte auf die Provokation des Verbrechens zu reagieren hätten": einerseits den "Gewinn an Kontextsensibilität in der Anwendung von Rechtsnormen", andererseits die "Erweiterung der Rechtsnormen um die Dimension der materiellen Chancengleichheit" (Honneth 2003: 91f.). Für unseren Fall käme der erste "Lernschritt" in Frage, wenn das chewsurische Kollektiv sich darauf einlassen würde, Aludas Auslegung der Rechtsnormen zu akzeptieren, und bereit wäre, den "moralischen Horizont" zu erweitern. Der Oberpriester Berdia und die Chewsuren nehmen die Tat Aludas aber so, wie Berdia bereits angekündigt hat. Durch das Verbrechen sieht das chewsurische

Kollektiv seine Integrität von innen gefährdet. Sie aktivieren den repressiven Apparat, um die kosmische wie die soziale Ordnung, die ihrer Ansicht nach durch Aludas Verbrechen verletzt wurde, wiederherzustellen. Aluda wird die Usurpation der Rechte des Priesters und das Opfer für den Ungläubigen angelastet und ausgeschlossen. Das Verhalten des chewsurischen Kollektivs und das Kollektiv selbst möchte ich als homöostatisch bezeichnen. Auf gesellschaftliche Verhältnisse übertragen, bedeutet Homöostase, dass die Erhaltung eines bestimmten Zustandes angestrebt wird und Abweichungen ausreguliert werden. Als Zustand wird hier das in "unwandelbare[r] Dauer" (Assmann 1983: 79f.) genommene, durch Gesetz und Tradition geheiligte Überleben einer Gemeinschaft bezeichnet. Wegen des religiösen Ursprungs des Gesetzes und der Traditionen ist der Verstoß als Sakrileg und als Störung der kosmischen Ordnung aufzufassen. Um sein sakralisiertes Überleben zu sichern, reagiert ein homöostatisches Kollektiv auf die Verletzung der Integrität entweder so, dass es seine Mitglieder, die gegen das Gesetz verstoßen, zum Gehorsam zwingt, oder so, dass es sie aus dem Kollektiv ausschließt. Die starke Homogenität eines solchen Kollektivs ist unter anderem durch die Intoleranz gegenüber dem nicht gesetz- und traditionskonformen Denken gewährleistet. Die Erweiterung des moralischen Horizonts ist für ein homöostatisches Kollektiv nicht möglich.

III Überwindung der kollektiven Desintegrität

Giwi Margwelaschwilis postmoderne Bearbeitung des Aluda-Sujets in seinem Roman *Muzal*, der als dissidente Auseinandersetzung mit der UdSSR gelesen werden kann, ist nicht auf die Erweiterung einer zu eng gefassten kollektiven Integrität, sondern auf die Überwindung einer kollektiven Desintegrität gerichtet. Sein Erzählkonzept, das die Handlung des *Aluda Ketelauri*-Gedichts in den Rahmen der Buch-metapher (als postmoderne Chiffre für die literarische Reflexion) verlegt, verfährt allerdings parabolisch statt realistisch. Von zentraler Bedeutung ist dabei die Metapher der Aufführung: Durch die Verlagerung der Geschichte in die "Buchwelt", wird der ontologische Status des Geschehens verändert. Jedes mal, wenn *Aluda Ketelauri* gelesen wird, müssen die "Buchpersonen" zur "Vorstellung" antreten und das Sujet "aufführen". Wenn das Buch nicht gelesen wird, führen sie ihr eigenes Leben. Die Buchpersonen sind "unsterblich":

> Der Tod [...] ist kein absolutes Verschwinden, sondern ein verborgenes Dableiben der Buchperson in ihrem jeweiligen Gedicht- oder Geschichtsgebiet, eine Form von getarnter Bereitschaft für die nächste thematische Runde: für die nächste Buchöffnung durch einen neuen realen Leserkopf. Mit dem Buchschluss [...] schlägt [...] die große Stunde der Wiederauferstehung (Margwelaschwili 1991: 18f.).

Die Gemeinschaft der Buchpersonen basiert anders als in der Realwelt nicht (oder nicht nur) auf der Blutsverwandtschaft, sondern hat "immer ein Thema zur Grundlage" (Margwelaschwili 1991: 7, in diesem Fall das "Thema" des *Aluda Ketelauri*). Das Thema wird in der Buchwelt auch "Themi" genannt. Durch die Verknüpfung des "Themas" mit dem "Themi" (ein georgisches Wort, das "Gemeinde" bedeutet) betont Margwelaschwili die Bedeutung des (durch Integration) identitätsstiftenden Mechanismus: Die Gemeinschaft ist nicht nur formal basiert, sondern sie wird auch vom "Thema" zusammengehalten. Wenn die Gemeinschaft zunächst mit Walzer als "eine Heimstatt für Zusammenhaltung, Bindung und Erzählvermögen" (Walzer 1993: 161) zu verstehen ist, dann verkehrt sich das Verhältnis im chewsurischen "Themi", das beispielhaft für die traditionalistische Gemeinschaft stehen kann, indem nicht der Text von der Gemeinschaft, sondern die Gemeinschaft von dem Text *erzeugt* und zusammengehalten wird. Der Text ("Thema") verbindet die Gemeinschaft mit der Ewigkeit, sichert ihre Identität und schützt sie vor dem Wandel. Der Text kann in diesem Fall, wie im "Themi", zum "Gesetz" werden und muss dann nicht nur gelesen, sondern auch gelebt und aufgeführt werden. Die Gleichsetzung von "Thema" und

"Themi" nach diesem Modell sakralisiert die Buchgemeinschaft: Das "Thema" ist "allen heilig"; [...] "[n]iemand würde jemals wagen, dagegen zu verstoßen oder es beispielsweise zu ignorieren" (Margwelaschwili 1991: 11).

Die Handlung des Buches setzt etwa 100 Jahre nach dem Erscheinen des *Aluda Ketelauri* (1888) ein, als das Thema nach Auskunft des Erzählers bereits zu devalvieren beginnt. Das Buch wird immer seltener geöffnet und die Buchpersonen geraten immer mehr aus dem "Thema oder Themi". Das auf dem "Thema" basierte "Themi" muss zunächst durch mnemotechnische, später aber auch durch repressive Maßnahmen der Diskurspolizei (Foucault 1977)[4] zusammengehalten werden.

> Was wir machen müssen, das wissen wir, weil es leichter zu behalten ist, immer noch ganz gut, was wir aber sagen müssen, besonders der genaue thematische Wortlaut, das kommt uns in unserem immer länger geschlossen bleibenden Buch allmählich aus dem Sinn (Margwelaschwili 1991: 12).

Die Ziegenhirten (Diskurspolizisten) verteilen zu diesem Zweck Spickzettel mit dem thematischen Wortlaut. Aus diesen Spickzetteln, die auf Holzklötze geklebt werden, wird ein Spiel: "Thomino"; ein Worthybrid aus Themi und Domino. Die Klötzchen müssen zusammengestellt werden, und als Sieger wird derjenige anerkannt, "dem es durch geschicktes Ausspielen der Klötzchen gelingt, den ganzen Text in irgendeiner seiner Äußerungen im Themi wortgetreu aufzubauen" (Margwelaschwili 1991: 13).

Die Anerkennungskämpfe, in deren Zentrum der von Aluda getötete Kiste Muzal – der Icherzähler des Romans – steht, werden auf drei hierarchisch geordneten ontologischen Ebenen, des Spiels (Thomino), der Gesellschaft (Themi) und der (aus der Buchweltperspektive) metaphysischen Ebene der Leser ("Realköpfe"), ausgetragen. Mit Muzal ist der "Fremde" im chewsurischen Themi von Anfang an präsent. Muzal, der "einem nach Rasse, Sprache und

---

4   "[W]ir müssen es hier mit einer Art von geheimer, über unser gesamtes Themi eingesetzter, Wachmannschaft zu tun haben" (Margwelaschwili 1991: 12).

Religion völlig verschiedenen Bergstamm" angehört, ist im "Themi" ein missachteter Außenseiter, ein Fremder:

> Niemand würde [...] einen Fremden wie mir irgendwelche große Bedeutung zumessen [...] Viele steinalte Buchpersonen im unserem Gebiet können es auch bis heute noch nicht verdauen, dass ich mit zu ihrem Themi gehöre [...] (Margwelaschwili 1991: 16).

Es ist aber nicht das Themi, sondern Muzal, der trotz seiner Marginalisierung durch das Themi ein integraler Bestandteil des Themas und sogar, wie er glaubt, die wichtigste Buchperson ist und als solcher die Initiative ergreift. Der Weg der Revolte und der Gewaltanwendung scheint für Muzal ausgeschlossen zu sein. Weil er glaubt, der reale Gedanke sei viel verderblicher als eine Bombe (Margwelaschwili 1991: 139), sieht er eine Möglichkeit, seinen Status im Themi zu verändern, darin, die realen "unthematischen" Gedanken über Innovationen im Thomino in das Themi hineinzuschmuggeln. Das Thominospiel, eine Widerspiegelung des Themis, wird zu einer Reflexionsebene, auf der die Zusammenhänge im Themi erkannt werden können. Auch Muzal wird sich seiner Rolle im Themi erst über das Thomino bewusst:

> Ich übertreibe nicht, wenn ich sage, dass die meisten Klötzchen sich ihrem Text nach entweder direkt [...] oder indirekt auf mich beziehen, dass jeder größere Einsatz [...] mit mir zusammenhängt [...] und folglich ohne mich [...] kein Thomino und zweifellos auch gar kein Themi zustande käme (Margwelaschwili 1991: 15).

Muzal, dem es um seine "Anerkennung" im engeren und um die Anerkennung des Fremden im weiteren Sinn im "Themi" und "Thomino" geht, führt neue Spielbegriffe ein, die nicht nur für das "Thomino", sondern auch für das "Themi" wichtige Folgen haben: "Schisch" (Das Handabschneiden) und "Händedruck", die zunächst "keinerlei Entsprechungen im Themi haben" (Margwelaschwili 1991: 21), werden zu den zentralen, die Verhältnisse im "Themi" erklärenden und strukturierenden Metaphern. Die Gestaltungsfreiheit im Spiel stellt Muzal dem kanonischen Starrsinn des "Themas" gegenüber. Die alternativen Entwürfe des "Themas" (und damit auch des "Themis") können zunächst auf der Spielebene ausprobiert werden. Das Spiel wird damit zum Polygon der Innovationen. Mit der Auflockerung der thematischen Zusammenhänge auf der Spielebene durch die "unbegrenzten Kombinationsmöglichkeiten der Klötzchen im Thomino" erlangen die Mitglieder des "Themi" eine Interpretationsfreiheit, allerdings zunächst auf der Spielebene. "Es [das Thomino – Z.A.] bekam, einmal von allen seinen eintönigen Richtlinien befreit, den neuen faszinierenden Sinn der Erlösung aller leidenden Buchpersonen, [...] also den Sinn der geschichtlichen Verbesserung dieser Personen" (Margwelaschwili 1991: 141). Durch sein Umschreibprojekt stellt Muzal aber nicht nur die Spielregeln im "Thomino", sondern auch das "Thema" und somit auch das "Themi" in Frage. Neue Spielregeln verändern die Verhältnisse im "Themi" insofern, als die Erkenntnisse, die man im Spiel gewinnt, auf das "Themi" übertragen werden. So wird Thomino, das anfänglich als ein mnemotechnisches Instrument für die Stärkung des Themis und Themas diente, von Muzal unter günstigen Voraussetzungen der Differenzierung von Thema und Themi zunächst unter dem Primat des Themas, dann in bewusster Traditionspflege von Seiten des Themis, schließlich im daraus hervorgehenden freien Thomino-Spiel subvertiert und in sein Gegenteil verwandelt.

IV Kollektive Integrität als Faktor oder Hindernis der Integration?

Der Sinnverlust des Themas in seiner Eigenschaft als identitätsstiftender und integritätsverbürgender Mechanismus führt dazu, dass die Mitglieder in Margwelaschwilis Kollektivs es nicht mehr rational nachvollziehen und folglich auch nicht mittragen können. Diese Entfremdung führt zu einem Verlust der kollektiven Identität. Damit verschwindet aber zugleich auch die "Stelle", die den Anspruch auf Unverletzlichkeit erheben kann. Wenn wir die Erhaltung als das Ziel einer Gemeinschaft akzeptieren (MacIntyre 1993; Taylor 1997), dann können wir anhand der Texte von Wascha-Pschawela und Giwi Margwelaschwili zwei strategische Modelle zur Erreichung dieses Ziels rekonstruieren. Das erste (homöostatische) Modell strebt das Bestehen der Gemeinschaft in unwandelbarer Dauer an. Das Gesetz (Brauch, Sitte) resp. das Thema, das von religiöser Wertigkeit ist, schmiedet die Mitglieder des Kollektivs zu einer "Ganzheit" zusammen. Es fordert von ihnen Gehorsam und unreflektierte Affirmation. Dieses Gesetz ist der einzige Identitätspol für die Mitglieder wie für den Zusammenhalt der Gemeinschaft. Es begründet den kollektiven wie den individuellen Integritätsanspruch. Wenn Verstöße dagegen nach innen allein durch Sanktionen und Ausschließungen, also durch eine restaurative *restitutio in integrum*, geahndet werden, ohne die verändernde Kraft des Verbrechens im Sinn Honneths zu nutzen, dann entfällt die Möglichkeit, Fremdes oder auch nur anderes zu integrieren, aber auch die Möglichkeit, sich in Fremdes oder Anderes zu integrieren.

Im zweiten (transformatorischen) Modell wird das Gesetz desakralisiert. Der Anspruch auf Integrität wird nicht mehr aus dem Gesetz, sondern aus der freien, den gesellschaftlichen Zusammenhalt konstituierenden Entscheidung der Mitglieder des Kollektivs begründet, die das Gesetz debattieren und verändern können. Die traditionelle Form (das Thema) kann nur "überleben", wenn sie für die Mitglieder der Gemeinschaft eine überzeugende Kraft behält. Die Individuen behalten die Option, alternative Entwürfe zu konstruieren, fremde Impulse zu integrieren oder auch sich in fremde Entwürfe zu integrieren (Habermas 1997: 258ff.). Das Fremde wird nicht als eine Bedrohung, sondern als Impuls zur Veränderung und – im Innen- wie im Außenverhältnis – zur progressiven *restitutio in integrum* im Honneth'schen (Honneth 2003a: 218) oder auch Habermas'schen (Habermas 1997: 7) Sinn angesehen. Muzal träumt von einer "Gemeinschaft der Fremden", einem Neben- und Miteinander der Lebensentwürfe und Narrationen, die nicht formal (und damit anders als im liberalen Konzept), sondern informell, lediglich durch den Händedruck, d.h. durch die Bereitschaft, das Fremde und das Andere in seiner Fremd- und Andersheit zu akzeptieren, organisiert ist. Die Integrität wird nach diesem Modell nicht thematisch oder durch Sujets festgeschrieben, sondern abhängig von einem "täglich zu vollziehenden Plebiszit" (Renan 1996: 35) performativ erzeugt.

Wenn Margwelaschwili in seinem Roman die beiden Modelle in eine zeitliche Relation zueinander setzt und damit für die Transformation der traditionellen, archaischen in eine freiheitliche, moderne Gesellschaft plädiert, ist nicht zuletzt die Kontroverse zwischen Kommunitaristen und Liberalisten ein Beleg dafür, dass Elemente des homöostatischen Gesellschaftsmodells nicht nur traditionelle, sondern auch moderne und demokratische Gesellschaften nach wie vor mitbestimmen. Gerade wenn sich Kollektive im Hinblick auf Nachbarkollektive relationieren und im globalen Rahmen der Weltgesellschaft zu einem Ganzen zusammenschließen wollen, werden sich die Integrationsprozesse nicht allein auf formal-rechtlichem Wege organisieren lassen, sondern auch durch Interferenzen von homöostatischen und transformatorischen Operationen bestimmt sein müssen.

ZITIERTE LITERATUR

Assmann, Jan (1983): "Das Grab als Vorschule der Literatur im alten Ägypten". *Schrift und Gedächtnis. Archäologie der literarischen Kommunikation.* Eds. Aleida und Jan Assmann, Christian Hardmeier. München: Fink, 64–94.

Forst, Reiner (1993): "Kommunitarismus und Liberalismus – Stationen einer Debatte". *Kommunitarismus. Eine Debatte über die moralischen Grundlagen der modernen Gesellschaft.* Ed. Axel Honneth. Frankfurt am Main, New York: Campus, 181–213.

Foucault, Michel (1977): *Die Ordnung des Diskurses. Inauguralvorlesung am Collège de France, 2. Dezember 1970.* Trans. Walter Seitter. Frankfurt am Main u.a.: Ullstein.

Habermas, Jürgen (1997): "Kampf um Anerkennung im demokratischen Rechtsstaat". *Einbeziehung des Anderen. Studien zur politischen Theorie.* 2. Aufl. Frankfurt am Main: Suhrkamp, 237–277.

Hegel, Georg Wilhelm Friedrich (1969): *Jenaer Realphilosophie: Vorlesungsmanuskripte zur Philosophie der Natur und des Geistes von 1805–1806.* Hamburg: Meiner.

Honneth, Axel (1992): "Individualisierung und Gemeinschaft". *Kommunitarismus in der Diskussion.* Hg. Christel Zahlmann. Berlin: Rotbuch Verlag, 16–24.

Honneth, Axel (2003): *Kampf um Anerkennung. Zur moralischen Grammatik sozialer Konflikte.* Frankfurt am Main: Suhrkamp.

Honneth, Axel (2003a): "Umverteilung als Anerkennung. Eine Erwiderung auf Nancy Fraser". *Umverteilung als Anerkennung? Eine politisch-philosophische Kontroverse.* Hgg. Nancy Fraser, Axel Honneth. Frankfurt am Main: Suhrkamp, 129–225.

MacIntyre, Alasdair (1993): "Ist Patriotismus eine Tugend?" *Kommunitarismus. Eine Debatte über die moralischen Grundlagen der modernen Gesellschaft.* Hg. Axel Honneth. Frankfurt am Main, New York: Campus, 84–103.

Margwelaschwili, Giwi (1991): *Muzal. Ein georgischer Roman.* Frankfurt am Main: Insel.

Mead, George H. (1972): *Mind, Self, and Society. From the Standpoint of a Social Behaviourist.* Chicago, London: The University of Chicago Press.

Renan, Ernest (1996): *Was ist eine Nation? Rede am 11. März 1882 an der Sorbonne* mit einem Essay von Walter Euchner. Hamburg: Rowohlt.

Rorty, Richard (1988): "Der Vorrang der Demokratie vor der Philosophie". *Solidarität oder Objektivität? Drei philosophische Essays.* Trans. Joachim Schulte. Stuttgart: Reclam.

Rössler, Beate (1992): "Gemeinschaft und Freiheit. Zum problematischen Verhältnis von Feminismus und Kommunitarismus". *Kommunitarismus in der Diskussion.* Hg. Christel Zahlmann. Berlin: Rotbuch Verlag, 74–86.

Sandel, Michael J. (1982): *Liberalism and the Limits of Justice.* Cambridge: University Press.

Taylor, Charles (1993): "Aneinander Vorbei: Die Debatte zwischen Liberalismus und Kommunitarismus". *Kommunitarismus. Eine Debatte über die moralischen Grundlagen der modernen Gesellschaft.* Hg. Axel Honneth. Frankfurt am Main, New York: Campus, 103–131.

Taylor, Charles (1997): *Multikulturalismus und die Politik der Anerkennung.* Frankfurt am Main: Fischer.

Taylor, Charles (2004): "Wieviel Gemeinschaft braucht die Demokratie". *Wieviel Gemeinschaft braucht die Demokratie? Aufsätze zur politischen Philosophie.* Frankfurt am Main: Suhrkamp, 11–30.

Taylor, Charles (2004a): "Die Beschwörung der Civil Society". *Wieviel Gemeinschaft braucht die Demokratie? Aufsätze zur politischen Philosophie.* Frankfurt am Main: Suhrkamp, 64–93.

Walzer, Michael (1993): "Die kommunitaristische Kritik am Liberalismus". *Kommunitarismus. Eine Debatte über die moralischen Grundlagen der modernen Gesellschaft.* Hg. Axel Honneth. Frankfurt am Main, New York: Campus, 157–181.

Wascha-Pschawela (1964): *Aluda Ketelauri.* Gesammelte Werke in zehn Bänden. Hg. Giorgi Leonidze. Bd. 3. Tbilissi: Sabchota Sakartvelo, 58–74.

Zahlmann, Christel (1992): "Vorwort". *Kommunitarismus in der Diskussion*. Hg. Christel Zahlmann. Berlin: Rotbuch Verlag, 7–16.

MATTHIAS BEILEIN

Auf diesem Markt ist Österreich.
Doron Rabinovicis *Ohnehin*

Vor annähernd zwanzig Jahren konstatierte Karl-Michael Brunner, dass Identität der "Inflationsbegriff Nr. 1" geworden sei, gut zehn Jahre später erklärte Hans-Ulrich Wehler Identität zum "Modewort par excellence" (Brunner 1987: 63; Wehler 1998: 130). Seitdem ist der Identitätsbegriff in keine Krise geraten, sondern behauptet sich gleichermaßen in ernst zu nehmenden wie in überflüssigen Diskussionen um das soziale Sein von Individuen oder Kollektiven. Sobald von Identität die Rede ist, ist indes die Krise nicht weit, besonders dann nicht, wenn es sich um so fragile und hybride Konstrukte wie nationale Identitäten handelt. Gerade in Bezug auf die Fragwürdigkeit überkommener Selbstdefinitionen stößt der Begriff "Identitätskrise" jedoch schnell an die Grenzen seines Erklärungspotentials. Wenn etwa die Münchner Politologin Susanne Frölich-Steffen in ihrer jüngst erschienenen Dissertation über *Die österreichische Identität im Wandel* die Diskussionen, die sich anlässlich der so genannten Waldheim-Affäre entwickelten, als "Identitätskrise" bezeichnet (Frölich-Steffen 1993: 129), so verdeckt der Begriff mehr als er enthüllt. Der Streit um Gründungsmythen und Geschichtsbilder, der – eine Fülle an Publikationen um das "Jubiläumsjahr" 2005 zeigt dies[1] – noch lange

---

1 Exemplarisch sei einerseits auf die hitzige Debatte um Robert Menasses Artikel über den Ständestaat (*Warum der Februar nicht vergehen will*, Menasse 2005) hingewiesen, die Österreichs Medien monatelang beschäftigte, andererseits auf das vom österreichischen Bundeskanzleramt herausgegebene *Lesebuch zum Jubiläumsjahr* (St. Pölten/Salzburg: Residenz, 2005), in dem Wolfgang Schüssel haarscharf daran vorbei manövriert, Österreich noch einmal zum ersten Opfer der Nationalsozialisten zu erklären (vgl. ebd., S. 55).

nicht beendet ist, hat die kollektive Identität vom "Land ohne Eigenschaften" (Menasse) ganz ohne jeden Zweifel zur Debatte gestellt, aber induzieren Diskussionen unweigerlich ein Krisenbewusstsein? Sind sie nicht vielmehr ein Indiz dafür, dass gerade diese Debatte die Notwendigkeit der Modifizierung des österreichischen Selbstverständnisses deutlich gemacht hat? Lösen Modifizierungen stets ein Krisenbewusstsein aus?

Selbst in einem Staat, der bis weit in die 1990er Jahre von der konfliktminimierenden sozialpartnerschaftlichen Verhandlungspraxis geprägt war, haben Verhandlungen über die kollektive Identität nicht die Identität des Landes an sich bedroht. In Verbindung mit den geographischen und politischen Veränderungen in Europa seit 1989 veränderte sich aber vor allem das Debattenfeld, in dem die kollektive Identität Österreichs nach wie vor ein zentrales Thema ist. Erheblichen Anteil an diesen Diskussionen hatten die österreichischen Intellektuellen, darunter vor allem eine Generation jüngerer Schriftsteller, die die Debatten um die österreichische Identität nutzen konnten, um sich im literarischen Feld zu positionieren (Beilein 2003). In nichtfiktionalen (Feijóo 2002) wie in fiktionalen Texten hat eine Gruppe meist jüngerer Autoren dafür gesorgt, dass die vermeintliche Identitätskrise Österreichs, die nichts anderes ist als eine Diskursivierung von jahrzehntelang Verdrängtem, in der Öffentlichkeit präsent bleibt. Im Folgenden soll am Beispiel von Doron Rabinovicis Roman *Ohnehin* gezeigt werden, wie die österreichische Gegenwartsliteratur dabei den "symbolischen Kampf um Anerkennung, um Zugang zu einem sozial anerkannten Sein" (Bourdieu 2001: 310),[2] zu einem der zentralen Themen innerhalb der Verhandlungen über die österreichische Identität macht.

Der 1961 in Tel Aviv geborene österreichische Schriftsteller Doron Rabinovici debütierte 1994 mit dem Erzählungsband *Papirnik*,

---

2   Siehe ferner Axel Honneth, *Kampf um Anerkennung. Zur moralischen Grammatik sozialer Konflikte*, Frankfurt am Main: Suhrkamp, 1994. Zur Einführung in die Terminologie von Honneth siehe Wolfgang Ranke (2005): "Integrität und Anerkennung bei Axel Honneth". *Monatshefte* 97, No.2, 168–183.

dem 1997 und 2004 die Romane *Suche nach M.* und *Ohnehin* folgten. Während die beiden erstgenannten Bände das Problem der Integritätsverletzung vornehmlich am Beispiel von Figuren zeigen, die der Zweiten Generation jüdischer Österreicher angehören, erweitert er diesen Topos in *Ohnehin* um weitere kulturelle Minderheiten, die in den "Vorstellungen anderer Landsleute, wie ein echter Österreicher auszusehen hatte" (Rabinovici 2004: 157), eine marginale oder gar keine Rolle spielen. In keinem anderen Text der zeitgenössischen Literatur begegnet einem ein Österreich, das so kosmopolitisch und polyglott wäre wie der Freundes- und Bekanntenkreis um die Hauptfigur Stefan Sandtner: Lew Feininger, dessen Eltern von Moskau erst nach Tel Aviv, dann nach Wien übersiedelten, Patrique Mutabo, Sohn eines kongolesischen Diplomaten, Flora Dema, eine Filmemacherin aus dem Kosovo, und ihr Freund Goran Bošković, ein serbischer Deserteur, der Shoah-Überlebende Paul Guttmann aus der Bukowina, der als displaced person in Wien geblieben war und dort ein erfolgreicher Geschäftsmann wurde. Selbst Sophie Wiesen, die einzige gebürtige Wienerin in Sandtners Freundes- und Bekanntenkreis, ist mit ihrer "Sehnsucht nach Urbanität und Moderne, nach New York und London" (Rabinovici 2004: 20) ganz Kosmopolitin: Sie hatte in Wien das Lycée française besucht.

Wie ernst es Rabinovici um die internationale Herkunft seiner Figuren ist, zeigt sich noch an Nebenfiguren, die der Text nur erwähnt, ohne dass sie für die Romanhandlung von Bedeutung wären: Florentina Rosales, eine Sängerin aus Rio, Roberto Klauber, ein Chemiker aus São Paulo, Beatrice, eine Künstlerin aus Kolumbien, und ein namenlos bleibender Schweizer Cineast sind Statisten der transitorischen "Nicht-Orte" (Augé 1994), der transnationalen Schauplätze, auf denen sich zu einem großen Teil die Handlung abspielt: Kaffeehäuser, Restaurants und vor allem der Wiener Naschmarkt. In Rabinovicis Roman wird der Naschmarkt zum global village:

> Im Fenster eines orientalischen Händlers sah er [Stefan Sandtner, M.B] Hunderte Gewürzsäckchen [...]. Er ging vorbei an japanischen Sushibuden, an chinesischen Delis, an einem marokkanischen Restaurant, einem indischen, einem persischen, türkischen, an einem Espresso und einer italienischen Pizze-

ria. Vor dem Wiener Gastwirt und dem Würstelstand ekelte ihn an diesem Augustmorgen [...] (Rabinovici 2004: 17).

Der überstaatliche Charakter dieses Ortes beschränkt sich dabei durchaus nicht aufs Kulinarische, sondern findet seine Entsprechung in den dort arbeitenden Menschen. Dem Leser begegnen polnische und slowakische Marktangestellte, der georgische Händler Mosche Dawaraschwili, die türkischen Obst- und Gemüseverkäufer Mehmet und Yelda Ertekin und die aus Zypern stammende griechische Marktfamilie Alexandrus, die nach und nach dem Personenensemble hinzugefügt werden. Auf dem Naschmarkt hat der Internationalismus Tradition: "In dieser Gegend war bereits seit Jahrhunderten nicht bloß deutsch, sondern ebenso italienisch, jiddisch, griechisch, türkisch, tschechisch, serbisch oder polnisch gesprochen worden [...]" (Rabinovici 2004: 178).

Diese Vielfalt kollidiert auf der Ebene der Schauplätze mit der Wohnung des ehemaligen SS-Offiziers Herbert Kerber, der, durch eine pathologische Gedächtnisstörung hilflos geworden, das Haus nicht mehr verlassen kann. Der Kontrast wird noch dadurch verstärkt, dass sich im Verlauf des Romans dieser Ort in den Schauplatz der privaten Tribunale zwischen Kerber und seiner Tochter Bärbl verwandelt (Rabinovici 2004: 130ff.). Es wäre freilich falsch, den durch diesen Kontrast noch freundlicher wirkenden Markt als die multikulturelle Vision eines unproblematischen *anderen* Österreichs zu deuten. Dies wird schon dadurch verhindert, dass der Roman eine klare Grenze zwischen Wien und einer Terra Incognita der Provinz zieht. *Ohnehin* ist in diesem Sinne kein österreichischer, sondern ein Wiener Roman. Wie schon in Robert Schindels *Gebürtig* (Schindel 1992: 118ff.)[3] fühlen sich die Protagonisten in *Ohnehin* "irgendwie verlo-

---

3   Schindel, der von sich selbst sagt, dass ihm "die österreichische Provinz unheimlich ist" (Kaindlstorfer, Günther (1992): "Auf Wiederschaun, Herr Schindel". *Falter*, 32/1992) hat auch in seinem lyrischen Werk diese Dichotomie zur Sprache gebracht, vgl. das Gedicht *Vineta 1*: "Dies Wien liegt dennoch nicht im Österreiche / Und wer noch glaubt, dass diese Stadt, die herzensbleiche / Dem Land der Hauptsitz ist vom schroffen Alpenbunker / Der soll vom

ren", sobald sie "die Grenzen Wiens" überschreiten und "die österreichische Provinz" betreten" (Rabinovici 2004: 94). Die Stadt-Land-Dichotomie des österreichischen Anti-Heimat-Romans wird hier fortgeschrieben, mit dem Unterschied freilich, dass sich die Handlung von der Peripherie ins Zentrum verlagert. Damit ist nicht gesagt, dass Wien die Insel der Glückseligkeit einer multikulturellen Urbanität wäre. Selbst wenn "auf der Wienzeile" sich "alle Landsmannschaften" (Rabinovici 2004: 182) vermengen und der Naschmarkt für manche der dort Arbeitenden zur "eigentliche[n] Heimat" wird (Rabinovici 2004: 162): Die Vorstellung vom friedlichen Nebeneinander der Kulturen ist letztlich ein "Klischee", das "Trugbild einer Stadt", nicht mehr als "ein idyllisches Bild [...] von bunter Vielfalt und froher Harmonie" (Rabinovici 2004: 178). Rabinovicis Naschmarkt in *Ohnehin* ist nur scheinbar ein Locus amoenus des kulturellen Pluralismus. Weder auf dem Naschmarkt[4] noch im Wien jenseits der Wienzeile bleibt "das Andere" des "homo austriacus" (Wodak 1998: 121ff.)[5] von der alltäglichen Missachtung in Wien unbedroht, was gleichermaßen kulturelle Minderheiten wie Grenzgänger hybrider Identitätsentwürfe trifft. Der Roman zeigt einerseits das multikulturelle Panorama der österreichischen Hauptstadt, führt aber gleichzeitig ein ganzes Spektrum unterschiedlicher Formen der "Herabwürdigung von individuellen oder kollektiven Lebens-

---

Transalpinen kommen da herunter / Möge uns geben den Devisenklunker / Und in der Hofburg riechen Östreichs beste Leiche" (Schindel 2004: 295).

4 Vgl. den hier nicht thematisierten Konflikt zwischen der türkischen Familie Ertekin und der griechischen Familie Alexandrus.

5 Laut dieser Autorin dominiert in den Selbstbildern der Österreicher die Vorstellung einer "naturwüchsige[n] Abstammung", die selbst dann "einem Nativismus verhaftetet bleibt", wenn sie gelegentlich "im Kleid einer multikulturellen Deszendenztheorie" auftritt (Wodak 1998: 485). "Ethnische Minderheiten finden [...] im österreichischen Selbstverständnis der nur deutschsprachigen Mehrheitsbevölkerung so gut wie keinen Platz. Außer von den Minderheitenangehörigen selbst werden sie kaum wahrgenommen. [...] Die Multikulturalität ist nur als historisch verklärte wichtig (Vielvölkerstaat, 'Völkergemisch')" (Wodak 1998: 489f.).

weisen" vor (Honneth 1994: 217), die dem Aufbau kollektiver hybrider Identitäten oder einem multikulturellen Pluralismus in Wien entgegenstehen. Rabinovici belässt es nicht dabei, die Missachtungen aufzuzeigen, sondern beschreibt ebenso den "Kampf um Anerkennung" der Missachteten, die Versuche, ihre personale Integrität zu restituieren bzw. abzusichern. Patrique Mutabo, der seit seiner Kindheit in dem Bewusstsein lebt, in Österreich seiner Hautfarbe wegen "stigmatisiert" (Rabinovici 2004: 157) zu sein (Goffman 1994), wehrt sich gegen die Versuche, auf sein Anderssein festgeschrieben zu werden. Er sei kein Ausländer, sagt er zu Theo Alexandrus, sondern "ein Österreicher. Ein echter. Ein waschechter" (Rabinovici 2004: 163), womit er das politische Schlagwort vom "echten Österreicher", das spätestens seit Kreiskys Kandidatur für das Bundeskanzleramt antisemitisch und rassistisch aufgeladen ist (Rabinovici 2001: 146ff.), dekonstruiert. Weil er zweisprachig aufgewachsen ist, hat Mutabo ein besonderes Sensorium für die deutsche Sprache entwickelt. Er weiß genau, "was auf gut deutsch gemeint ist", wenn im Alltag auf Redewendungen zurückgegriffen wird, die auf rassistischen Stereotypen basieren, und setzt sich "im heimischen Tonfall" (Rabinovici 2004: 158) dagegen zur Wehr. Rabinovici illustriert an dieser Figur außerdem, dass die gesellschaftliche Missachtung von kulturellen Minderheiten auch dann eine Gefahr ist, wenn in Primärbeziehungen diese Ressentiments nicht geteilt werden. Stefan Sandtner ist mit Patrique Mutabo befreundet, hat aber die an sich harmlose charakterliche Schwäche, zu Verabredungen immer zu spät zu kommen. So unbedeutend es für andere sein mag, an einem transitorischen Nicht-Ort wie dem U-Bahn-Aufgang am Wiener Resselpark eine Zeitlang auf einen Freund zu warten, so bedeutend ist es für jemanden, der wegen seiner Hautfarbe als Stigmatisierter gilt. "Es gehe hier, sagte Patrique, einmal nicht um Stefans Neurosen. Er möge gefälligst auf seine Situation in dieser Stadt Rücksicht nehmen" (Rabinovici 2004: 156f.). Hält sich ein Schwarzafrikaner für längere Zeit dort auf, so verliert dieser Platz seinen Charakter als Nicht-Ort: Der Resselpark wird dann "Zentrum der Drogen und ein Ort einschlägiger Polizeiübergriffe" (Rabinovici

2004: 156), wobei Dunkelhäutige besonders an diesem Ort unter dem Generalverdacht stehen, Drogendealer zu sein (Misik / Rabinovici 2000). Wie schon in *Suche nach M.* macht Rabinovici auch in *Ohnehin* die Integrität der österreichischen Juden zu einem der wichtigsten Themen. In seinem ersten Roman zeigte er (Beilein 2005), wie die Verletzung der personalen Integrität "die Identität der ganzen Person zum Einsturz bringen kann" (Honneth 1994: 213). Dabei waren seine beiden Protagonisten jedoch nicht unmittelbar antisemitischen Angriffen ausgesetzt, vielmehr verlief der Erkenntnisprozess über die Solidarisierung mit anderen missachteten Minoritäten. Erst das Sich-Erkennen im Anderen, also die Einsicht, dass es den österreichischen Juden genauso ergehen könnte wie den österreichischen Türken oder den Schwarzafrikanern, löste dort jenen Prozess aus, der die eigene Identität zunächst in Frage stellte und sie in der Aktion gegen die Missachtung wieder restituierte (Rabinovici 1997: 47). Einige Jahre zuvor hatte schon Peter Henisch in seinem unter dem unmittelbaren Einfluss der Waldheim-Affäre entstandenen Roman *Steins Paranoia* (1988) ein ganz ähnliches Aktionsmuster beschrieben, mit einem wesentlichen Unterschied: Während in *Suche nach M.* ausländerfeindliche Übergriffe der Auslöser für einen Prozess sind, der die eigene Selbstbeziehung in Frage stellt, ist es in *Steins Paranoia* antisemitisches "Gerede" (Henisch 1988: 5), das diesen Prozess auslöst. Stein, der an diesem im Text unausgesprochen bleibenden Satz und an seiner Unfähigkeit, darauf anders als mit Schweigen reagieren zu können, verzweifelt, revidiert seinen eigenen Lebensentwurf. Er hatte zuvor Österreich gegenüber seinem Vater, der aus dem kanadischen Exil nicht nach Österreich zurückgekehrt war, stets verteidigt und dort, wo doch alles "vergangen" (Henisch 1988: 17) sei, was noch bedrohlich sein könnte, ein Leben geführt, das auf Unauffälligkeit und Konfliktvermeidung angelegt war. Nun aber nimmt er den "Ressentimentfluß" (ebd. 65) in Österreich wahr, der auf "Itaker" (ebd. 56), "Tschuschen" (ebd. 68) und "Krüppel" (ebd. 70) ebenso abzielt wie auf Juden, und gelangt dadurch zu einer "*Umkehr*" (ebd. 70): "[V]ielleicht kam es nur darauf an, sich die *leidende Form* nicht *gefallen zu lassen* und aus ihr auszubrechen, aufzubrechen, in eine Form zivilcouragierter Aktivität" (ebd. 69). Die Erkenntnis der "gemeinsamen Diskriminiertheit" (ebd. 72) steht bei Henisch am Ende einer durch Integritätsverletzung ausgelösten Infragestellung der personalen Identität, während sie bei Rabinovicis *Suche nach M.* am Anfang steht und die eigene Infragestellung der Identität erst in Gang setzt.

In *Ohnehin* fällt zunächst auf, dass die jüdischen Figuren dem Antisemitismus mit einer gewissen Gelassenheit begegnen. Als beispielsweise dem jüdischen Unternehmer Paul Guttmann zu Ohren kommt, dass sein Angestellter Welch, ein Wiedergänger von "Herrn Karl", mit dem Carl Merz und Helmut Qualtinger schon Anfang der 1960er Jahre der österreichischen Gesellschaft einen Spiegel vorgehalten hatten, im Warenlager "Judenzoten zum Besten" gibt (Rabinovici 2004: 35), reagiert er pragmatisch. Obwohl er keinen Anlass hat zu glauben, dass Welch kein Antisemit ist, entlässt er ihn nicht, sondern macht ihm in einer kurzen Aussprache klar, dass seine Ressentiments weniger eine Bedrohung für Guttmann, sondern vor allem für die Arbeitsabläufe in seiner Firma sind. Damit gelingt es ihm, Welch in die Firma zu integrieren, ja zu einem "der kollegialsten im Depot" zu machen. Für Guttmann kann es "keine Entschädigung für die Verfolgung" geben, "ebenso keine Rache" (Rabinovici 2004: 36). Er reagiert rational, nicht emotional auf die Missachtung und nimmt ihr damit den bedrohlichen Charakter.

Auch der aus Russland stammende Jude Lew Feininger handelt ähnlich. Dass sein Nachname immer wieder ausgerechnet zu "Weininger" verballhornt wird (Rabinovici 2004: 101, 117), nimmt er fast gleichgültig hin, ebenso wie er sich schon damit abgefunden zu haben scheint, dass an seinen Deutschkenntnissen gezweifelt wird (Rabinovici 2004: 95). Wodurch er sich aber missachtet fühlt, ist der Philosemitismus.[6] Als Bärbl, die unter der Vergangenheit ihres Vaters lei-

---

6 Über den Philosemitismus sagte Rabinovici in einem Interview: "Mich stört im Alltag der Philosemitismus mehr als der Antisemitismus. Es kommen so weniger Antisemiten, um mir auf die Schulter zu klopfen". Paul Jandl (1998):

det, versucht, ihre Schuldgefühle durch eine Solidarisierung mit "den Juden" zu sublimieren, reagiert Lew gereizt:

> Du würdest am liebsten eine antifaschistische Pyjamapartie veranstalten und in Häftlingskleidern herumlaufen. Du bist kein SS-Opfer. Hörst du? Und mich wirst du auch zu keinem machen. Ich bin kein Opfer. Meine Verwandten waren welche, gewiß. Ich nicht. Verstehst du? Ich nicht. Was hast du gesagt? 'Wir Kinder von Opfern und Tätern'? Meinst du, wir wären eine einzige große Familie? Eine Art Mischehe aus Juden und Nazis? Eine Täteropfermischkulanz ... Die Mischpoche von Auschwitz? Wir Kinder? Ich will kein Kind mehr sein. Ich bin erwachsen. Du auch. Es ist an der Zeit (Rabinovici 2004: 119).

Rabinovici zeigt hier, dass Missachtung nicht auf Ressentiments beruhen muss, sondern auch eine Folge der unkontrollierten Reaktionsbildung sein kann, Integritätsverletzungen sich also auch dann einstellen können, wenn in der sozialen Interaktion die besten Absichten verfolgt werden.

Dies gilt für die Integrität von Kollektiven (Philosemitismus) ebenso wie für personale Integritäten. Stefan Sandtners Liebesbeziehung zu Flora Dema zerbricht daran, dass er unfähig ist, sich in ihre Lage zu versetzen. Während Flora auf ein Zeichen von ihm wartet, das ihr signalisieren würde, dass er zu ihr steht, verheimlicht Sandtner vor ihr, dass er sich um eine gemeinsame Wohnung und eine Aufenthaltsgenehmigung für sie gekümmert hat, weil er sie damit überraschen möchte. Sandtners Zögern kann sie nur als Desinteresse an ihrer persönlichen Situation und ihrem aufenthaltsrechtlichen Status verstehen, und tatsächlich macht Flora ihm in ihrem letzten Gespräch deutlich, dass er im Grunde nichts von ihr weiß (Rabinovici 2004: 226–233). Als ihm Flora mitteilt, dass sie Wien verlassen wird, ist es zu spät für seine Überraschung. In der kurzen Zeit ihrer Beziehung hat ihr Stefan nie zu verstehen gegeben, dass er sich wirklich für ihr Schicksal interessiert. Flora, die in ihrem Filmprojekt einen Kampf

---

"Ein Gepeinigtsein von Peinlichkeiten. Jüdisch sein in Österreich – Ein Dreiergespräch". *Neue Zürcher Zeitung*, 11.7.1998 [Interview mit Robert Schindel, Robert Menasse und Doron Rabinovici].

um Anerkennung der in Österreich lebenden Sans Papiers führt, hält sich selbst nicht illegal in Österreich auf. Sie führt diesen Kampf vielmehr stellvertretend für ihren Kameramann Goran, der keine Aufenthaltsgenehmigung hat und schließlich verhaftet und abgeschoben wird, wofür sich Flora die Schuld gibt (Rabinovici 2004: 232). Sie war jedoch ihrerseits unfähig, ihre "Anerkennungserwartungen" (Honneth 1994: 261) Sandtner so deutlich zu machen, dass er angemessen darauf hätte reagieren können. Die Ursache dafür ist die Missachtung, die sie aus dem Kosovo vertrieben hat. Diese Verletzung ihrer persönlichen Integrität hat sie versucht zu verdrängen, und das Scheitern dieses Versuchs führt zum Scheitern ihrer Beziehung zu Stefan: "Ich hätte dir das alles erklären sollen. Goran hat mich immer wieder dazu gedrängt, mit dir zu reden. Aber ich wollte lieber mit dir einfach nur die Zeit genießen. Einmal nicht davon sprechen. Einfach vergessen" (Rabinovici 2004: 233).

Der Wunsch, vergessen zu können, ist das Leitmotiv des Romans, das die Geschichten von Kerber, dem liebeskranken Sandtner, seiner neuen Freundin Flora und vielen anderen Figuren des Romans verbindet. *Ohnehin* ist auch ein Roman über das für Österreich so besondere Jahr 1995. Vor dem Hintergrund der Ereignisse dieses Jahres, 50 Jahre Kriegsende, 40 Jahre Abzug der Alliierten und Neutralitätserklärung, der Beitritt zur EU, die Serie der Briefbombenattentate, der Bombenanschlag auf die Sinti in Oberwart, das Attentat auf Yizchak Rabin, die Fortdauer des Krieges im ehemaligen Jugoslawien, macht der Roman auf die kulturelle Vielfalt Österreichs aufmerksam, die längst schon einen irreversiblen Prozess der Hybridisierung in Gang gesetzt hat, und positioniert sich damit in den laufenden Debatten um die österreichische Identität.

ZITIERTE LITERATUR

Augé, Marc (1994): *Orte und Nicht-Orte. Vorüberlegungen zu einer Ethnologie der Einsamkeit.* Übersetzt von Michael Bischoff. Frankfurt am Main: S. Fischer.

Beilein, Matthias (2003): "Wende im Entweder-und-Oder: Österreich und die engagierte Literatur seit 1986". *Engagierte Literatur in Wendezeiten.* Hgg. Huntemann, Willi u.a. Würzburg: Königshausen & Neumann, 209–221.

Beilein, Matthias (2005): "Unter falschem Namen. Schweigen und Schuld in Doron Rabinovicis 'Suche nach M.'" *Monatshefte* 97, No.2, 250–269.

Bourdieu, Pierre (2001): *Meditationen. Zur Kritik der scholastischen Vernunft.* Übersetzt von Achim Russer u.a. Frankfurt am Main: Suhrkamp.

Brunner, Karl-Michael (1987): "Zweisprachigkeit und Identität". *Psychologie und Gesellschaftskritik* 44, 55–75.

Feijóo, Jaime (2002): "Die Verstörung der Zweiten Republik. Schriftsteller-Essays über Österreich". *1945–1989–2000: Momentos de lengua, literaturas y culturas alemanas. Actas de la X Semana de Estudios Germánicos.* Hgg. Acosta, Luis A. u.a. Madrid: Ed. del Orto, 231–244.

Frölich-Steffen, Susanne (1993): *Die österreichische Identität im Wandel.* Wien: Braumüller [Diss. Phil. München 1993].

Goffman, Erving (1994): *Stigma. Über Techniken der Bewältigung beschädigter Identität.* Übersetzt von Frigga Haug. Frankfurt am Main: Suhrkamp.

Henisch, Peter (1988): *Steins Paranoia.* Salzburg/Wien: Residenz.

Honneth, Axel (1994): *Kampf um Anerkennung. Zur moralischen Grammatik sozialer Konflikte.* Frankfurt am Main: Suhrkamp.

Menasse, Robert (2005): "Warum der Februar nicht vergehen will". *Das war Österreich. Gesammelte Essays zum Land ohne Eigenschaften.* Frankfurt am Main: Suhrkamp, 421–426.

Misik, Robert / Rabinovici, Doron (2000): "Vorwort. Aufbruch der Zivilgesellschaft". *Republik der Courage. Wider die Verhaiderung.* Hgg. Misik, Robert / Rabinovici, Doron. Berlin: Aufbau Taschenbuch Verlag, 9–14.

Rabinovici, Doron (1997): *Suche nach M.* Frankfurt am Main: Suhrkamp.

Rabinovici, Doron (2001): "Tracht und Zwietracht. Oder Politik als Folklore". *Credo und Credit. Einmischungen.* Frankfurt am Main: Edition Suhrkamp, 130–155.

Rabinovici, Doron (2004): *Ohnehin.* Frankfurt am Main: Suhrkamp.

Schindel, Robert (1992): *Gebürtig.* Frankfurt am Main: Suhrkamp.

Schindel, Robert (2004): *Fremd bei mir selbst. Die Gedichte.* Frankfurt am Main: Suhrkamp.

Wehler, Hans-Ulrich (1998): *Die Herausforderung der Kulturgeschichte.* München: Beck.

Wodak, Ruth u.a. (1998): *Zur diskursiven Konstruktion nationaler Identität.* Frankfurt am Main: Suhrkamp.

HORST TURK

"Mooristan" und "Palimpstine".
Die Integration Europas ein Vabanquespiel säkularisierter Monotheismen?

Konstellationen implizieren Loyalitäten, die auf geteilten Integritätsstandards basieren. In diesem Sinn lässt sich von nationalen und "postnationalen" (Habermas 1998), aber auch – wenn man den Rahmen weiter spannt – von europäischen und globalen Konstellationen sprechen. Letztere sind wie die ersteren durch Grenzziehungen und Grenzüberschreitungen auf das Vabanquespiel säkularisierter Monotheismen im "Kampf um Anerkennung" (Honneth 2003)[1] bezogen, was deutlich wird, sobald man sich externen Debattenschauplätzen, etwa: Salman Rushdies "Mooristan" und "Palimpstine" (Rushdie 1995: 371) in *The Moor's Last Sigh*, zuwendet.

I Mythen und Genealogien. Die Nation als Familie

Mit Rushdies Bombay-Romanen betreten wir ein Terrain, das seit den 70er Jahren des 20. Jahrhunderts nicht nur in identitätspolitischer, sondern auch in sicherheitspolitischer Hinsicht zu den Krisenherden

---

1 Vgl. dazu Wolfgang Ranke (2005): "Integrität und Anerkennung bei Axel Honneth". *Integrität. Europäische Konstellationen im Medium der Literatur.* Special Issue der *Monatshefte für deutschsprachige Literatur und Kultur.* Eds. Hans Adler et al., 97.2, 168–183.

des Postkolonialismus zählt. Die Mehrfachkodierung des "Indian country" (Rushdie 1995: 414) als India und als Indianerland eignet sich daher zur Exposition der Identitätsproblematik aus der Perspektive des Kindes in besonderer Weise, bereitet aber auch bereits die Lösung des Problems im Zeichen der "islamic bomb" (Rushdie 1995: 341) aus dem Standpunkt des Erwachsenen vor. "In Indian country", heißt es im Rückblick des fiktionalen Autobiographen, "there was no room for a man who didn't want to belong to a tribe, who dreamed of moving beyond [...]" (Rushdie 1995: 414). In der Konfrontation mit der "islamic bomb" vollzieht er die Emanzipation von seinem "Daddyji", indem er sich vor dem Hintergrund einer politisch und ideologisch kontrovers aufgeladenen Abstammung für die jüdische Zugehörigkeit entscheidet: "I took a breath, and plunged: 'I guess you must know who-all this bomb is meant to blow into more bits than poor Rajiv, and where?' [...] 'excuse me, but I find that I'm a Jew'" (Rushdie 1995: 336f.). Die Bedingungen für seine soziale Ortlosigkeit und die Gründe für seine Entscheidung sind familiärer, politischer und moralischer Natur. Mumbay – zu dem Zeitpunkt noch Bombay – kann als prominentes Beispiel der erfolgreich in Angriff genommenen Industrialisierung und Demokratisierung gelten. Gekoppelt an eine exemplarisch ausgeprägte postkoloniale Hybridität, nimmt das Sujet die Gestalt eines Zeit- und Familienromans an, der, in der Genealogie auf paradigmatische Eckdaten der Geschichte bezogen, das Projekt einer globalen Neujustierung reflektiert. Dabei werden gezielt Loyalitätsbindungen ausgetestet, unter anderem auch subsidiär eingeworbene, die Leerstellen besetzen oder auch durch autochthone Besetzungen verdrängt werden.

So findet sich gleich zu Beginn eine Anspielung auf den Protestantismus – "'Oh, you Moor, you strange black man, always so full of theses, never a church door to nail them to'" (Rushdie 1995: 3) –, der einen festen Platz in der abendländischen Säkularisierung und Nationenbildung hat. Auf indische Verhältnisse übertragen, muss sich die Säkularisierung jedoch einen Code-Wechsel gefallen lassen. Denn hinduistisch statt christlich agiert, hat der Nationalismus sein Idol nicht an *vater*ländischen Verkörperungen – etwa: Moor als literarische

Inkarnation Gandhis oder Nehrus mit Rama im Hintergrund –, sondern an maternalen Verkörperungen: Aurora in der Pose der "*Mother India*" (Rushdie 1995: 137) als literarische Inkarnation Indira Gandhis mit Kali im Hintergrund. Darüber hinaus ist Aurora "as much the incarnation of the smartyboots metropolis" (Rushdie 1995: 139); ihr wird in Komplettierung der "expandierten Familienmetapher" (Schultheis 2004: 105ff.)[2] ein gleichermaßen modernisierter Exponent der "paternal family" an die Seite gestellt: Abraham als literarische Inkarnation des okzidentalen Kapitalismus mit Jahwe im Hintergrund: "*I am that I am* ... yes, indeed, she had made a study of the Old Testament god" (Rushdie 1995: 88). Zwischen den beiden steht – als Sujet der Geschichte wie der Kunst und am Ende auch des Geschäfts, zugleich abtrünnig und in einem höheren Sinn solidarisch – der Stammhalter mit unsicherer Abkunft: Moor als Inkarnation des deregulierten Wachstums mit Boabdil, dem effemisierten letzten Sultan von Granada, im Hintergrund. Die Konstruktion trägt deutliche Züge des aktualisierten *displacement*, indem die verwendeten Referenzen nach Maßgabe der geteilten indisch-europäischen Kolonialgeschichte neu gemischt und ausgelotet werden. Dabei kommt es zu unverhofften Konvergenzen und Divergenzen, insbesondere was die religiösen Vorstellungsbildungen als Medien der Überzeugungsbildung und Loyalitätsbindung angeht.

Aurora ist als eine geborene da Gama (Rushdie 1995: 29) katholisch, und sie desavouiert sich und die jüdische Kolonie in Cochin, indem sie eine Mesalliance mit Abraham, dem jüdischen Exportbuchhalter der Firma, eingeht. Es ist dies eine Affäre, die durch das leere Grab (Rushdie 1995: 93) des portugiesischen Entdeckers hindurch die konfessionellen Einwände der jüdischen wie der christlichen Seite außer Kraft setzt, indem zugleich die verheimlichte

---

2   "*The Moor's Last Sigh* details the failure of those unified visions through an expanded metaphor of the nation as family. Playing off the rich associative traditions of the Western paternal family and Mother India, Rushdie shows their conflicted attempts to forge unity out of historical, ethnic, religious, caste, and linguistic difference" (Schultheis 2004: 131).

muslimische Teilidentität Abrahams aufgedeckt wird. Der Effekt dieser Bloßstellung der Identitäten im Begehren (Rushdie 1995: 414) ist weder der adamitischen Erkennung nach dem jüdisch-christlichen Sündenfallmythos noch der ödipalen Erkennung nach dem sophokleischen griechischen Mythos nachempfunden, sondern als Suspension der "Mosaischen Unterscheidung" angelegt. Durch sie wurde, folgt man in diesem Punkt Jan Assmann, der "Raum des jüdisch-christlich-islamischen Monotheismus" als "geistiger und kultureller Raum konstruiert", den die Europäer "seit fast zweitausend Jahren" bewohnen (Assmann 1998: 17f.) und der für den Orient und für Asien nicht gleichermaßen verbindlich ist:

> Did you ever see your father's cock, your mother's cunt? Yes or no, doesn't matter, the point is these are mythical locations, surrounded by taboo, put off thy shoes for it is holy ground, as the Voice said on Mount Sinai, and if Abraham Zogoyby was playing the part of Moses then Aurora my mother sure as eggs was the Burning Bush (Rushdie 1995: 88).

Der Erzähler dekonstruiert diesen Raum, hält sich dabei jedoch keineswegs an den Gegensatz von "feminized tradition und masculinized modernity" (Schultheis 2004: 135), sondern versichert sich beider Pole auf dem Entwicklungsstand der Moderne, während er den profangeschichtlichen Rahmen zugleich auf ein Eckdatum der europäischen Kolonialgeschichte, den Fall von Granada, ausrichtet. "We all eat children [...] If not other people's, then our own," (Rushdie 1995: 125) lautet das Bekenntnis Auroras, als sie sich, gestützt auf ihr Renommee als "giant public figure" und "national heroine" in der Pose der Muttergottheit und Boabdils Mutter – "Well may you weep like a woman for what you could not defend like a man" (Rushdie 1995: 80) – der nationalen Bewegung zur Verfügung stellt und aus dieser Position einen jährlichen Tanz gegen die Götter am Unabhängigkeitstag aufführt. Sie widerspricht damit der nationalistischen Tendenz der *Mumbay Axis*. Denn diese betreibt eine Homogenisierung im Zeichen "göttlicher Rechte" und strebt nicht nur eine Säuberung des Landes von allen "invaders" (Rushdie 1995: 299), der islamischen Fremdherrschaft wie der englischen Kolonialherrschaft, an, sondern auch den Aufbau einer "sparkling, up-to-date powerloom industry" (Rushdie 1995: 307), die unter der Bedingung einer wiederhergestellten nationalen Souveränität nach europäischem Vorbild die bourgeoise Regulierung durch das Establishment, aber auch die sozialistische Revolution konterkarieren soll.

Das Verfahren, das Rushdie einschlägt, um den Austrag sozialer Konflikte im globalen Rahmen zu reflektieren, ist wesentlich durch die kritische Auseinandersetzung mit dem Unverletzlichkeitsanspruch interagierender und konkurrierender kultureller Gewalten geprägt. Statt sein zeitgenössisches, zugleich fremdkulturell geprägtes Personal postfigurativ in ästhetische, ideologische, literarische oder mythische Paradigmen eintreten zu lassen, um es daran zu messen und gegebenenfalls einer *revanche de Dieu* zu überantworten, legt der Ich-Erzähler den Akzent nach der Art des performativen Kulturenvergleichs auf die Funktionswerte der Gewalten im *enactment*, um die Deutungsvorgaben des *emplotment* wie des *commitment*[3] einschließlich ihrer Loyalitätsbindung kulturell und historisch an den Effekten ihrer Regulierungsleistung zu messen. So bedient er sich z.B. einer ganzen Kaskade von Höllen (Rushdie 1995: 165) und Strafphantasien – von der jüdischen gegenweltlichen (Rushdie 1995: 113) über die christliche überweltliche bis zur hinduistischen innerweltlichen (Rushdie 1995: 368) –, wobei die Bezugsgrößen und ihnen gemäß auch die Motive und Intentionen wechseln und als Substanz nur die "flayed and naked unity of the flesh" (Rushdie 1995: 414) auf dem Platz bleibt. So benutzt er, der Lutherreminiszenz vergleichbar, das Paradigma des "Merchant of Venice" nicht, um Aurora, Flory und Abraham in das Deutungsschema des europäischen Antisemitismus einzurücken, sondern zu dessen Sprengung unter den Bedingungen der indischen Moderne. "Aurora was no Porcia", heißt es unter demonstrativer Herausstreichung des Unterschieds:

---

3 Zur Implementierung literarischer Texte mit Szenarien auf der Ebene des *enactment*, Handlungsmustern auf der Ebene des *emplotment* und Überzeugungen auf der Ebene des *commitment* vgl. Turk 2003: 140–157.

I do not mean it wholly as a criticism. She was rich (like Portia in this), but chose her own husband (unlike in this); she was certainly intelligent (like), and, at seventeen, near the height of her very Indian beauty (most unlike). Her husband was – as Portia's could never have been – a Jew [...] (Rushdie 1995: 115).

Als generelle Bedingung der Fehlläufe in der Geschichte wird der Austritt aus der regulierten in die deregulierte Sich-selbst-Gleichheit auf verschiedenen Ebenen angesehen. So wird in Aurora zunächst statt des erstgeborenen Sohns, auf den die jüdische Gemeinde, solange Flory lebt, Anspruch erhoben hat, ein "[g]enius born [...] filling the empty spaces in her bed, her heart, her womb. She needed no-one but herself". Und auch für Abraham gerät die Trennung der "diverging paths" (Rushdie 1995: 116) zum Auslöser, sich am Gründungsmythos des modernen Indien zu beteiligen. Etwa zeitgleich verlagern sich die Wirkungsfelder Abrahams und Auroras von der Peripherie ins Zentrum der Entwicklung nach Bombay, wo sie ihre Karrieren aufnehmen. Sie reüssiert als Malerin und Mutter in Manifestation der "Mother India" nach ihren beiden Aspekten, dem rettenden und dem vernichtenden,[4] er als Autokrat des Marktes und eifersüchtiger Gatte in der Selbstvergötterung eines "shadow-Jehovah" (Rushdie 1995: 336), beide getrennt und vereint nach der Art des *juste milieu* in einer "complicity of silence" (Rushdie 1995: 107).

II "Complicity of silence". Rushdies Analyse des postkolonialen Establishments

In Rushdies Roman sind es nicht die Götter, die Vergeltung üben, indem sie in die "complicity of silence" einbrechen, sondern die

---

[4] Zur Kali-Qualität ihrer selbst und der *Mother India*-Imago vgl. Liddle, Joshi 1986: 55.

"perversit[ies] of humankind" (Rushdie 1995: 124), die, von der Sanktionsgewalt der expandierten Familienmetapher befreit, in der ästhetischen Würdigung und Kritik zum Ort der Integritätsrestitution avancieren. Im Zentrum der Malerkarriere Auroras steht die Entdeckung des Palimpsests durch Vasco Miranda, ihren Protegé und auf Distanz gehaltenen Geliebten aus Goa. Beide haben Moor als umstrittenes Sujet im Visier. Vasco erweist sich als Parteigänger der "Mother Portugoose" anstelle der "Mother India" (Rushdie 1995: 156) in der kompromittierenden Ausführung eines Porträtierungsauftrags vor Moors Geburt: Aurora "sitting cross-legged on a giant lizard under her chhatri, cradling empty air. Her full left breast, weighty with motherhood, was exposed" (Rushdie 1995: 158). Genötigt durch Abrahams eifersüchtigen Protest, bringt er die leere Luft durch Übermalung des Bildes historisch und ikonographisch im Selbstporträt auf den Nenner der kolonialistischen Identifikation: *"The Artist as Boabdil, the Unlucky (el-Zogoybi), Last Sultan of Granada, Seen Departing from the Alhambra"* (Rushdie 1995: 160). Wenn Aurora sich durch den Affront anregen läst und Moor in ihrem Œuvre als rehabilitierter Boabdil figuriert, dann teilt sie mit Miranda das Sujet, die Ikone und die Rückführung auf das historische Eckdatum, übertrifft ihn aber, indem sie den Komplex naiv und authentisch statt sentimental und kitschig (Rushdie 1995: 408) auffasst. Insbesondere "her last, unfinished, unsigned masterpiece" im Zyklus der "so-called 'dark Moors'": "The Moor's Last Sigh" besticht durch diese Qualität:

> It was a picture which, for all its great size, had been stripped to the harsh essentials, all its elements converging on the face at its heart, the Sultan's face, from which horror, weakness, loss and pain poured like darkness itself [...].

Als Maßstab der Restitution fungiert der Blick der klassischen Moderne: "a face in a condition of existential torment reminiscent of Edvard Munch" (Rushdie 1995: 218). Dieser Blick bringt auf der Ebene visionärer Neuerfindung die "identity of all men" geradeso zur Geltung wie der Roman die Entblößung der "flayed and naked unity of the flesh" (Rushdie 1995: 414) auf der Ebene erzählter Geschichten. Hinter den Bildern verbirgt sich allerdings der Antagonismus zweier allein auf sich gerichteter Loyalitäten, deren Decouvrierung Sache der postmodernen dekorativen "airport art" (Rushdie 1995: 253) bleibt, während sich die Integritätsrestitution der Loyalitäten an der klassischen Moderne orientiert. Im Fall Mirandas erwächst die Decouvrierung aus dem Ressentiment sozialer Unterprivilegierung seit dem Anschluss Goas und dem Ressentiment des Glaubensverlusts im Zug der ästhetischen Säkularisierung. Er hält sich durch Annihilation an den ikonographischen und historischen Repräsentanzen ebenso schadlos wie an der Kunst selbst und agiert religionskritisch gesehen aus "Ressentiment" im Sinn Nietzsches, jedoch mit einer geheimen Erlösungshoffnung im Sinn Schopenhauers. In Auroras Selbstdarstellung erwächst die Restitution aus einer mythomanen Identifikation: ebenfalls "somewhat blasphemously" (Rushdie 1995: 220). Sie malt ein Bild für Menschen, die ihre Götter aufgegeben haben, jedoch zugleich so, wie es sich Abraham Zogoiby erhofft haben mochte: "as a godless madonna with child", erhöht zu einer "mythomanic gem" (Rushdie 1995: 220). Die Übereinstimmung mit Abraham betrifft die rückhaltlose Loyalitätsbindung: bei Abraham an die Macht und damit an ihn selbst, bei Aurora an das Leben und damit an sie selbst. Beide Positionsnahmen stehen in der Notwendigkeit, Allianzen zu schließen, wie sie in der Population benötigt werden.

III "People make the alliances they need".
Die Unzuverlässigkeit von Konstellationen

Rushdies Kalkül transformierter Loyalitätsbindungen geht auf, sobald man sich der Unzuverlässigkeit historischer Konstellationen zuwendet. Gegen die Exzesse der nationalen Homogenisierung stehen die Postmarxisten (Rushdie 1995: 338) und Frauenrechtlerinnen (Rushdie 1995: 362), das Establishment und die ästhetische Moderne, steht aber auch das organisierte Verbrechen (Rushdie 1995: 331), in das die bedrohte Minderheit der einstmaligen Eroberer abgewandert ist, und steht ebenfalls der imagologische Nachwuchs, Nadia Wadia als Schönheitskönigin und Idol der Nation. Sie ist als Miss World wie Moor über die Grenzen hinweg auf globalisierte Anerkennungsprozesse bezogen, allerdings nicht in der Form des Palimpsests persönlich betroffen, wohl aber medial und auf diese Weise wie Moor ein Ausdruck, Faktor und Indikator, schließlich Opfer des Schauplatzes, nämlich Bombays als "bastard child of a Portuguese-English wedding, and yet the most Indian of Indian cities" (Rushdie 1995: 350). Sie wirkt wohltuend auf Moors rebellisches Sein, sein "true, unnamed, amoral self," seine "secret identity" (Rushdie 1995: 337), obwohl die Vermählung mit ihm scheitert, weil Abrahams diplomatischer Versuch, die muslimischen Gangs des organisierten Verbrechens zu vereinigen (Rushdie 1995: 331), von Erfolg gekrönt ist und den Dingen eine andere Wendung gibt. Sie wird vom Erzähler als "dark, ironic victory for India's deep-rooted secularism" gewertet mit einem Seitenhieb auf Raman Fieldings theokratische Vision:

> The truth is almost always exceptional, freakisch, improbable, and never normative, almost never what cold calculations would suggest. In the end people make the alliances they need. They follow the men who can lead them in the directions they prefer. It occurred to me that my father's pre-eminence over Scar and his colleagues was a dark, ironic victory for India's deep-rooted secularism. The very nature of this inter-community league of cynical self-interest gave the lie to Mainduck's vision of a theocracy in which one particular variant of Hinduism would rule, while all India's other people bowed their beaten heads (Rushdie 1995: 331 f.).

Damit ist das Stichwort gefallen, in dessen Horizont der Sinn des *enactment* deutlich wird. Es kommt zum Endkampf zwischen Mainduck und Abraham, nationalistischer und kapitalistischer Solidarisierung, ein Kampf, der entweder in puristisch basierter Loyalität der Mehrheit oder in palimpsestisch basierter Solidarisierung der Minderheiten, sei es paternal, sei es maternal, eine Emanzipation von den "communal ties" (Rushdie 1995: 336) – mit Max Weber würde man sagen: von einer traditionsverbundenen "Brüderlichkeitsethik" (Weber 1986: 542ff.) – zur Folge hat. Die Emanzipation kann säkular in sozialen oder konfessionell in religiösen Vorstellungsbildungen, aber auch fundamentalistisch in versetzt wiederhergestellten religiösen Vorstellungsbildungen Platz greifen. In der Krise können indessen auch unerwartete Konvergenzen und Divergenzen aufscheinen. Rushdie lässt Abraham im Rekurs auf die Bibel und Homer – die beiden Grundtexte der abendländischen Zivilisation – nach der "Unsterblichkeit" greifen. Sie ist für ihn weniger eine Sache der "Schönheit" oder der Religion als eine Sache des Lebens. Von dessen Säulen, "*God, family and money*", ist ihm nach Auroras tödlichem Absturz beim Tanz gegen die Götter, den er selbst veranlasst hat, nur noch eine geblieben. Er benötigt jedoch "*a minimum of two*" und reflektiert nun in Anspielung auf aktuelle politische Tendenzen in Indien sowie in Analogie zur Säkularisierung nach dem Muster der europäischen Konstellation – beidemal abweichend von der jüdischen Tradition – auf die Unsterblichkeit des eigenen Namens, statt sich mit der Unsterblichkeit im Volk (Cohen 1978: 350) bzw. im Gottesnamen (Derrida 1985: 174) zu begnügen:

> The devote rejoice in death [...]. They think it's the door to God's chamber of glory. But that's an empty room. Eternity is here on earth and money won't buy it. Immortality is dynasty. I need my outcast son (Rushdie 1995: 318).

Folgerichtig verfällt die Reflexion unter den Bedingungen des Liebes- und des Schönheitsentzugs auf die Dynastie als alternativen Weg in die Unsterblichkeit. Doch in Moor greift eine andere Loyalität Raum (Rushdie 1995: 336), die nicht die Loyalität des nächst höheren, historisch existierenden, aber auch nicht die Loyalität eines kategorial höheren,[5] utopischen Kollektivs[6] ist, sondern die Loyalität eines

---

5 Etwa des externen europäischen oder auch des internen in seiner staatlichen Organisation. Vgl. in diesem Sinn George H. Mead, *Mind, Self, and Society. From the Standpoint of a Social Behaviourist.* Chicago, London: Univ. of Chicago Press, 1972, 199, 286 und 167f., nach der Rekonstruktion von Tugendhat 1993: 279f.

6 Etwa im Habermas'schen Sinn einer immer weiter hinausgeschobenen "Gemeinschaft". Habermas 1996: 7. Vgl auch Honneth 2003: 89.

nächst höheren Kollektivs in den widerstreitenden historisch existierenden Kollektiven, und er bedient sich dabei einer Variante, die genuin in der europäischen Konstellation eingeschrieben ist. Moor positioniert sich im Rekurs auf Abrahams jüdische Abstammung als Jude. Er aktiviert damit eine Gestalt des abendländischen Kosmopolitismus (Albrecht 2005), aktiviert sie jedoch nicht im Namen der Ethik mosaisch, sondern – zu seiner Überraschung – im Namen der zerstörten "communal ties":

> Surprise, because after all I had been raised in *Elephanta*, where all communal ties had been deliberately disrupted; in a country where all citizens owe an instinctive dual allegiance to a place and faith, I had been made into a nowhere-and-no-community man – and proud of it, may I say. So it was with a keen sense of the unexpected that I found myself standing up to my formidable, deadly father (Rushdie 1995: 336).

Die Peripetie der Romanhandlung spielt auf drei Ebenen. Stilistisch gesehen ist der ironische Sieg "for India's deep-rooted secularism" einer Polyvalenz zu danken, insofern der Säkularismus sowohl physisch wie auch ethisch wie auch materiell "verwurzelt" sein kann. Weltanschaulich gesehen wird eine Restitution der "reality of our being" hinter den "Maya-veils of unknowing and illusion" in dem Sinn bemüht, dass sich die Maja-Schleier selbstherrlich zur Offenbarung ("Revelation") aufgespreizt haben, statt ihren Sinn in der Enthüllung ("revelation") preiszugeben (Rushdie 1995: 334f.). Politisch gesehen ist der Sieg weder kommunitaristisch im Sinn der "communal ties" noch liberalistisch in Sinn des "nowhere-and-no-community man" zu deuten. Vielmehr stellt er eine Lösung des Problems wechselseitiger Erkennung und Anerkennung dar, in der die einschlägigen Integritätsstandards mehrseitig abgeglichen und aus der regional bedingten Position und dem regional bedingten Interesse in ein integratives Konzept des "generalised other" eingefügt werden.

IV "Mooristan" und "Palimpstine". Orte der europäischen *restitutio in integrum*

Dabei rückt der Islam – nach der historischen Konstellation seit dem Fall von Granada in der schwächsten Position – nach dem pluralisierten Kalkül eines Agons konvergierender Semantiken in die stärkste Position einer Solidarität "of shame" ein. Sie ist positional und nicht essentiell zu verstehen – "[s]hame is not the exclusive property of the East" (Rushdie 1995a: 29) –, verdrängt aber als universelle Determinante die Schuld, sobald man sich auf die Position eines "deep-rooted secularism" einlässt.

Das "fig-leaf of shame" einer humangesellschaftlichen, vermeintlich vorgeschützten Solidarität, nicht die fleischliche Erkennung als Erkennung des Ursprungs wird verboten:

> Abraham became stone. He was ice, and flame. He was God in Paradise and I, his greatest creation, had just put on the forbidden fig-leaf of shame. 'I am a business person,' he said. 'What there is to do, I do.' *YHWH. I am that I* am (Rushdie 1995: 336).

Genau besehen haben wir es mit einem Vabanquespiel dreier paternal kodierter Theokratien gegen ihre Wiedergeburt aus einer maternal kodierten Kosmokratie zu tun: die judaische das genaue Gegenteil *und* Komplement der Kosmokratie, die christliche abgefallen in die "hundred-percent fakery of the real" (Rushdie 1995: 184), die islamische der Ort der Integritätsrestitution in der Solidarität "of shame". Die drei sind integraler Bestandteil der europäischen Konstellation, "Mainduck's vision of theocracy" ist, ihr nachgebildet, in Wahrheit nur "one particular variant of Hinduism" (Rushdie 1995: 332).[7] Was Bestand hat, ist Moors Verlangen nach der verlorenen Mutter: "in long art, if not short life" (Rushdie 1995: 324). Das Verlangen richtet sich sowohl

---

7 Vgl. Randeria 1996: 53.

auf Mirandas mariologische Porträtierung unter muslimischer Übermalung – wie auch auf Auroras letztes, "unfinished, unsigned masterpiece". Es ist ein Bild unverstellter menschlicher Qual und Mutterliebe, losgelöst von aller religiösen Ikonographie, das einer hommage an Moor in der Imago des verunglückten Sultans und damit an den ehemaligen vertriebenen "invader" gleichkommt:

> in which she turned, at last, to the one subject she had never directly addressed – facing up, in that stark depiction of the moment of Boabdil's expulsion from Granada, to her own treatment of her only son (Rushdie 1995: 218).

So erfüllt sich – als Quintessenz des *emplotment* wie des *enactment* und des *commitment* – eine in der Komposition angelegte lancierte *captatio benevolentiae* für den erneut unterlegenen Mohammedanismus im Namen der in ihm vertretenen "humanity":

> the painting they found on her easel was about me. In that last work, *The Moor's last Sigh*, she gave Moor back his humanity. This was no abstract harlequin., no junkyard collage. It was a portrait of her son, lost in limbo like a wandering shade: a portrait of soul in Hell. And behind him, his mother, no longer in a separate panel, but re-united with the tormented Sultan. Not berating him – *well may you weep like a woman* – but looking frightened and stretching out her hand. This too was an apology that came too late, an act of forgiveness from which I could no longer profit.

Auroras "masterpiece" hat Moor, wenn auch für das Leben zu spät, die Menschlichkeit *zurück*gegeben sowie dem Buch, in dem es vorkommt, den Titel *vor*gegeben: "The Moor's Last Sigh" (Rushdie 1995: 315 f.).

Das ästhetische Gelingen oder Scheitern der Unternehmung hing nicht vom geglückten Leben des Protagonisten, wohl aber von der geglückten Aushebelung und Wiedereinsetzung der europäischen Konstellation durch ihn aus der Position eines externen Debattenfeldes ab. In diesem Sinn kommen nicht Jerusalem (Rushdie 1995: 376) oder Rom als *lieux de mémoire* (Nora 1997) in Frage – sowenig wie der neue Adam (Rushdie 1995: 343) als Hoffnungsträger –, sondern "Mooristan" und "Palimpstine" (Rushdie 1995: 371) als wieder aufgesuchte Flucht- und Endpunkte der Reconquista (Rushdie 1995: 390) und Moor selbst als Kind der "expandierten Familienmetapher", das seine Geschichte dort abfasst und niederlegt. Der Ort – Benengeli unweit Granada – ist ein Reservat des internationalen "riff-raff" und ehemaliger Falangisten (Rushdie 1995: 392), Vasco Miranda ihr "greatest and most dreadfull inhabitant" (Rushdie 1995: 393), darauf fixiert, "in his 'Little Alhambra', the fabulous multiple culture of ancient al-Andalus" zu erneuern (Rushdie 1995: 398). Dorthin ist außer Vascos Palimpsest mit der übermalten Aurora auch die wiedergeborene Mutter, unterlegt mit dem Porträt ihres Mörders, verbracht worden. Es ist der zuständige Ort für eine – wenn nicht buchstäbliche, dann doch metaphorisch rückübertragene – *restitutio in integrum* als Wiedereinsetzung der europäischen Konstellation in den vorigen Stand eines erneut aufzurollenden Prozesses durch die Anamnese, allerdings um den "deep rooted secularism" und die "shame" als Medium der wechselseitigen Anerkennung erweitert. Die Ablösung des "tearful equestrian chocolate-box picture" (Rushdie 1995: 324) ist dazu der eine, die Durchleuchtung von Auroras unvollendetem Meisterwerk der andere Weg. Das Palimpsest der Eltern – "each with one of my parents hidden underneath?" (Rushdie 1995: 419) – bleibt als *"testament [...] to that most profound of our needs"* erhalten: *"our need for flowing together, for putting an end to frontiers, for the dropping of the boundaries of the self"* (Rushdie 1995: 433). Damit schließt das Projekt einer *restitution in integrum* am zuständigen Ort und vor einem zuständigen Gremium.

ZITIERTE LITERATUR

Albrecht, Andrea (2005): *Kosmopolitismus. Weltbürgerdiskurse in Literatur, Philosophie und Publizistik um 1800*. Berlin: de Gruyter.

Assmann, Jan (1998): *Moses der Ägypter. Entzifferung einer Gedächtnisspur.* Wien: Hanser.

Cohen, Hermann (1978): *Religion der Vernunft aus den Quellen des Judentums.* Hg. Bruno Strauß. Wiesbaden: Fourier.

Derrida, Jacques (1985): "Des Tours de Babel". *Difference in Translation.* Ed. Joseph F. Graham. Ithaca: Cornell Univ. Press, 165–207.

Habermas, Jürgen (1996): *Einbeziehung des Anderen. Studien zur politischen Theorie.* Frankfurt am Main: Suhrkamp.

Habermas, Jürgen (1998): *Die postnationale Konstellation. Politische Essays.* Frankfurt am Main: Suhrkamp.

Honneth, Axel (2003): *Kampf um Anerkennung. Zur moralischen Grammatik sozialer Konflikte.* Frankfurt am Main: Suhrkamp.

Liddle, Joanna und Joshi, Rama (1986): *Daughters of Independence. Gender, Caste and Class in India.* New Brunswick: Rutgers Univ. Press.

Nora, Pierre (1997): *Les lieux de mémoire.* Paris: Gallimard.

Randeria, Shalini (1996): "Hindu-'Fundamentalismus': Zum Verhältnis von Religion, Geschichte und Identität im modernen Indien". *Religion – Macht – Gewalt. Religiöser 'Fundamentalismus' und Hindu-Moslem-Konflikte in Südasien.* Hgg. Christian Weiß u.a. Frankfurt am Main: IKO Verlag für Interkulturelle Kommunikation, 25–57.

Rushdie, Salman (1995): *The Moor's Last Sigh.* London: Jonathan Cape.

Rushdie, Salman (1995a): *Shame.* London: Vintage.

Schultheis, Alexandra W. (2004): *Regenerative Fictions. Postcolonialism, Psychoanalysis, and the Nation as Family.* New York: Palgrave Macmillan.

Tugendhat, Ernst (1993): *Selbstbewußtsein und Selbstbestimmung. Sprachanalytische Interpretationen.* 5. Aufl. Frankfurt am Main: Suhrkamp.

Turk, Horst (2003): *Philologische Grenzgänge. Zum Cultural Turn in der Literatur.* Würzburg: Königshausen und Neumann.

Weber, Max (1986): *Gesammelte Aufsätze zur Religionssoziologie,* Bd. 1, 8. Aufl. Tübingen: Mohr.

Part III

Identitary Processes in European Literatures

J. MANUEL BARBEITO, JORGE SACIDO

The Ghost of the Empire and the 'English' Postcolonial Identity

When Tony Blair pronounced the title 'the People's Princess' on the occasion of Lady Diana's death, he was invoking the ghost of a *fairy queen* to metamorphose into a secular saint and preside over a nation that would realise his dream of the Third Way. The hypothesis of this paper is that the loss of the empire produced a ghost that has kept returning and that affects the construction of *Englishness* by demanding *third ways* to restore former greatness and world leadership. In doing so, it haunts the relationships of the old metropolis with the ex-colonies and the social integration of immigrants coming from them. Both these relationships and processes of integration vary depending on the existing international status of the ex-colonies, that is, their position of superiority or inferiority in the international arena.

I

In 1944 George Orwell wrote an essay entitled "The English People". The moment of the essay is framed by two relevant dates for England and the world geopolitical map: it was finished in May, the month before the Normandy landings, and published in 1947, the same year of India's independence. In "England your England" (1941), Orwell had already reflected on "The Essence of Englishness" and the "distinctive and recognizable" features of "English civilization" (Orwell 1962: 65). The use of England in the title of this earlier essay acquires its full ideological sense in the expression "The English People" of the 1944/47 essay. Although in the latter "British" is consistently associated with the empire and both "British" and "English" with nation, by choosing "English" in favour of British in the title, Orwell indicates a return to the essences.

The notion of *Englishness* underwent a profound transformation in the last third of the nineteenth century propelled by the desire to achieve the unity of the nation under the leadership of a bourgeoisie that saw itself destined to guide both the nation and the British Empire (Philip Dodd 1999; Eagleton 1983). Right in the middle of the twentieth century, Orwell thought it opportune to separate the essence of the nation, 'The English People', both from the dominant class and from the Empire, nevertheless maintaining the connection between 'British' and 'nation' when the inclusion of Wales and Scotland was deemed convenient. Half a century later, Blair wisely avoided embarrassing terminology when he invited his countrymen to both an inward and outward movement: in his phrase, "people" obviously refers to the English people, but were there not millions of people from the world over who shared the whole nation's grief and contemplated in awe and respect the State funerals of the idol whom they had come to know in TV programs and in the tabloids? This double movement is an important feature of the English political ideology of the second half of the twentieth century. More specifically, one of the nation's dreams has been that a deeper understanding of its own values would lay the basis for its status as a world leader. Orwell's essay, which has much inspired both John Major and Tony Blair, offers an excellent starting point for the exploration of some of the most important aspirations and fears of the English collective consciousness of the second half of the twentieth century.

Orwell's essay is a mixture of organicism, traditionalism, historicism and pragmatism. A detached unbiased observer in contact with "ordinary, useful, unspectacular people," would easily grasp "the salient characteristics of the English common people": "artistic insensibility, gentleness, respect for legality, suspicion of foreigners, sentimentality about animals, hypocrisy, exaggerated class distinctions, and an obsession with sport" (Orwell 1987:16). Other defining features are added to these as the argument develops: democratic feelings; anti-totalitarianism instilled by tolerance, itself linked to lack of interest in intellectual issues (Orwell 1987: 27); the desire for profound peaceful changes which are in tune with respect for legality (Orwell 1987: 30); and equally important, the English language as the great distinctive feature that must be rescued from the dangers of the dissemination it is exposed to by territorial expansion and the simplicity of its use. Significantly, the remedy for the dangers of dissemination is neither standard English nor great literature, but the revitalisation of language by the common people: "The people likeliest to use simple concrete language, and to think of metaphors that really call up a visual image, are those who are in contact with physical reality" (Orwell 1987: 43).

Orwell is aware that these defining features of English identity are not really natural or permanent: actually, some are fairly recent – in the middle of the nineteenth century, for instance, brutality, not gentleness, he says, was characteristic of English life (Orwell 1987: 20) – and it is quite difficult to find a common thread that connects the English from the sixteenth to the twentieth century. Nevertheless, they *feel* that such a thread exists and that it connects Shakespeare, Lawrence, Blake, and Chesterton. In the absence of permanent timeless features, tradition emerges as the force that strengthens the bonds that time dissolves. The English are not phlegmatic by nature; rather, it is in tradition that this behaviour takes root. This means that phlegm should not be considered a superficial pose, as the people's behaviour during the blitz clearly showed. However, tradition is not indelible and immutable. In fact, the English desire for profound, even revolutionary, changes threatens its stability. Tradition is not perfect either: it has positive aspects, as phlegm proved to be in wartime, and negative ones, like the exaggerated class distinctions, the disappearance of which Orwell welcomes. While, on the one hand, you cannot do without tradition because it is the soil in which your character takes root, you must, on the other hand, decide which traces of the past should be kept and which criteria should be applied to select them. These criteria are provided by a project about the future, which Orwell, tracing a circle, derives from the English identity features described both in "England your England" and "The English People". The idea was to offer the world a specific product, distilled out of the characteristics of the English people, a product which was indispensable in the international situation in the middle of the twentieth century. This imagined future, though, as we shall see, was haunted by the past.

The last part of "The English People" focuses on "The Future of the English People". In order to accomplish their destiny, the English must both correct inertias and make the best of their character: the birthrate, social equality, and respect for the intellect must all increase, and centralisation must be reduced (Orwell 1987:48). Above all, the English people must take "their destiny into their own hands" (Orwell 1987: 55) and thus transform formal democracy into real democracy. The detached observer has been left behind to contemplate the distinctive English features discussed in the first part of the essay; at the moment of projecting the future of the English people it is the concerned citizen, with his own prejudices, that must come to the fore and speak.

Two major assumptions underlie Orwell's proposal: the existence of 'the English people', and their potential for leadership ("If the English took the trouble to make their own democracy work, they would become the political leaders of western Europe, and probably of some other parts of the world as well", Orwell 1987: 47–48). Orwell associates this capacity with the idea of inherited greatness. 'Greatness', though, cannot be permanently guaranteed; in fact, this issue is going to be decided soon: "by the end of another decade it will be finally clear whether England is to survive as a great nation or not" (1987: 55).

The first great assumption – that such a thing as 'the English people' exists – is crucial for the project, for if England is to remain a great nation, "it is the common people who must make it so" (Orwell 1987: 55). The notion of the common people has been linked to the emergence of nationalisms since the nineteenth century in Europe (Burke 1996), but this association was significantly belated in England. Towards the end of the nineteenth century the notion of Englishness was not connected with 'the people' in England, but with the dominant class, and one of the aims of educational institutions was to guarantee the belief held by the elite that the ideal of national identity was incarnated in the *gentleman* (Dodd 1999: 91–92). In this sense, using the term "people" suggests replacing an imperialist ideology by a nationalist one. Thus *Englishness* is no longer associated with the dominant class and it is in the common people where the essence of the nation is placed. When those characteristics on which the existence of 'the people' is founded are in danger of extinction, there are two possible ways to go: either ideology naturalises tradition stating the existence of a timeless essence, or a project is proposed which takes it as a starting point but also makes its transformation possible. Orwell took the second path.

Orwell tried to take advantage of the unity induced by the external enemy and to incite the English people to embrace a common project by inviting them to look beyond the catastrophe of the war and by showing them in advance the role they could play on the post-war world stage. Orwell rejected both pessimism – the assertion that England was finished – and nostalgia – the dream of the return of the glories of the past (Orwell 1987: 55). England had to discover its own destiny, something characteristically 'English', yet that could at the same time be offered as a staple product with competitive advantages in the market. And Orwell thought that he had discovered it: what the world needed was a guide capable of providing an alternative, a true third way, to the two opposing political ideologies (American materialism and Russian totalitarianism) that would be dominant from then on (Orwell 1987: 48). England's greatness depended on its ful-filling its true destiny and serving as the moral guide in times of trouble: "give the example that millions of human beings are waiting for", i.e., an alternative both to chaos and dictatorship (Orwell 1987: 55). This potential for leadership derived from a particular historical experience: England had learned that one nation alone could not rule the Earth (something that the Germans and the Japanese had already learned by 1947, andthat Russians and Americans had yet to learn, the latter still lagging behind in this apprenticeship). Furthermore, Orwell continues, England was in a position to teach others how to solve internal problems in a decent human manner, as the English had in the past shown their capacity to realise revolutionary changes without bloodshed (Orwell 1987: 47). Alas, Orwell decided to ignore Cromwell, Ireland, India; or, was "the end of the Empire [...] a sort of gentleman's agreement between old pals at the club," as some popular films of the early 80's suggest? (Rushdie 1992: 101).[1]

Taking Orwell's central thesis that England's destiny depends on the common people, it is first necessary to consider the changes that its demographic composition has undergone since the end of World War II. There are many people living in England today who were not born there, whose ancestors were not originally from the British Isles, and who have not received or do not accept the cultural heritage that Orwell projects into the future. A particular feature distinguishes the immigrant population in England from that of other countries on the Continent, such as those in Germany or Switzerland: an important part of the immigrants in England are natives from former colonies of the once greatest world's empire, the first migratory wave taking place in 1948, just one year after the publication of Orwell's essay. One then wonders if the idea of greatness of the English nation that dominates Orwell's project may not be haunted by the ghost of the Empire.

As national identity is both public and intimate, both collective and a modification of the ego, it will be useful to ask, in psychoanalytical terms, whether England has really accepted the loss of the empire as a necessary first step for adopting a new identity. This can help us to understand Orwell's effort and, more importantly, to find the source of the force behind his message. Using Nicolas Abraham and Maria Torok's terminology, we may ask whether the lost object has been "introjected" or "incorporated"? (1978) Introjection, the normal process of mourning, begins with accepting the loss of the object and ends with the displacement of desire to other objects. Incorporation, on the contrary, consists of denying the real loss and of an imaginary *swallowing up* of the object itself. Consequently desire remains fixed to

1   Or, as Eagleton put it: "The renowned moderation of the English spirit does not spring from a history of peace and civility; it is rather a reaction to a British history of bloodshed and sectarian strife" (2005: 97).

this object. In a sense, one could say that Orwell succeeded in conceiving an introjection type of project: on becoming the moral guide of the world, the English people would accept the material loss of imperial power and devote itself to a new ideal. Nevertheless, it remains to be seen if "greatness" is not an indelible trace of the Empire, which threatens to turn the dream into a nightmare. This is the reason why Salman Rushdie states that the magnificent idea of greatness is just "filth" (1992: 131). The English should obviously clean this stain, but liberation from it is all the more difficult as power and greatness are linked to narcissism; hence, the strong appeal the invocation of greatness still has and the corresponding need for the insistent call on the English from representative immigrant voices to give up all dreams related to the Empire.

II

In the second half of the twentieth century, the danger of a negative reaction of the incorporation type increased with the arrival of immigrants from the colonies, as they disturbed the dream of the people as an organic whole. It is worth asking how popular imagination dealt with the arrival of these immigrants, to what extent and under which conditions they have been integrated into 'the English people', and what ghosts have haunted the process. Has the loss of the old colonial relationship been accepted or was it confined to a sort of *crypt*, as Nicholas Abram and Maria Torok would call it, where it remained encysted with all its ghosts? This is what Rushdie denounces in "The New Empire within Britain":

> The same attitudes are in operation right here as well, here in what E. P. Thompson has described as the last colony of the British Empire. It sometimes seems that the British authorities, no longer capable of exporting governments, have chosen instead to import a new Empire, a new community of subject peoples of whom they think, and with whom they can deal, in very much the same way as their

predecessors thought of and dealt with 'the fluttered folk and wild', the 'new-caught, sullen peoples, half-devil and half-child', who made up, for Rudyard Kipling, the White Man's Burden (1992: 130).

The dream of greatness affects English society internally as well as externally in terms of its image in relation to other countries. Hence, one may also ask the following questions: What ghosts haunt the relationship with an object that has long been lost and has come to embody the very idea of superiority and greatness? How does the popular imagination deal with and represent the relationship with the USA? Are the States seen as the heir onto whom dreams of greatness are projected and lived out vicariously, or does the fear of becoming a sort of Whitehouse aide upset those dreams? Perhaps both aspects are two sides of the same coin, so that the *special relationship* so dear to English politicians inevitably and simultaneously awakens both the pride of power and the ghost of submission.

II. 1

A brief look at four well-known and fairly representative literary landmarks provides a good starting point to tackle the issue of the relationship between the colonisers and the colonised. The modern period has seen different justifications for the abandonment of western humanitarian scruples towards colonised people. The colonised (if conceived as *human* at all, which itself has sometimes been a matter for debate) have been considered culturally backward and morally wrong in their customs and principles, which called for the white coloniser's intervention to teach and guide them. As Edward Said put it, the mission of all empires is to "educate, civilise, and expand order and democracy" (2003: 8). There is always something else involved in justifying domination and subjugation: the colonised are dangerous, and all the more so the more their master's welfare depends on them. Othello, Caliban, Heathcliff, Bertha all contribute to their masters' welfare, but this source of material well-being that comes from below is also a source of misgivings and suspicion for their masters. These characters share four other important traits: First, all of them are displaced people and immigrants, except Caliban, who is an exile in his own country. Second, all of them know how to curse, which is morally wrong and very convenient when it comes to classifying and discriminating them (they become much more dangerous when they can also speak correctly as Othello and Heathcliff can, both of them inclined and able to woo young women belonging to the elite). Third, in each of the four cases a sexual menace is lurking in the background. Finally, the normal solution for the social integration of the sexual instinct into the social order is out of the question; marriage that has so often symbolised the ideal agreement between opposed interests is unfeasible in this case bringing ghastly consequences to the coloniser who dares to challenge the taboo.

The dangerousness attributed to immigrants is a powerful and ready-at-hand weapon against them, and it has two inseparable effects for the social order: it prevents their integration and, consequently, makes the very integrity of 'the people' impossible. Immigrants, like ghosts, *are* and *are not* (part of 'the people'); they belong to the people as a source of material prosperity, but they are not true members of the community. This simultaneous "to be/not to be" represents a sort of metaphysical menace to ideology for according to it things are always what they are. In order to examine the activity of the English *native* popular imagination regarding national identity, the ghosts that haunt it, and the strategies used to exorcise them, let us consider some symptomatic examples taken from advertisements and films. While doing this, we will also pay attention to the proposals of alternative national identities imagined and expressed by representative immigrant voices.

II. 2.

The analysis of a piece of electoral propaganda allows us to see the price that immigrants are forced to pay for their integration, which also functions as a way of exorcising the ghosts of their origins. The caption of one Tory poster of the 1983 elections read: "Labour say he is black, we say he is British". The first part of the message aims at distorting the progressive ideal of integration – respect for difference – and transforms it into disdain, if not into a sign of racism; the second part asserts that the Tories accept blacks into the British community. This verbal message accompanies a visual one: a black man impeccably dressed in city style. The conservative aspect of the message becomes obvious: the primary condition for admission is assimilation, that is, the immigrant's renunciation of his/her difference. One might ask what would happen if, instead of bearing city attributes, the man bore signs of tribal or class distinction. Referring to his own easy integration in England, Salman Rushdie relates it to "my social class, my freak fair skin and my 'English' English accent. Take away any of these, and the story would have been very different" (Rushdie 1992: 18). In the absence of respect for difference that the conservative message makes fun of, the black man will be inevitably rejected. Or, as Caryl Phillips put it: "no afros, no dashikis, no beads, no shoulder bags, only a suit, tie and briefcase, thank you very much" (2002: 247–48).

The assimilation of the other to the conservative ideal performs, then, the incorporation of the imperial relationship in a cyst. In a properly 'cryptic' way, the ghost of tribal and racial contempt for the *inferior* other haunts the poster caption, at the same time that the explicit message itself tries hard to win the immigrant vote by offering an ideal that is perfectly adequate to the system; something s/he must be ready to fight and die for as a member of the nation. As the title of Orwell's essay states, what is being offered here is that 'England' be 'your England', on condition that the immigrant must give up his/her own identity before really belonging to the English people. "That seems quite reasonable", someone might say who has decided to ignore the historical irony that an immigrant coming from the colonies contributed to the construction of that very same 'England' that is now imposed on him/her. If this is taken into account, though, Orwell's words acquire a different tone as an expression of the conditions that the immigrant is forced to accept: "The suet puddings and the red pillar-boxes have entered into your soul. Good or evil, it is yours, you belong to it" (Orwell 1962: 65). But, as Said wrote, "history can't be wiped out as if it were a blackboard, so that 'we' can write our future on it and impose our ways of life on inferior peoples" (2003: 8). The crucial question then is in what way and to what extent can immigrants, without renouncing their own selves, be allowed to participate in projecting the future of 'England'?

The highest expression of the exclusion camouflaged in this offer of conservative integration is, obviously, that it is not the black man who speaks, but rather a 'we' who does; this 'we' only includes the members of the conservative party but also aspires to take in the majority of the British. Referring to the speech in which Margaret Thatcher eulogised the Falklands victory in renewed imperial tones, Rushdie makes the sense of this 'we' clear: "her use of the word 'we' was an act of racial exclusion, like her other speech about the fear of being 'swamped' by immigrants (Rushdie 1992: 131). The silence of blacks is the final condition for their incorporation. If Othello had kept quiet he would have never conquered Desdemona; this would have been impossible too if he could only curse like Caliban, whose attempts at capturing Miranda are doomed to fail. In the voice of the immigrants, in their expression of their own desires, aspirations, and manner of integration lies a real danger. For, do these coincide with the conservative ideal, with the progressive ideal, or with neither of them?

II. 3

Immigrant representative voices denounce that British society remains caught up in the dreams of the past, which makes it unfit to meet the basic conditions for integration, and warn against the double risk of confrontation and ghettoisation. One of these unfulfilled necessary conditions is the acceptance of the reality principle: Hanif Kureishi, in "The Rainbow Sign", stated that the English have not learned that "British isn't what it was" (1986: 101). And Anthony Barnett entitled a TV program *Let's take the Great out of Britain*, which is a step that, according to Rushdie, must be taken as "the idea of a Great Britain [...] has bedevilled the actions of all post-war governments" and constitutes a motive of confrontation: "until you, the whites, see that the issue is [...] simply the business of facing up to and eradicating the prejudices within almost all of you, the citizens of your new and last, Empire will be obliged to struggle against you" (Rushdie 1992: 138). Only if deep changes take place in British identity can this danger be conjured up.

III

Before considering some proposals aimed at bringing about these changes, we shall pay attention to the way in which the relationship between England and the USA is imagined, to what extent the ghost of the loss of the Empire haunts the imagination, and how it is dealt with in popular art. Two recent successful British comedies, which can be taken as complementary, are relevant here: *Notting Hill* and *Love Actually*. Two facts should be taken into account. First, racial difference does not involve discrimination in either of them; the focus now is that the ex-colony has become the new imperial power with which the former Empire aspires to maintain a *special relationship*. Second, the sexual game is a relevant connecting thread in both films.

Bertha Mason (*Jane Eyre*) and Anna Scott/Julia Roberts (*Notting Hill*) have something in common on which the difference between them stands. In both cases a woman coming from a place with either a colonial present or past brings wealth home. Yet, depending on whether the colonial relationship still exists or not, their character is positive or negative, as if the romantic sublime had been split up into two and the horror went all to Bertha, while the glamour went all to Anna/Julia: one is a devil, the other an angel. This positive side associated with the American star is the consequence of the change in the position of the former colony, which has become a superpower. Anna/Julia's wealth does not come from below, from the slave, but from the master. And masters, of course, propitious though they may be, demand presents, 'fruits'. England seems to have them ready at hand

– tradition, human relationships, the cosy old home – and offers them through the person of the owner of a bookshop who still sells his goods in the old way, in a face-to-face relationship with his customer. Someone arrives at this shop who is also engaged in the cultural business, but in this case on a large colonising scale. She is the bride of America and a radiant film star whose earnings leave the character of the English broker – a friend of the bookseller – speechless. However, the world of massive money and business on a worldwide scale is too impersonal – her face circulates in posters advertising the film – and lacks just what the bookseller can offer: a warm human relationship, a real home. This home, though, is not symbolised by the bookseller's own house (as he lives with an extravagant Scot), but by a married couple formed by an ideal English woman and her husband (she had kindly refused to marry the bookseller, though they continue to be fond friends). In this way, two possible inter-British relationships are suggested and treated with light irony and tenderness. On the one hand, Scotland is represented by an extravagant, inoffensive and congenial pal who marries the equally extravagant sister of the book-seller; on the other, the relationship between the married couple serves as a good example of true and tender love, though one should not forget that the ideal English woman, wealthy and modern (she is a judge) as she is, is symptomatically on a wheelchair.

Julia-America has amassed enough power and money to be prepared to retire from impersonal business and to appreciate the personal human encounter. To this relationship, America brings the economic and military control over the world, capable of invading countries and imposing governments; whereas England brings tradition, home, a moral dimension. Unfortunately, the happy side of this alliance is coupled with another, darker one. The innocent and naïve William Thacker (Hugh Grant) conquers the American *belle*, and is of course conquered by her. A completely normal outcome, and yet the conquest by America is potentially disturbing, though this feeling is almost successfully repressed in the film. After dinner in the ideal English married couple's house, where the film star exorcised the ghost of her artificiality and humanised herself by confessing that she has been on a diet for many years and has had surgery, the protagonists take a night walk. She sees a beautiful garden and decides to go inside, despite her companion's reluctance to trespass private property. The young woman climbs the gate in the wink of an eye and suddenly she invades the territory that neither Napoleon nor Hitler were able to: the English garden, that space to which every English person aspires, according to Orwell. The English chap, respectful of the law and a bit podgy, climbs over to the other side with great difficulty, following her lead.

In this way, at the very centre of the story we come across an allegory of the violation of intimacy – associated with the traditional object of English love, the private garden – as well as a representation of the English willingness to follow America (though reluctantly) in its international adventures. This is a paradoxical kind of violation since there is no violence involved here. In fact, it inverts the rules of the battlefield; now the conquered is the one that conquers and the conqueror is trapped. Once inside the garden, the couple inhabits a ghostly atmosphere, a space deeply appealing to the actress. Apart from the peace and tranquillity that contrasts with her way of life, this place offers her the possibility of a walk into the past. Tradition is embodied in the very bench she sits on which bears the names of the married couple who once owned it thus taking them beyond life and death.

The English offer is thus complete. Tradition emerges as the suitable space for a close, warm, stable family relationship, one of the American dreams, one of the most recurring, the more the destruction of the family institution increases over there. Accordingly, in the last scene of the film we see a now pregnant Anne Scott lying on a park bench and resting her head on her husband's lap while he reads quietly.

The ghost of English decadence has thus been exorcised in a way: with Anne/Julia comes both new economic sap and political relevance in the international arena. The reverse of the coin of this *special relationship* with the USA, which enables England to vicariously experience imperial power, is of course to suffer American imperialism in its own flesh.

This is an aspect that briefly emerges in *Love Actually*. In this film, the American visitor is not the bride of America but the president of the United States himself. England is not represented here by a man but by the girl the prime minister has fallen in love with. Though beautiful, she is not the fascinating superstar of *Notting Hill*, but a middle-class girl who has not made herself by accumulating wealth. Taking advantage of his position, the American president tries to make the best of his stay, and he would have succeeded in turning the cosy drawing room of 10 Downing Street into a second Oval Office had the prime minister not come upon the scene. This is an inversion of the garden scene in *Notting Hill* where tradition charms the beautiful invader. *Love Actually* stages the danger of invasion of the very seat of English political power, as a result of England being charmed by the Superpower. The prime minister's intervention takes political form the following day during the press conference when he affirms English autonomy before the American president. Even though such strong self-affirmation may no longer have a really firm base, it provokes the enthusiasm of the audience. The lack of this base is compensated for by the union of political power and the people, as in Orwell's dream: crossing social borders, the Prime Minister runs to meet his beloved in a middle-class neighbourhood at the end of the film.

We are thus back to the people, a move repeated in P. M. Tony Blair's phrase 'the People's Princess'. At the beginning of this chapter, we took the liberty of a certain irony at the expense of Blair's ideal of the people presided over by the spirit of the princess. Jessica Evans (1999) has explained that this invocation is the expression of a dream of a magical union with the people, of bypassing the mediation of institutions, i.e., the traditional political and social representation. Blair's dream of a union with the people that would restore England to its condition as moral world leader finds its nightmare in the justification of the invasion of Iraq by Bush's invocation of a revengeful ghost, much more potent than the one of the unfortunate princess: God himself will lead the forces of good against evil. In the face of this, it is difficult to disagree with Rushdie's diatribe against politicians in "Outside the Whale": "if writers leave the business of making pictures of the world to politicians, it will be one of history's great and most abject abdications" (1992: 100).

These two films' use of humour to exorcise the ghost of the Empire is most relevant. It is this way of dealing with ghosts, rather than the wishful thinking of a *special relationship* that affords vicarious enjoyment of power, which can contribute to the liberation from those ghosts of the past that can only haunt and undermine the future.

IV

Let us leave the dreams of politicians aside, for the moment. If we pay attention now to the representative voices of groups not taken into account in the Orwellian dream, silenced in the conservative poster and astonishingly ignored in Blair's speeches on his way to 10 Downing Street (Blair 1997), we can see that they point in the direction of an "openly interactive and mutable concept of national identity" (Kureishi 1986: 102). This identity model promises to prevent both the isolation of the British in their essential identity and of the immigrants in theirs as well as the imposition of assimilation as a condition for integration and absolute relativism. We will briefly examine now the existing material conditions and the devices that these proposals use to achieve their goal.

On a planetary scale, the accelerating process of continuous change which modernity consists of constantly turns those practices, institutions and ways of life obsolete that tie individuals to the past. The problem is how to appropriate these transformations for meaningful human change, in this case, for the integration of immigrants. We can call *processors* the agents entrusted with this appropriation in some of the proposals. The range of these goes from the individual to the writer to the family to the local group to the global community. The nation, one should notice, has been relocated in the margins. Instances of the above mentioned *processors* can be seen respectively in Caryl Phillips's *A New World Order* (2002), in Rushdie's *The Satanic Verses* (1988), in

Gurinder Chadha's film *Bend it like Bekham* (2002), in Zadie Smith's *White Teeth* (2000), or in Marshal Berman's (1996) reading of Rushdie. All these *processors* and their viability must be examined in detail, though it is beyond the scope of the present essay to do so. We will concentrate instead on the great importance that all these alternatives to nationalism attach to recognition as the condition to building a human community.

For some, the first step for England to adopt a new identity is that the members of British society become 'multicultural individuals'. Phillips, for instance, affirms that "A truly multicultural society is one which is composed of *multicultural individuals; people who are able to synthesise different worlds in one body* and to live comfortably with these different worlds" (Phillips 2002: 279–80. Our emphasis). Thus, it is the individual that must process the synthesis of cultures. This basic element of western ideology, though, has already proved too weak to perform the tasks it was entrusted by ideology itself.

In *Bend it like Beckham*, Guinder Chadha makes an alternative proposal. Individuals cannot process the changes on their own, for they must take the group they are part of into account. More specifically, the family is conceived as an authentic and versatile mediator both between the past and the present and the present and the future; it is the family that instils tradition in its members and also what makes the individual's non-traumatic break with the old models possible. The condition for this to occur is family love, which guarantees the triumph of respect for the other over personal interests and convictions and also prevents the tragic ending of the conflict of beliefs and generations. This reaches its highest expression in the scene in which the daughter gives up her own interests for the sake of her parents and the father reciprocates by pushing his own conventions to the background. As usual, the spirit of comedy is haunted by the ghost of tragedy: ideally, the family performs the synthesis, and by means of love succeeds in processing the socio-cultural changes that lead to the abandonment of the old prejudices that hinder personal realisation and free human relations. This is not a quiet dream, as two dangers threaten its tranquillity. First, filial love that drives the girl to give up her plans may also serve as a means to subject her to the clan. Second, this is very likely to happen when the group reacts against change and sticks to its traditional beliefs and ways of life, an attitude represented in the film by Muslims, which is the reason why they are excluded from marriage alliances. The film ends with an alliance between marginal sectors. The football manager, of Irish origins, plays cricket in a typical English landscape with the father of the Hindu girl he loves. Thus an alliance is represented between marginal groups that accept being transformed and at the same time appropriate English tradition, also in the process of transformation. Paradoxically, a proposal like this made from the margins stigmatises a marginal sector, the Muslims.

Unlike what happens in this film, in Rushdie's *The Satanic Verses* relationships between parents and their children are characterised by strong tensions and the predicament of being unrooted is dramatised in them. Both the characters and the narrator may suffer because of this rupture in Rushdie's work. Using the story of his governess as an excuse, the narrator of one of the short stories in *East, West*, writes a portrait of the artist as a young man that, in contrast with the social integration reached in the conventional *Bildungsroman*, culminates in the writer's refusal to belong to any country in particular. The story of the governess shows a possible way out of the inner struggle over conflicting feelings of belonging and provides a contrast with the irresolution of the conflict experienced by the writer: like his governess, the narrator also has "ropes around the neck ... pulling in this and that direction, East and West, the knot tighten demanding: choose, choose"; but, unlike her, the narrator cries "I won't choose any of them, I choose both, do you hear. I refuse to choose" (Rushdie 1994: 211).

Unrootedness in Rushdie finds compensation in cosmopolitism. Rushdie thinks that his condition of immigrant enables him to say something of particular relevance, both concrete and universal. If always, and specially in modernity, human beings have experienced the break with the past, immigrants experience a double loss because of the physical distance which separates them from their origins. It is in this sense that, according to Marxal Berman, Rushdie is a 'modernist', because he gets rid of the old dogmas and expresses the condition that is common to all inhabitants of modernity. As the narrator of *The Satanic Verses* stated, "Modern life is universal after all ... because we are as tragically uprooted and fragmented and twisted as they" (Berman 1996: 53).

In this cosmopolitic dimension individuals are rescued from their impotence, but the question is *how*. What is the engine of this cosmopolitic community united in unrootedness? For Berman, modernity is characterised not only by a process of continuous transformation but also by the production of a culture that contradicts bourgeois calculation and that expands propelled by the ongoing process of internationalisation. Berman believes that this fissure between culture and capitalist calculation opens up the possibility for an alternative discourse to materialise in mass movements that make historical change meaningful at certain moments, as happened in 1989. According to Berman, then, capitalism generates a historical dynamics that, even if it does not cause its breakdown, still it prevents the total domination of discourses intentionally at the service of power and helps to struggle against radical scepticism and hopelessness about political struggle.

Said and Rushdie are salient examples of the refusal to accept scepticism: both try to take advantage of the potential of the individual by placing him or her in an institutional context. The individual still plays an important part as the processor of synthesis, but only to the extent that the role of the writer establishes a bond between the individual and the collective. The writer is not any individual: his or her position in the world of communication allows him to contribute to form and to form part of communities that rescue him or her from isolation and thus empowers his or her stance. The writer's intervention both against imperial and communitarian dogmas is indispensable in a world where so much is at stake in the production of discourses. As Said affirms concerning the Iraq war, "without that deliberate creation of a feeling that people from those countries are not like 'us', and that they could not appreciate 'our' values – the base of the Orientalist dogma – the war would not have taken place" (Said 2003: 8). The material link that transnational communication provides between the individual and the cosmopolitan community and the permanent production of a renewed humanism (the title of Said's essay from which these quotations are taken is "Humanism as resistance") gives a glimmer of hope.

In the face of recent events, one must admit that the promotion of discourses like Rushdie's or Said's has been less effective and powerful than that of those intellectuals denounced by Said for having renounced their true social function and collaborating with imperial power. Even so, those moments in which people gather to make history their own give sense to daily efforts of resistance and instil a sober optimism, unquestionably not devoid of uncertainty. The aesthetic moment of being here takes on historical relevance:

> 1989 was not only a great year, but a great modernist year. First, because millions of people learned that history was not over, that they had the capacity to make their own history – though not, alas, in circumstances chosen by themselves. Second, because in the midst of their motions, those men and women identified with each other: even in different languages and idioms, even thousands of miles apart, they saw how their stories were one story, how they all were trying to make the modern world their own. I fear that vision has faded from our public life. Maybe it will return, in ways we can't foresee. Meantime, I want to fight to keep the memory and the hope alive (Berman 1996: 55).

Rushdie is a symbol of modernity for Berman because his everyday engagement is an extraordinary exercise in responsibility.

Zadie Smith proposes a union "in the common recognition of a single human race", as well (Head 2003: 117). Like Rushdie, Smith also wants to transcend national boundaries, though her project takes root in the local. Hers is not a traditional local space occupied by only one culture, but rather a multicultural one providing a common home for a diverse citizenship whose members are able to share the problems of diversity. Ideally, this space, which demands everyday practice in recognition for the solution of shared problems in a local context, is the processor of changes and allows the insertion of individuals in the global community.[2] Whereas Rushdie rests on the modernist impulse to a global citizenship, Smith tries to find support in transformed local identities. Both leave nationalism aside to find support in one aspect of contemporary reality.

V

When we compare these proposals to Orwell's and to that made in the Tory electoral poster, it is tempting to establish an opposition between the category of recognition as used by cosmopolitans and that of identification as used in English nationalist discourse. Let us fall into temptation and conclude with a brief general reflection on what is at stake here, which involves issues even larger than the integration of immigrants. Recognition as used by cosmopolitans obeys the principle of respect for difference and acceptance of similarity between human beings, in contrast with nationalist ideology, the darkest side of which is the repression of internal difference and of similarity with the other. Marshal Berman's cosmopolitan ideal relies on the structural contradiction between culture and bourgeois economic calculation and on the existence of impersonal forces that tend to internationalisation. In this scheme, collective forces are mainly left hanging in suspension waiting for the moment to act. Consequently, human control of the ongoing daily process of change is largely waved, and all we can do regarding collective participation, so Berman admits, is little more than to lie in wait for the moment when identification with a common cause takes place and the masses walk the streets again and give sense to changes, as happened in 1989, a great modernist year for Berman. Nationalist identification, on the contrary, takes advantage of the modification of

---

2   For a less optimistic reading of Smith's text from the perspective of the aftermath of the 7th July attacks, see McLeod (2005).

the ego it produces and gathers a collective force that intervenes, in a more or less organised way, in everyday life.

As long as recognition of the other and identification with the same are held in opposition, they help to expose each other's weaknesses: respect for difference and acceptance of similarity between human beings is a pharmakon against parochial repression of internal difference and of similarity with the other; the necessity of daily organised action fuelled by identification warns against the weakness and uncertainty of universalist aspirations. But recognition and identification may ideally complement each other. On the one hand, the modifications of the ego produced by identification are part of historical and cultural processes. This means that there is nothing in nature to prevent a process that could build an ego for whom the human community would be a dimension as intrinsic as the group in which the individual was born can be. On the other hand, one should not forget that for recognition of the other to take place, a moral act of good will is not enough. Hegel has shown that the drama of recognition is dominated by violence, all the more so when the stage is haunted by an 'other' historically represented as an enemy. This is one reason why there cannot be authentic recognition until 'we' learn how to deal with our own ghosts. In sum, recognition is not possible if the ego is not produced as, paraphrasing Hegel, "an 'ego' which is a 'we' and a 'we' which is an 'ego'". It will remain a merely idealist program unless a historically human dimension is built where a modification of the ego can be produced that enables different subjects to identify with each other as a part of a common 'we'. Utopian? Yes, but perhaps only then it will be possible for us living in a commodified world to be more attracted by the human image than by our own reflected on the polished surface of a new car.

It can be argued that at present historical forces and international affairs do not seem to lead in this direction. But, before embracing scepticism and retiring from the political arena, one should remember that there are people like Said, Rushdie, and Eagleton whose work provides reasons for refusing to embrace the ideology implied in the phrase "things are what they are once and for all", and who do all they can to keep the flame of memory and hope burning, not just while we lie in wait for the moment of collective vision to come (though this is better than nothing), but while we study strategies and possibilities of intervention and assume our responsibility to make the best of our positions to promote justice in daily life.

WORKS CITED

Abraham, Nicolas and Maria Torok (1980): "Introjection-Incorporation". *Mourning* or *Melancholia*. Serge Lebovici and Daniel Widlöcher. New York: International University Press, 3–16.

Berman, Marshal (1996): "Why modernism Still matters". *Modernity and Identity*. S. Lash and J. Friedman, eds. Oxford: Blackwell, 33–58.

Blair, Tony (1997): *New Britain: My Vision of a Young Country*. London: Westview Press.

Burke, Peter (1996): "We, the People: Popular Culture and Popular Identity in Modern Europe". *Modernity and Identity*. S. Lash and J. Friedman, eds. Oxford: Blackwell, 293–308.

Dodd, Philip (1999): "Englishness and the National Culture". *Representing the Nation: A Reader: Histories, Heritage and Museums*. David Boswell and Jessica Evans, eds. London: Routledge, 87–108.

Eagleton, Terry (1983): *Literary Theory: An Introduction*. Minneapolis: The University of Minnesota Press.

Eagleton, Terry (1995): *Heathcliff and the Great Hunger*. London: Verso.

Eagleton, Terry (2005): *The English Novel: An Introduction*. Oxford: Blackwell.

Evans, Jessica (1999): "Nation and Representation". *Representing the Nation: A Reader: Histories, Heritage and Museums*. David Boswell and Jessica Evans, eds. London: Routledge, 1–8.

Kureishi, Hanif (1986): *My Beautiful Laundrette and the Rainbow Sign*. London: Faber & Faber.

McLeod, John (2005): "Revisiting Postcolonial London". *The European English Messanger* 14.2: 39–46

Orwell, George (1962): "England Your England". *Inside the Whale and Other Essays*. Harmondsworth: Penguin, 63–90.

Orwell, George (1987): "The English People". *The Collected Essays, Journalism and Letters of George Orwell*. Vol 3. Sonia Orwell and Ian Angus, eds. Harmondsworth: Penguin, 15–56.

Phillips, Caryl (2002): *A New World Order: Selected Essays*. London: Vintage.

Rushdie, Salman (1992): *Imaginary Homelands: Essays and Criticism 1981–1991*. London: Granta Books/Penguin.

Rushdie, Salman (1994): *East, West*. New York: Random House.

Said, Edward (2003): "El humanismo como resistencia". *Babelia*. 23 August 2003: 8–9.

BRAD EPPS

"No todo se perdió en Cuba": Spain between Europe and Africa in the Wake of 1898

I Introduction

It seems that it is time, long time, as Carlos Serrano has argued, to move beyond the story of modern Spain in which "el Desastre" and "la generación de 1898" are the dominant signs of a wrenchingly metaphysical meditation on a nation, in José Ortega y Gasset's formulation, made and unmade by Castile (Serrano 1998: 48). "It is a matter of apprehending," Serrano asserts, "the turn of the century in its globality, contradictory and profuse, in its richness and its limitations, as tension and movement, and not of making yet another visit to the icy pantheon of old mummified glories" (Serrano 1998: 340). Serrano's proposal for a "global vision" in which the upheaval of "the Disaster" and the brooding soulfulness of "the generation of 98" would be put into critical perspective implicates another sign, one whose claims to a more imperious if no less profuse and contradictory sort of globality are far from inconsequential: namely, "Europe". For if there is a signifier by which modernity, progress, and the discourse of democratic rights are at once grounded and mobilised in turn-of-the-century Spain, and against which Spain is often as not measured and deemed "disastrous" and/or all too "soulful," it is "Europe". The object of considerable dispute among those associated with the equally disputed "generation of 98," Europe, as both site and signifier, gleamed in opposition to the presumed obscurantism, backwardness, and primitivism of other parts of the world, Spain ambivalently included. The gleam of "Europe," though dimmed by two world wars and genocide, still endures and marks a wide array of cultural, political, and economic projects whose appeal during and after the transition from Franco's dictatorship to democracy has a lengthy history. 1898 and, more amply, the turn of the nineteenth and twenty centuries constitute a particularly charged moment of this history, the study of which is shadowed by the present moment of global postcolonial migrations, just as Europe, then as now, is shadowed by other geopolitical sites and signifiers: the Americas, obviously enough; and much less obviously Asia, which tended to be figured primarily in terms of despotism and decorative exoticism; but also Africa, the site of colonial projects and presences that, persisting in the wake of the war of 1898, continue to this very day.

As I have noted elsewhere, the oft-repeated claim, a sort of school-book truism, that Spain lost its last colonial possessions in 1898 is patently false, but in its falsity it signals something unsettlingly true: unlike the pearls of the Pacific and the Caribbean, the so-called dark continent seemed to matter little, or not enough, or for all the wrong reasons, and conjured up, for many a Spaniard, a never-never land that was at once slavish and indomitable, indolent and wild, sensual and fanatic (the title of a travel memoir by Catalan writer Aurora Bertrana), and resistant to both an increasingly secularised modernity and the "eternal traditions" of Christian humanism – to use a phrase dear to Miguel de Unamuno in *En torno al casticismo* (1895, 1902). Spanish Guinea, including the islands of Fernando Poo (present-day Bioko), Elobey, Annobón, Corisco, and the mainland Río Muni (all of which now comprise the Republic of Equatorial Guinea); Western or Spanish Sahara (today the non-recognised Saharawi Arab Democratic Republic, claimed by Morocco); and, most notably, Morocco, constituted another colonial sphere, one that sputtered on through wars, trading ventures, missions, and mismanagement until Spain's ramshackle withdrawal from Western Sahara in 1976, and whose last, still contested remnants are Ceuta and Melilla, dotted on the Moroccan coast. Splintered between the North African and the Sub-Saharan, and minor in comparison with the holdings of France, Great Britain, Belgium, Portugal, Germany, and Italy, Spain's African colonies have also been splintered from their Caribbean and Pacific counterparts, whose fate has so dominated Spanish studies that even many of the most historically sensitive critics continue to present 1898, all too sweepingly, as the date of the loss of Spain's colonies and of its Imperial pretensions. In what follows, I will first examine some recent historical revisions of "the Disaster" and "the generation of 1898" that strive to put them in perspective by emphasising the competitive centrality of turn-of-the-century Europe and by claiming that the impact of the war of 1898 has been "exaggerated". Then, I will turn to some older, largely literary and geographic reflections on the role of Africa in Spain's embattled colonial aspirations and European projections.

II (In)adequate Measures, (Im)proper Signs, and Comparative Critique

The general ignorance of, or indifference to, the Spanish presence in Africa contrasts with the awareness of, and interest in, the Spanish absence in the Caribbean and the Pacific. Then again, as historian José Álvarez Junco remarks, the awareness among Spaniards of the loss of the Caribbean and the Pacific colonies also contrasts with the relative lack of attention that accompanied the loss of 98% of Spain's possessions 70 or 80 years before (Álvarez Junco 1998: 411). According to Álvarez Junco, the Spanish intellectual and political elites of the 1820s were fixated on the struggles between absolutism and enlightenment and not, as in the 1890s, on the "affirmation of the nation in a European context of competition for world dominion" (Álvarez Junco 1998: 411–412). The European context of competition and domination, implicating as it does the world as a shattered whole, is critical to understanding the impact that the defeat in 1898 had on many Spaniards, for in many respects much remained the same as before. The defeat did not entail, that is, any major change in the

Spanish government, the monarchy, the Constitution, or the party system; any significant depression, run on the banks, or state bankruptcy; or any great national novel or painting – at least not in any directly discernible way (Pan-Montojo 1998: 10). And yet, the loss of Cuba, Puerto Rico, the Philippines, and Guam, rendered official with the Treaty of Paris, had profound psycho-symbolic ramifications, enshrined not only in formulations such as "the Disaster" and "the generation of 1898" but also in popular phrases such as "más se perdió en Cuba," or "more was lost in Cuba," by which Spaniards indicated that a loss, failure, or problem was, when compared to the loss of Cuba, really not so great. The comparative logic behind the phrase "más se perdió en Cuba" will prove significant to our examination of recent assessments of modern Spanish history and culture by Serrano, Álvarez Junco, and others who question how much was *really* lost in Cuba, but for the moment suffice it to say that Cuba, outshining Puerto Rico and the Philippines, all but eclipsed Africa and remained, long after being "lost," uncannily "present" to a handful of Spaniards who found it difficult, if not downright impossible, to affirm the nation without it – and the imperial clout that it commanded.

As José Varela Ortega observes in his introduction to Joaquín Costa's *Oligarquía y caciquismo* (1902), Cuba "had always been a special colony, in many respects richer than Spain itself [...], overflowing with immigrants from the Peninsula," many of whom were staunchly opposed to Cuban independence (Costa 1998: 29). Debatable as the idea of Cuba's superior wealth surely is, the same cannot even be ventured of Spain's African territories, poor, lacking in modern infrastructure, and on the whole sparsely populated, with few Spanish immigrants. The differences, which comparative analysis throws into relief (problematically, as I hope to show), bear on the status of Spain in "a European context of competition for world dominion," even as the "European context" proves to be also American and Asian, under the hegemony of the United States and Japan. Whatever the exact parameters of the competition for world dominion, the conflicts *among* European nations were obviously accompanied by conflicts *between* Europe, as a profoundly uneasy union, and entire regions, even continents, such as Africa, whose partitioning in the late nineteenth century came on the heels of the unification of Germany and Italy. The "scramble" or "race" for Africa, as it came to be called in 1884, the year of the Conference of Berlin in which Europe came together (along with the United States and the Ottoman Empire) to take Africa apart, more or less coincided with protracted military conflicts between Spain and Cuba (F.-Fígares 2003: 36). Thus, while most of the European nations had their sights set on Africa and Asia, Spain was struggling to keep its hold on its last American and Pacific colonies, even though, or perhaps precisely because, it had already lost "much more".

The idea that "more was lost" *before* Cuba was lost has led Álvarez Junco to claim that

> [t]he *Disaster* of 1898 is a clear case of exaggeration or of an overblown perception of events of limited importance that are experienced, however, as a collective misfortune of cataclysmic proportions. An erroneous perception based [...] on the nationalist climate proper to the end of the nineteenth century and on the problems with the construction of Spanish identity throughout the century" (Álvarez Junco 1998: 411).

What was 'lost in Cuba' was not, in this view, something of great material value (though others, as we have seen, would beg to differ), but an illusion, an imperial dream, the fiction of still being one of the world's great colonial powers (Álvarez Junco 1998: 411). And yet, the illusion of Empire was, for Álvarez Junco, likewise overblown. Putting things into presumably proper historical perspective, comparing one event and response with another, Álvarez Junco, for whom the loss of Cuba was an exaggeration in economic and territorial terms, effectively bolsters Serrano's claims that "the Disaster" was also an exaggeration in literary and cultural terms. For Serrano, the Spanish defeat of 1898, despite its notoriety, did not produce any major work of Spanish art, literary, pictorial, or otherwise. There was, to be sure, a "literature of war" and, more prominently, a welter of essayistic reflections by Unamuno, Costa,

Ramiro de Maeztu, Ángel Ganivet, and others on the "problem of Spain" and its "regeneration," but there was not, Serrano maintains, "the creative work that really took up the theme of the abandonment, and the defeat, of the illusions – if they indeed existed – regarding the future of Spain overseas" (Serrano 1998: 335). If the dearth of creative works explicitly centred on the Spanish defeat in 1898 renders "the generation of 1898" questionable, the fact that many of the most celebrated texts on the national problem were penned *before* the defeat likewise raises questions about the significance of said generation or, for that matter, about the generational model in general. Many scholars have questioned the validity of "the generation of 1898," and Serrano is thus on well-trodden ground when he says that "the crisis of consciousness that is typically seen as the consequence of the defeat of 1898 had begun before and in the margins of the defeat" (Serrano 1998: 338). It had begun, furthermore, to different effects in different parts of Spain, especially in Catalonia and Euskadi, where industrialisation, linguistically charged cultural revival, and geographic proximity to France – and thus, synecdochically, Europe – fuelled alternative national movements. Part and parcel of these alternative national movements were alternative generational conceptions, such as the Catalan "generation of 1901," which Jaume Vicens i Vives presented as the flipside to the Spanish "Disaster" of 1898, something like the dawn of one nation amid the twilight of another (Vicens i Vives 1958: 296). If "the Disaster" is arguably far from self-evident, so too is the "generation" to which it has been fused; both terms, in short, may well be powerful misnomers.

The upshot of the preceding remarks should be clear: Serrano and Álvarez Junco, two of the most perceptive contemporary scholars on Spain, strive to foster a "global view" of 1898 that goes beyond the "the conventions of a critical history petrified into a painful, Spanish nationalist vision" (Serrano 1998: 340) – that is to say, "the Disaster" – and that engages a more broadly European understanding of the *fin de siècle* by presenting the Spanish defeat of 1898 as neither as economically and politically momentous nor as culturally exceptional as many have argued and even more have assumed. Of course, the defeat obviously *did* involve human suffering and hardship, but it also involved the perception of Spanish particularity, peculiarity, or *difference* that was infamously recast in the 1960s, under the direction of the Francoist minister Manuel Fraga Iribarne, into a commercial lure for foreign tourists. Juan Pan-Montojo, editor of an insightful collection that includes the aforementioned essays by Serrano and Álvarez Junco, rejects, like them, the notion of Spanish singularity and presents "the *Desastre* as a variant of a generalised intellectual or ideological crisis in the West and a crisis of national identity," likewise generalised (Pan-Montojo 1998: 10). The emphasis on a generalised Western crisis, with the European nation-state at its centre, does indeed place Spain in a circuit that gainsays the rhetoric of singularity, but it also reiterates the Europeanist position of some of the most famous thinkers linked to "the generation of 1898" and reaffirms, *albeit in a more expansive, global mode,* the tendency to generalise a failure of a specific government into a problem of the nation. The 1898 defeat has been spun, in short, into a more or less general crisis (more inasmuch as all of Europe is implicated; less inasmuch as Spain alone is implicated) that outstrips governmental and military particulars. As Varela Ortega states, "once the conflict was over, the *Disaster* was perceived as a problem of the entire country and not just of a few politicians or even a regime. As a result, the Spanish 98 came to manifest itself more as a national revulsion than as a nostalgic hangover for lost Empire" (Costa 1998: 33).

Yet the crisis, let alone the revulsion, of the nation is here, in the disastrous generational rhetoric of 1898, inseparable from an "imperial hangover". After all, by the late nineteenth century, the concept of the nation had become so bound to the concept of Empire that even many proponents of aspirant nation-states envisioned an imperial future, one that had already been realised by a nation-state as small and new as Belgium. Enric Prat de la Riba, whose *La nacionalitat catalana* (1906) has been extraordinarily influential in modern Catalan – and Spanish – politics, was on this score adamant: "imperialism is the triumphant period of nationalism, the nationalism of a great people" (Prat de la RIba 1978: 108). Prat's view of a modern Catalan Empire – or more precisely of a modern Spanish or Iberian Empire under Catalonia's direction – was at once elegiac and rosy, harkening back to a time of splendour and striving to bind imperialism not to militarism but to a non-coercive practice of "civilisation." By the time Prat was writing, Belgium's Leopold II had already deployed similar civilising rhetoric to devastatingly disingenuous effect in the Congo, where ivory, rubber, and slavery effectively trumped freedom, enlightenment, and progress. Prat's conception of a civilising imperialism was not, however, that of the regal Leopold, and brought him instead, enamoured as he was of the Mediterranean, to the decidedly non-Mediterranean United States. Praising Theodore Roosevelt and calling for Catalans to Americanise rather than Europeanise themselves, Prat not only advocated a way out of the Spanish-European binary that was pervasive at the turn of the century and that marked, for instance, the public correspondence between Ganivet and Unamuno (Spain as whole unto itself; Spain as part of Europe), he also explicitly likened Catalonia to a European colony. In Prat's formulation, Spanish imperialism was not merely a foreign affair, something that happened beyond the Iberian peninsula, but a phenomenon that saturated the metropolis – without really binding it together. Little wonder, then, that someone as different from Prat as Ortega y Gasset, who declared in 1921 that "by 1900, the Spanish body had returned to its native peninsular nakedness," would see in "the falling away of the last overseas possessions [...] the sign of the beginning of intrapeninsular dispersion" (Ortega 1997: 45).

The loss of the colonies in the Caribbean and the Pacific, the "last overseas possessions," did not foreshadow for Ortega the loss of the colonies in Africa, but rather of the so-called peninsular peripheries themselves. In this, he followed Unamuno, who declared in 1898 that, "once our colonial Empire collapses the problem of decentralisation [...] will emerge with force" (Ganivet 1998: 159). The possibility of intrapeninsular dispersion (Ortega's fear), no less than the possibility of a reconfigured Spain or Iberia (Prat's desire), was another symptom of a general national revulsion, crisis, or disaster that manifested itself in a "coming home" that, eliding or discounting Africa, was experienced by many Spanish nationals as a "coming apart". Yet the very notion that there *was* an "experience" or "feeling" of general national revulsion, crisis, or disaster was something that others, writing immediately after the war, contradicted. In a chronicle from early 1899, the great Nicaraguan modernist, Rubén Darío, expressed admiration for the dynamism of the Catalan capital but consternation over the lack of reverberations that the war had had on the Spanish capital. In the process, Darío suggested that Spain, through provincial indifference, stagnation, and self-complacency, had already lost its colonies before it had fought for them and, moreover, that it risked doing the same *vis-à-vis* Catalonia. Darío's perception of indifference to the defeat is a far cry from contemporary critics' assessment of an exaggeration; and yet, interestingly, the first may give credence to the second: perhaps the citizens of Madrid were "indifferent" to the aftermath of the war because, as Álvarez Junco contends, relatively little economic and material was at actually stake. Or perhaps, the perception of indifference says more about Darío, the select foreign poet, than about the reality of the Spanish citizenry in general. Or perhaps it is the contemporary reading of exaggeration itself that bears reflection.

Common as it is, the use of one historical event or period to measure another is troubling, remitting as it does to a transhistorical scale that allows one to speak of exaggerated and non-exaggerated, inadequate and adequate, improper and proper, responses in the first place. To say that the "feeling" of disaster around 1898 was an exaggeration because less land and money, fewer goods and inhabitants, were at stake than in the earlier wars of American independence is, in other words, to suggest that a non-exaggerated, adequate, or proper response – not just by historians who studied the defeat but also by the people who lived it – would take into account earlier periods in a way that would respect a constant emotional standard or norm. According to this normative logic, the *non-exaggerated* perception, the *right* response, would have meant comparing 1898 from the very outset to earlier moments, disjoining "fact" and "feeling," and contending, in a manner that parents are fond of telling their children, that things were not, in reality, as bad as they had been before. The idea of a disjuncture between the economic and political, on the one hand, and the psychic and symbolic, on the other, or between facts and feelings, entails the idea of a juncture, a coming together, correspondence, or correlation. In some respects, it is as if Álvarez Junco and, more implicitly, Serrano had transferred T. S. Eliot's artistic understanding of an "objective correlative" (or rather the lack thereof, which is how Eliot defines "excess") to the realm of history: Hamlet, in brooding and killing, was "excessive" in his reaction to his mother's "guilt;" Spaniards, in resorting to the term "Desastre" and in binding it to an entire "generation," were "exaggerated" in their reaction to the loss of Spain's last American and Pacific colonies.

There is, however, another mode of "exaggeration". As Darío suggests, what was "too much" was the *lack* of revulsion over the war and its implications. After all, although exaggeration and excess normally signify "too much," they can also signify "too little," as in "the response was exaggeratedly subdued or excessively calm". As different as Darío's (contemporaneous) perception of indifference is from Álvarez Junco's (retrospective) perception of exaggeration, in a profound sense they come to the same thing: the ability or authority of one person – here, a poet and a historian, respectively – to determine what the emotional or psycho-symbolic response of others *should be* or *should have been*. The point is important inasmuch as it implicates the previously expressed assertion that the Spanish presence in Africa has been largely ignored, forgotten, or elided, and, moreover, that it *should not be so*. Structurally, such an assertion (that is to say, mine) recalls Darío's assertion that the loss of the Caribbean and Pacific colonies was largely ignored, forgotten, or elided, and that it *should not have been so*. With the passing of time, however, Darío's reading, taken up, amplified, and "corrected" by others, has issued in a markedly different reading, one that, as we have seen, has deemed the response to the defeat to be exaggerated in the sense of "too much," not "too little". Accordingly, even as an objective correlative, or rather its lack, is shadowed forth, and hence even as a referential principle of reality is deployed (without which history, as conventionally practiced, would be hard pressed to be), it is a non-referential principle of discursivity that comes to the fore. In other words, and as Michel Foucault has argued with respect to the "repressive hypothesis" in the domain of sexuality, there is a veritable discursive explosion in which the silence that supposedly attended the defeat of 1898 in the Spanish capital becomes strident and the dearth of attention overabundant.

The discursive explosion that renders Darío's post-war complaint that "the fall had no reverberations" (Darío 1998: 90) premature and hence "exaggerated" simply does not obtain, however, for the Spanish territories in Africa. Indeed, if what was lost in Cuba was not really as great as the rhetoric of disaster and national revulsion would indicate, what was retained – and later lost, abandoned, or surrendered – in Africa has scarcely been recognised, *comparatively* speaking. To complain about this lack of attention, to strive to reverse it, raises, however, the questions about measure, nomenclature, and comparative critique that we have been considering regarding "the Disaster" and "the generation of 1898". For there can be little doubt that the African territories *were* less important, materially *and* symbolically, than the Caribbean and Pacific territories, however "exaggerated" their value and importance may have been. Miguel Martín, writing in 1973 on the Spanish presence in Morocco and noting the scarcity of studies on Spanish colonial practice (as distinct from colonial uprisings, rebellions, and wars), declares that Cuba alone has merited examination, and even then insufficiently. For him, "perhaps the commotion that the loss of Cuba produced among intellectuals explains the minimal attention" (Martín 1973: 5) that Morocco and other parts of Africa have received. Whatever the case, as Martín goes on to say, "the few exceptions ... confirm the rule of silence" (Martín 1973: 12). While the silence that Darío found so disturbing in relation to "the Disaster" of 1898 soon gave way to a discursive explosion (with Darío's complaints thus functioning as part of a broader "incitement to discourse"), the silence that Martín signals in relation to Africa has proved considerably more intractable.

Of course, the silence is overdetermined. Although the hubbub that attended the war in the Caribbean and the Pacific seems to have overwhelmed many, though not by any means all, of those who wrote and spoke about Africa, Spain's African territories were not only poorer and less populated by Spanish immigrants than its other overseas territories, they also had a different legal status. An important instance of this difference is articulated in the Constitution of 1812, which explicitly included the "African possessions" as part of "Las Españas" – literally, "the Spains" – but which did not grant their inhabitants full and immediate rights of citizenship. Although article 18 of the Constitution declared that, "those Spaniards are citizens who by both lines [maternal and paternal] originate from the Spanish dominions of both hemispheres and who are settled in any town in the same dominions," article 22 specified that Africans "still have open the door of virtue and merit by which they can be citizens". What was elsewhere and for others a birthright was for those born in Spanish Africa achieved by performing "qualified services to the fatherland or by distinguishing themselves for their talent, commitment, and conduct," provided that they were legitimately born and "exercise[d] a useful profession, office, or industry with their own capital". Given the political turmoil of the times, the Constitution of 1812 was only intermittently in effect, but the distinctions it drew between the territories in Africa and elsewhere are nonetheless significant. In the Constitution of 1876, in effect until 1923 and hence during the Spanish-American War, there is no direct reference to Africa, only to Cuba and Puerto Rico. The "rule of silence" that held for Africa, and that extended at times to the Pacific, clearly antedates the Spanish defeat in 1898; the commotion that the loss of Cuba produced among intellectuals does not therefore *explain* the minimal attention that the African colonies received, as Martín contends; it merely confirms it – resoundingly.

At this point, after tracing some of the debates and disagreements around nomenclature ("the Disaster" and "the generation of 1898"), measure ("in the sense of both "too much" and "too little"), and comparative critique, it bears asking whether it is an "exaggeration" to maintain that the Spanish presence in Africa merits more attention than it has received or, for that matter, if the relative lack of attention itself is an "exaggeration". The questions are as crucial as they are complex. The call by some of the most subtle and substantive historians and cultural critics to put things "in perspective" and to foster a global vision; to speak in terms of a general Western or European crisis that outstrips a specifically Spanish "Disaster;" and to debunk "the generation of 1898" in favour of the *fin de siècle* (the French figuration is not incidental) or what José-Carlos Mainer, via Ricardo Gullón, has called an omnicomprehensive modernism (Mainer 1994: 61), is eminently reasonable and appealing, but nonetheless deeply, maybe even intractably, problematic. One of the problems, perhaps the greatest one, is that the presumably non-exaggerated response seems to be operable only from a distance and in hindsight, as the historian's prerogative. That the historians and cultural critics here under consideration are writing not only long after "the Disaster" but also long after the Spanish Civil War, let alone the Holocaust and other disasters of the twentieth century, arguably only heightens the sense of "exaggeration," one of whose instances is surely, as already noted, the persistent, almost rote claim that Spain lost its last colonial possessions and/or its imperial illusions in 1898. Inasmuch as both Serrano and Álvarez Junco adduce the loss, abandonment, or defeat of imperial illusions as what was "really" at stake in 1898, they too may incur in an exaggeration, for the illusion was *not* lost, at least not entirely. It was, after all, the fractured persistence of a dream of imperial power and, more euphemistically, of a "civilising mission" both before and *after* 1898 that accounted, at least in part, for the presence of Spain in Africa. And it was Africa, as we shall see more directly in the brief section that follows, that weighed heavily on debates in Spain about its singularity *and* its European pertinence, its ability or inability to compete in a European context of world dominion, and its relations to a putatively progressive modernity and a putatively primitive prehistory.

III Geography, National Identity, and Global Competition

Exaggerated or not, the defeat in 1898 exposed Spain's technological deficiencies and political shortcomings in a spectacularly international way, spurring many Spaniards to give themselves over to melancholic lamentations and regenerative ventures alike. The United States did not have a chivalric legacy or a castle-strewn countryside, but it did have state-of-the-art military equipment and a booming industrial, agricultural, and scientific infrastructure, and Spain, *in comparison*, appeared to many Americans torpid, retrograde, and even primitive. It was an image that was hardly new, for any number of Europeans had long viewed Spain as an exotic, quasi-Oriental other, "sensual and fanatic" in its own right. Critically minded Spaniards had similar views, with the obvious difference that they, unlike their European counterparts, were implicated in them. Joaquín Costa, writing shortly after the war of 1898, declared that, "Spain [was] still mired in the fifteenth century and [could not] compete or even live with the twentieth-century nations" (Costa 1998: 200). The defeats in Cavite (Philippines) and Santiago de Cuba led Costa, one of the most vocal and valiant opponents of oligarchy, to say that Spaniards were finally beginning to "wake up from their stupor, fully naked, aware that they had nothing, not even institutions" (Costa 1998: 202). So bad was the situation, so debilitated the monarchy, that Costa qualified the social state of Spain as "barbaric," its civilisation mere varnish, worse even than Morocco, whose "barbarism [was] organic, and as such naïve" (Costa 1998: 100). Joan Maragall, the premier Catalan modernist poet, was no less negative, going so far as to pronounce Spain, in 1897, a "dead thing" (Maragall 1988: 33) from which Catalonia, if it were to live, should sever itself. For Maragall, as for countless others (and not just in the potentially break-away states of Euskadi and Catalonia), the charges of death, stagnation, inertia, backwardness, and barbarism tended to mean – in the racialist and racist language that characterised the times – that Spain was more African than European. For Maragall, Spain's "flaminquisme," or stereotypically Flamenco culture, was something that "civilised people [could not] bear except as jokes and extravagancies of an African tribe" (Maragall 1988: 35). Dismissing the idea that Africa began at the Pyrenees, Maragall suggested instead that it began at the Ebro River, on the southern side of Catalonia. More imperially oriented others, whose language was no less racialist, argued, as we shall see, that Africa itself did not begin until the Atlas. The limits of Europe are as contested as the sweep of Africa. If Spain, a sovereign state, was shot through with intrapeninsular particularities that seemed to grow more intense as it lost its colonies, Africa, a continent, was buckled by particularities of its own – and of Europe's making. For many Spaniards, Morocco, like the rest of the Maghreb, retained a cultural appeal and elicited a fearful respectfulness as a land of warriors, scholars, and church fathers that did not hold for Sub-Saharan Africa, simplistically figured as "Black Africa," further from the peninsula in space and historical memory and hence further from the dubious accoutrements of "civilisation". When the main Spanish character of José Cadalso's *Cartas marruecas* (1789), Nuño, writes to the Moroccan Ben-Beley that he "would like to engage a wise African, because [... he is] fed up with all of the Europeans, except for a few who live in Europe as if they were in Africa" (Cadalso 2000: 112), he conveys an enlightened humanist appreciation of Morocco as a reservoir of wisdom that serves to underscore his disdain for the frivolity of Europe, particularly as represented by France. Cadalso's epistolary fiction places Spaniards and Moroccans in correspondence and reinforces an idealised vision of near brotherhood that goes back to medieval romances and the Golden Age gem *Abencerraje* (c. 1561) and that continues in the work of Juan Goytisolo today. In *Aita Tettauen* (1905), an historical novel that Goytisolo, in an essay included in *Crónicas sarracinas*, considers a model of interlocking identities and ethnic tolerance, Benito Pérez Galdós, Spain's most famous realist, reiterated the notion of a *fraternité manquée*. In the overly optimistic language of one of his characters: "[t]here is nothing easier than for a Moor to come here, learn the language in a short time and pass himself off as a native Spaniard. [...] The faces and ways of acting are the same here as there; and if it were as easy to change languages as it is to change clothes, the people themselves would be confused," melded together (Goytisolo 1989: 105). So close was the resemblance, so "confusing," that Galdós construed the war between Spain and Morocco in 1859–60 as a civil war (Goytisolo 1989: 106) – an assessment that would prove hauntingly ironic in the uprising, from Africa, that initiated the Spanish Civil War of 1936–39. Galdós' text appeared a year after France and Spain had partitioned the North African nation (an internationally contested decision that issued in the 1906 Conference of Algeciras) and only a few years before another military venture in Morocco in 1909, one that would spark acts of violent popular resistance known as the "Tragic Week," centred in Barcelona, a city weary of Spain's colonial pretensions. Spain would again be embroiled in war with Morocco in 1926, but it was the war of 1859–60 – by which, as Kathleen Davis notes, "O'Donnell's government was attempting to enhance Spain's international prestige and re-enter the arena of colonial power" (Davis 2005: 642) – that set the standard for critiques of militaristic patriotism. A "mixture of religious faith, chivalric madness, and haughty superstition", as Galdós put in *Aita Tettauen* (Pérez Galdós 2004: 134), the war of 1859–60 was also, in Álvarez Junco's estimation, "the most immediate international precedent to the war of 1898" (Álvarez Junco 1998: 434), one that was "pompously baptised the 'War of Africa'" (Álvarez Junco 1998: 433).

Pompous or not, the conflation of Morocco and Africa has a long history, as Cadalso's text indicates. In fact, Morocco is repeatedly taken as both a "natural" extension of Spain and as a gateway to the rest of Africa. Pedro Antonio de Alarcón, whose *Diario de un testigo de la guerra de África* (1859–60) Galdós turned upside down in *Aita Tettauen*, presented the African side of the Mediterranean as the site of "the treasure of lost Spanish grandeur" and as "the foundation for a future Iberia" (Alarcón 2005: 5). Alarcón anticipated post-1898 works on Spanish colonialism in the Americas and the Pacific by saying that "Spain should go to Africa to recover its talisman" and that it "should realise that the most natural function of its existence is constant expansion towards the South" (Alarcón 2005: 5). Ángel Ganivet, in his 1898 public epistolary exchange with Unamuno later published as *El porvenir de España*, also presented Morocco as the gateway to Africa and to a regenerated Spain. Despite his calls for Spain to turn inward, Ganivet saw Morocco, and through it Africa, as an exception to his isolationist rule, saying that although "it would be good to close all of the doors so that Spain does not spill out [literally 'escape'], he would nonetheless "leave one door ajar, that of Africa, thinking about the future" (Ganivet 1998: 139). Explicitly citing the Monroe Doctrine (and turning its anti-European dictum on its head), Ganivet posited Morocco, and through it "all of Africa," as the "'sphere of influence' or *hinterland*" (Ganivet 1998: 140) of Spain. More audaciously, he declared that, "if Spain had the strength to work in Africa, I would dedicate myself to inventing half a dozen new theories so that we could legally keep whatever we fancied" (Ganivet 1998: 141). To do so, he would enlist the Moroccan, and more generally the Arab, "governed by a superior spirit," as "an effective ally, the only one capable of raising up the African races without doing violence to their idiosyncrasy" (Ganivet 1998: 141). Although journalist and fiction writer Carmen de Burgos ridiculed the notion of a reliable Moroccan ally in her devastating account of the war of 1909, "En la guerra," Ganivet's appreciation of the Arab, which rankled the openly anti-Arabic Unamuno (who saw the Spanish presence in Morocco as "bad business," both financially and spiritually, for Spain, "Eso," Burgos 1989: 210), was far from gently fraternal, despite its humanistic rhetoric.

Whatever traces of a cross-cultural rapport there may have been in Ganivet's version of the Monroe Doctrine, he saw Spain's place in Africa as compensation for its looming displacement from the Americas and Asia. It was, to be sure, partial and ambivalent compensation, for if Ganivet asked if there could be anything "more beautiful than civilising savages," he also asked if there could be "anything more absurd than a colonial enterprise in Africa" (Ganivet 2003: 219). In what might be read as a proto-surrealist gesture, Ganivet chose *both* the beautiful and the absurd, and did so through a largely retrospective assessment of colonisation in the Americas and a prospective assessment of internal strife in Spain itself that led him to propose that Spain should look to the Mediterranean as its only legitimate colonial sphere (Ganivet 2003: 216–220). The proposal, as Ganivet knew, would not be easy to popularise. True, the Moroccan war of 1859–60 had generated widespread support as Spain's way to revive the "glories" of the Reconquest and to make its power known once again to Europe, but by the time of war and defeat in the Caribbean and the Pacific, Africa, with Morocco as its designated gateway, had receded into the *hinterland* of Spanish thought. "Our colonisation has almost been the stuff of novels," wrote Ganivet. "The majority of the nation has always been ignorant of the geographic situation of its dominions; it has been like Sancho Panza, who never knew where the island of Barataria was" (Ganivet 1998: 35). The exception, at least for the inhabitants of Spain's southern coast, was Morocco, which Alarcón had contemplated from atop the Sierra Nevada (from where he imagined that "the Moors sleep their historical death," Alarcón 2005: 4) and from which, over a century later, the narrator of Goytisolo's *Reivindicación del Conde don Julián* (1970), contemplating the Spanish coast from Tangiers, would launch a fantastically vengeful invasion of Francoist Spain. In the modern period, the only truly colonial invasion launched by Moroccans has been to the Western Sahara (partially occupied by Spain in late 1884, its borders were demarcated by France and Spain in late 1912), and it has hardly been to assist Spain, as Ganivet imagined, in securing "support in the African continent to maintain [its] personality and independence before Europe" (Ganivet 1998: 142). Rather, Spain repeatedly invaded Morocco, striving to have a role on a stage set primarily for Western eyes.

The eye is one of the first weapons of explorers and conquerors (the imagination is another), and it is little surprising that its ability to span space was enlisted to justify territorial expansion. For Ganivet, "what is most permanent in a country is the territorial spirit. The most transcendent act of our history is attributed to Hercules, when he came and with one blow separated us from Africa" (Ganivet 1998: 122). This fanciful historiography had received literary form in Jacint

Verdaguer's *Atlàntida* (1877), a modern Catalan epic poem that brings together the myth of Hercules and the history of Columbus, but it also marked a range of geographic and historical studies that argued that the Strait of Gibraltar was a geographic accident and that Spain, as a territorial unit, extended to the Atlas mountains in the southeast of Morocco. A striking example, long after "the Disaster," is Tomás García Figueras' *Africa en la acción española*, winner of the Premio África de Literatura in 1946 and rife with Francoist rhetoric, which asserts that, "in reality, the claim that *Europe ends in the Atlas* and not that Africa begins in the Pyrenees is perfectly exact" (García Figueras 1949: 11–12, emphasis original). The ideological malleability of territory was much in evidence in the nineteenth and early twentieth centuries, when geographic associations provided a scientific and humanitarian veneer to colonialist endeavours in which explorers, missionaries, soldiers, politicians, and businessmen alike intervened; it was also in evidence when Morocco, after Spain withdrew from the Sahara, used virtually the same arguments of territorial unity to buttress its colonialist claims (Ruiz Miguel, quoted in Martínez Milán 2003: 18). And yet, territory and those who inhabited it were also obdurately resistant to ideological manipulation. Not only were Spanish territorial claims on Morocco forced (in every sense of the word), but also, south of the Atlas, deep in Africa, Spain was truly "beyond itself". In the Gulf of Guinea, an epically inflected tale of a geographic cataclysm that separated Spaniard from Moroccan as European from would-be European was simply not operant, nor was a genealogically inflected tale of mixed brotherhood variously told by Cadalso, Galdós, Ganivet, and Goytisolo. There, the ideology of race imposed itself with a force that outstripped its increasingly charged deployments among Europeans and North Africans. The British explorer Sir Richard Burton, for a time consul in Spanish Guinea, had disguised himself as an Arab but could not disguise himself as a Guinean, and his views of Sub-Saharan Africans were accordingly "coloured" with a mode of racism that took the body as a barrier insusceptible to ideological malleability (Ridao 2005: 11–12).

"Black Africa" was, and remains, an indiscriminate mass for most Spaniards, most Europeans, most Americans (North and South), and its inhabitants the most visible embodiments of a Western-defined "difference". A recent article in the Spanish daily *El País* titled "Los 100.000 subsaharianos que todo el mundo ve" [The 100,000 Sub-Saharans that Everyone Sees] reports that although Black Africans comprise only 4% of the total number of immigrants to Spain, they are the most "visible" and hence the most susceptible to detention, harassment, and rejection – even as a paternalistic discourse of compassion is unfurled. As María Dolores F.-Fígares writes, "[t]he construction of the representation of Black people in the imaginary of Spanish society has its roots in the lost overseas Empire and in the struggles by abolitionists against slavery, which gives way to the discourse of compassion, the only one that is presented as an alternative to the discourse of superiority;" put more simply, the savage gives way to the child in need of protection, education, and control (F.-Fígares 2003: 18). This is the image that marks the end of Luis Martín-Santos' much-celebrated anti-Francoist *Tiempo de silencio* (1961), in which Spaniards are likened to Black Africans in order to underscore their difference from them: "We are not Blacks, we are not Blacks; Blacks jump, laugh, shout, and vote to elect their representatives to the United Nations. We are not Blacks, nor Indians, nor underdeveloped countries" (Martín-Santos 1988: 292). For all its ironic and hyperbolic feints, all its unprocessed racism, Martín-Santos' portrayal of Spanish backwardness recalls earlier portrayals by Costa, Maragall, and others writing at the turn of the century, for whom backwardness was synonymous with Africanness, be it Moroccan or, more resolutely, Sub-Saharan. Then as before, modernity, progress, and the discourse of democratic rights bore a European stamp that has had particularly devastating implications for Africa, whose perceived and presumed "primitiveness" has been marshaled as justification for its conquest, occupation, and protracted subjection to Western norms, including those of the post-Westphalian nation-state. Spain's role in the profoundly uneven propagation of the nation-state model in Africa may be "minor" when *compared* to that of other Western countries, but it is significant nonetheless, affecting not only Morocco and the Western Sahara (which Morocco claims), but also Equatorial Guinea, the only country in Africa where Spanish is an official language. Indeed, although Equatorial Guinea has received – in general and in the present article as well – far less attention than Morocco, a number of Guineans, writing in Spanish, generate responses, rebuttals, and forms of resistance that, expanding on travel, missionary, and other forms of literature, go to the heart of modern Spanish culture. An especially incisive response, some ninety years after "the Disaster," is uttered at the end of Donato Ndongo's *Las tinieblas de tu memoria negra* (1987), when the protagonist, a young man "educated" by Spanish missionaries, calls the smug, self-sure Whites "slaves of modernity" (Ndongo 2000: 162). How this compares with other assessments of colonialism in a European context of global domination and whether it is an exaggeration remains, however, to be seen. In the meantime, Europe, now almost fully constituted as a union, and the values for which it stands, will continue to be put to the test most powerfully at its southern borders.

WORKS CITED

Alarcón, Pedro Antonio de (2005): *Diario de un testigo de la guerra de África*. Sevilla: Fundación José Manuel Lara.

Álvarez Junco, José (1998): "La nación en duda". *Más se perdió en Cuba: España, 1898 y la crisis de fin de siglo*. Ed. Juan Pan-Montojo. Madrid: Alianza, 1998, 405–475.

Bárbulo, Tomás (2006): "Los 100.000 subsaharianos que todo el mundo ve". *El País* 6–11–2006, 6.

Bertrana, Aurora (1991): *El Marroc sensual i fanàtic*. Barcelona: Edicions de l'Eixample.

Burgos, Carmen de (1989): "En la Guerra (Episodios de Melilla)". *La flor de la playa y otras novelas cortas*. Madrid: Castalia/Instituto de la Mujer, 163–218.

Cadalso, José (2000): *Cartas marruecas/Noches lúgubres*. Ed. Emilio Martínez Mata. Barcelona: Crítica.

Constitución política de la Monarquía Española. Promulgada en Cádiz a 19 de marzo de 1812. http:// www.congreso.es /constitucion/

Constitución de 30 de junio de 1876. http://www.congreso.es/ constitucion/

Costa, Joaquín (1998): *Oligarquía y caciquismo: Como la forma actual de gobierno en España; urgencia y modo de cambiarla*. Introd. José Varela Ortega. Madrid: Biblioteca Nueva.

Darío, Rubén (1998): *España contemporánea*. Ed. Noel Rivas Bravo. Managua: Academia Nicaragüense de la Lengua.

Davis, Kathleen E. (2005): "Sons of Adam: Cultural Transference in Galdós' Aita Tettauen". *Bulletin of Spanish Studies*, 82.5, 641–654.

Eliot, T. S. (1975): "Hamlet". *Selected Prose of T. S. Eliot*. Ed. Frank Kermode. New York: Harcourt Brace Jovanovich.

Epps, Brad (2005): "Between Europe and Africa: Modernity, Race, and Nationality in the Correspondence of Miguel de Unamuno and Joan Maragall". *Anales de Literatura Española Contemporánea*, 30.1–2, 95–131.

Espinosa de los Monteros, Ramos (1903): *España en África*. Prologue by José Rocamora. Madrid: R. Velasco Imp., Marqués de Santa Ana.

F.-Fígares Romero de la Cruz, María Dolores (2003): *La colonización del imaginario: Imágenes de África*. Granada:

Universidad de Granada y Centro de Investigaciones Etnológicas Ángel Ganivet.

Foucault, Michel (1978): *The History of Sexuality: An Introduction.* Vol. 1. Trans. Robert Hurley. New York: Random House.

Ganivet, Ángel (2003): *Idearium español.* Ed. Fernando García Lara. Introd. Loretta Frattale. Granada: Diputación Provincial de Granada/Fundación Caja de Granada.

Ganivet, Ángel and Miguel de Unamuno (1998): *El porvenir de España.* Ed. Fernando García Lara. Introd. Pedro Cerezo Galán. Granada: Diputación Provincial de Granada/Fundación Caja de Granada.

García Figueras, Tomás (1949): *África en la acción española.* Madrid: Instituto de Estudios Africanos.

Goytisolo, Juan (1989): *Crónicas sarracinas.* Barcelona: Seix Barral.

Goytisolo, Juan (1970): *Reivindicación del Conde don Julián.* Mexico: Joaquín Mortiz.

Gullón, Ricardo (1990): *Direcciones del modernismo.* Madrid: Alianza.

Maeztu, Ramiro de (1997): *Hacia otra España.* Madrid: Biblioteca Nueva.

Mainer, José-Carlos (1994): "El modernismo como actitud". *Historia y crítica de la literatura española.* Francisco Rico, ed. Vol. 6.1. Modernismo y 98. Primer Suplemento. José-Carlos Mainer, ed. Barcelona: Grijalbo, 61–76.

Maragall, Joan (1988): "La independència de Catalunya". *Articles polítics.* Ed. Joan-Lluís Marfany. Barcelona: Edicions de la Magrana/ Diputació de Barcelona, 33–35.

Martín, Miguel (1973): *El colonialismo español en Marruecos (1860–1956).* France: Ruedo Ibérico.

Martín y Peinador, León (1908): *Estudios geográficos: Marruecos y plazas españolas, Argelia, Túnex y Tripoli, Sahara y Sahara Español, Guinea Continental e Insular Española, problema marroquí.* Madrid: Bernardo Rodríguez.

Martín-Santos, Luis (1988): *Tiempo de silencio.* Barcelona: Seix Barral.

Martínez Milán, Jesús María (2003): *España en el Sáhara Occidental y en la Zona Sur del Protectorado en Marruecos, 1885–1945.* Madrid: Universidad Nacional de Educación a Distancia.

Ndongo, Donato (2000): *Las tinieblas de tu memoria negra.* Barcelona: Ediciones del Bronce.

Ortega y Gasset, José (1997): *España invertebrada.* Madrid: Alianza/ Revista de Occidente.

Pan-Montojo, Juan (1998): "Introducción. ¿98 o fin de siglo?" *Más se perdió en Cuba: España, 1898 y la crisis de fin de siglo.* Ed. Juan Pan-Montojo. Madrid: Alianza, 9–30.

Pérez Galdós, Benito (2004): *Aita Tettauen.* Madrid: Ediciones Akal.

Prat de la Riba, Enric (1978): *La nacionalitat catalana.* Barcelona: Edicions 62.

Ridao, José María (2005): "Prólogo". *Richard Burton, cónsul en Guinea Española: Una visión europea de África en los albores de la colonización.* By Arturo Arnalte. Madrid: Catarata.

Serrano, Carlos (1998): "Conciencia de la crisis, conciencias en crisis". *Más se perdió en Cuba: España, 1898 y la crisis de fin de siglo.* Ed. Juan Pan-Montojo. Madrid: Alianza, 335–403.

Unamuno, Miguel de (1977): "Eso de Marruecos". *Crónica política española (1915–1923).* Ed. Vicente González Martín. Salamanca: Almar, 209–212.

Unamuno, Miguel de (1991): *En torno al casticismo*. Madrid: Espasa-Calpe.

Verdaguer, Jacint (1979): *L'Atlàntida*. Barcelona: Edicions 62.

Vicens i Vives, Jaume and Montserrat Llorens (1958): *Industrials i polítics del segle XIX*. Barcelona: Teide.

JAIME FEIJÓO

Deutsch-deutsche Identitätsfragen nach der Wende. Mit einer Lektüre von Christa Wolf und Wolfgang Hilbig

I Deutsche Identitäten

Betrachtet man die Werke, die nach 1989 die deutsche Literaturentwicklung wesentlich mitbestimmt haben, so wird man feststellen, dass die Vereinigung Deutschlands in einem beträchtlichen Teil von ihnen eine Rolle spielt. Sei es bei dem Versuch, den endgültigen "Wenderoman"[1] zu schreiben, sei es, dass die Vereinigung in vielen Texten den Hintergrund der Handlung darstellt,[2] das Thema ist überall präsent. Dabei spielen ostdeutsche Autoren eine Hauptrolle, sowohl diejenigen, die schon vor der Wende veröffentlicht hatten,[3] als auch solche, die erst danach bekannt wurden.[4] Ältere und jüngere ostdeutsche Autoren haben sich intensiv mit der DDR-Vergangenheit und mit der Frage ihrer *verlorenen* Identität auseinandergesetzt und dabei erreicht, dass beinahe zwei Jahrzehnte nach dem Fall der Berliner Mauer die Frage nach der nationalen Identität weiterhin ein Hauptthema der Gegenwartsliteratur und der gesellschaftlichen Debatte in Deutschland geblieben ist.

1 Vgl. dazu die Darstellung von Ledanff 1997.
2 Vgl. dazu Soldat 1997.
3 Dies ist z.B. der Fall von Christa Wolf, Christoph Hein, Brigitte Burmeister oder Monika Maron.
4 Gemeint sind Autoren wie Ingo Schulze, Thomas Brussig oder Reinhard Jirgl.

Statt ein gemeinsames kulturelles Selbstverständnis zu stiften, hat die politische Vereinigung das Problem der "inneren Einheit" erst recht virulent gemacht. Die nationale Identität, auf die sich die Leipziger Demonstranten am Vorabend der Wende mit der Formel "Wir sind ein Volk", so leicht meinten berufen zu können, muss wohl im Laufe von Generationen erst mühsam erworben werden. Vorerst gibt es mehr Anzeichen für zwei verschiedene, in einigen Hinsichten sogar entgegengesetzte Identitäten, die sich zudem erst in dem Moment herauskristallisieren, da "das gegenseitige Kennenlernen im vereinten Deutschland [...] die gegenseitige Fremdheit zutage" fördert (Simanowski 2000: 214).[5] Das Verhältnis zwischen Ost und West in der Berliner Republik motiviert offenbar nicht die Herausbildung einer *Kulturnation* sondern einen *Kulturkonflikt*, aus dem zwei gegensätzliche Identitäten, sozusagen zwei Kulturnationen, entstehen.

Die Ursachen dieses "deutsch-deutsche[n] Kulturkonflikt[s]" (Simanowski 2000: 219) reichen bis zur Herausbildung der beiden deutschen *nationalen Teilidentitäten* in der Nachkriegszeit zurück. Weil es damals "keine Möglichkeit für die Identifikation mit der nationalstaatlichen Idee gab", entstanden "Ersatzidentifikationen" (Arns 2001: 3), die sich dann im Laufe der Jahre verhärtet haben: im Westen eine schuldhafte "Holocaustidentität", deren andere Seite die "Wirtschaftswunderidentität" war, im Osten die "Antifaschismusidentität", verbunden mit der Idee einer übernationalen sozialistischen Identität. Beide Modelle stammen aus entgegengesetzten Prinzipien, die vor allem auch darauf angelegt waren, die jeweilige andere Identität in Frage zu stellen: So wie das Wirtschaftswunder gegen die Versäumnisse der Planwirtschaft, wird der Antifaschismus gegen den Fortbestand des Nazionalsozialismus in der Bundesrepublik angeführt. Diese "Ersatzidentitäten" bilden die Grundlage für die heutigen neuen Identitätsbildungen. Klaus Schlesinger (1998: 86) erinnert daran, dass die Wende im Osten "Der Umbruch" genannt wird: Aus der Perspek-

---

5 KritikerInnen der deutschen Vereinigung wie Daniela Dahn behaupten sogar, "daß der Prozeß der Annäherung [...] durch die Einheit abrupt unterbrochen" wurde (zit. n. Neuhaus 2002: 359).

tive des Ostens ist die Wende eine Art *Nachkriegszeit*, eine neue "Stunde Null"; im Westen sah man hingegen in der Wiedervereinigung vor allem die Chance für die Formulierung einer neuen gesamtdeutschen Identität, die jene "Holocaustidentität" überwinden sollte,[6] und vernachlässigte dabei eine ernsthafte Auseinandersetzung mit der Geschichte der DDR.

Aus der Sicht ostdeutscher Autoren haben gerade die Vereinigung und die damit verbundenen Konflikte zwischen Ost- und Westdeutschland dazu geführt, dass sich "post festum eine einheitliche DDR-Identität formuliert hat" (Simanowski 2000: 214). In einem Aufsatz über die Erinnerung an die DDR hat der Kulturhistoriker Dietrich Mühlberg den Ostdeutschen ein kulturelles Gedächtnis attestiert, dem die "professionelle[] Geschichtsdeutung von Westdeutschen" zuwiderläuft (Mühlberg 2002: 219). Mühlberg analysiert die Wende als eine große "Abrechnung [...], mit der den ostdeutschen Traditionsträgern das moralische Recht entzogen werden sollte, an der Erinnerungsarbeit der neuen Bundesrepublik teilzunehmen" (Mühlberg 2002: 224). Dieses "westdeutsche Umerziehungskonzept" (ebd. 229) ziele auf eine radikale Demontage der ehemaligen DDR, auf die "geistige Delegitimierung der fehlgeschlagenen sozialistischen Alternative durch ihre Entlarvung als Diktatur" (ebd. 229). Dabei seien "de[r] 17. Juni, de[r] 13. August 1961 und de[r] Mauerfall" (ebd. 229) als die entscheidenden Fakten der DDR-Geschichte gedeutet, die interne demokratische Wende und die "friedliche Revolution" im Herbst 1989 dagegen weitgehend ignoriert worden. Resultat dieser Geschichtsschreibung ist nach Mühlberg eine ostdeutsche "geistige

---

6 Vgl. z. B. die "Friedenspreisrede" von Martin Walser am 11. Oktober 1998 (und die anschließende Walser-Bubis-Debatte), in der der konservative Schrift-steller sich gegen die Instrumentalisierung und "Monumentalisierung" der nationalsozialistischen Schande in der gegenwärtigen deutschen Kultur empört und ein Ende der deutschen Auseinandersetzung mit der NS-Zeit verlangt. Das Holocaust-Thema läßt aber die deutsche Kultur bzw. Literatur nicht los, das bestätigt auch die Sicht auf jüngere Werke wie z.B. Marcel Beyers *Flughunde* (1995), Günter Grass' *Im Krebsgang* (2002) oder Uwe Timms *Am Beispiel meines Bruders* (2003).

Heimatlosigkeit", die durch eine *ostalgische* Reproduktion der verlorenen Heimat kompensiert wird. Dabei handelt es sich jedoch nicht nur um eine nostalgischen Anwandlung und um das retrospektiv idealisierte Bild einer humanen und solidarischen Gesellschaft, das als Trotzreaktion gegen die Verachtung und Bevormundung des Westens entsteht und die tatsächlichen Leiden der DDR-Existenz ins Positive verkehrt.[7] In einem Aufsatz in der Zeitschrift *Merkur* hat der Essayist Michael Rutschky 1995 auf die Entstehung einer "neuen DDR" hingewiesen, die den "Negativraum der Kolonisatoren Unterworfenen, Gekränkten" transzendiert: "Die neue DDR [...] ist feste, selbstbewußte Provinz. Diese DDR hat überhapt erst jetzt Gelegenheit zu entstehen, weil niemand sie nur gezwungenermaßen bewohnt. Jeder kann gehen. Deshalb ist man freiwillig hier" (Rutschky 1995: 864). Rutschky zeichnet das Bild einer neuen "Erfahrungs- und Erzählgemeinschaft, in der sich überlieferte Elemente, Spolien der untergangenen DDR erhalten und umbilden, in der neue Elemente entstehen, indem sie sich mit solchen Spolien verbinden" (Rutschky 1195: 856). Im Osten der Berliner Republik ist also eine neue kulturelle Identität entstanden, die zu einer allgemeingesellschaftlichen Auseinandersetzung zwingt.

Erinnern wir uns noch einmal daran, wie das Thema der nationalen Identität in der unmittelbaren Wende-Zeit aktualisiert wurde. Die Proteste im Herbst 1989, die das Ende der DDR einleiteten, gingen von universalistischen demokratischen Grundsätzen aus, bei denen die kollektive Identitätsfrage zunächst nicht im Vordergrund stand. Ihr Leitsatz "Wir sind das Volk" richtete sich gegen ein von seinen Bürgern immer weiter sich entfernendes kommunistisches Regime und beanspruchte das Recht auf eine wahrhaft partizipative Demo-

---

7 "Ostalgie entsteht, weil eine professionelle, medial wirksame Aufarbeitung der DDR, die nicht stigmatisierend ist, die zu differenzieren, abzuwägen und an den Alltagserfahrungen der Leute anzuknüpfen vermag, nicht stattfindet." (Ahbe, Thomas: „Gruppenbild mit Banane. Aus dem Kulturalmanach des vereinigten Deutschland." *Freitag*, 29.9.2000, zit. n. Mühlberg 2002: 227).

kratie, im Verständnis vieler einen "echten demokratischen Sozialismus", der die utopische Zielvorstellung vieler DDR-Schriftsteller und Intellektueller war.[8]

Aber bald wurde dieser *universale* Anspruch auf Egalität mit der *partikularen* Frage der nationalen deutschen Identität verbunden. Die Aussage "Wir sind das Volk" wurde durch die Formel "Wir sind ein Volk" ersetzt und damit gewissermaßen die universale Menschenwürde mit der besonderen deutschen Identität und dem kapitalistischen System der Bundesrepublik gleichgesetzt. Aus der Perspektive der kommunitaristischen Multikulturalismus-Theorie von Charles Taylor wurde dabei eine "Politik der allgemeinen Menschenwürde" ("a politics of equal dignity" Taylor 1992: 38), die auf die universale Gleichheit von Rechten und Immunitäten fußt, unvermittelt in eine "Politik der Differenz" überführt, die auf die einmalige Identität eines Individuums oder einer Gruppe, auf die Differenz gegenüber anderen setzt, ohne ihre Entgegensetzung weiter zu reflektieren.

Diese Gleichung erwies sich bald als eine falsche: Im Rahmen einer Politik der Differenz (in diesem Fall die Setzung der partikulären deutschen Identität) geraten die allgemeinmenschlichen Rechte des "Wir sind das Volk" in den Hintergrund, und damit auch das Ziel einer für jedermann gerechten Einheit. Die gesamtdeutsch-nationalistisch gesinnten Ostdeutschen bemerkten bald, dass die ersehnte Freiheit im kapitalistischen System der Bundesrepublik nicht unmittelbar soziale Gleichheit garantiert und identifizierten dann die allgemeinmenschliche Würde mit einer neu sich herausbildenden ostdeutschen "Teilidentität".

Wie aber wurden die neu entstehenden deutschen Identitätsentwürfe literarisch formuliert und wie reflektiert die Literatur dieses Dilemma zwischen Gleichheit und Differenz? Es bedarf einiger Anmerkungen über die literarische Entwicklung beider Literaturtraditionen, bevor wir auf die Wende-Debatten eingehen können.

---

8 Vgl. unten Teil II.

II "Kleine" und "große" deutsche Literatur

Im Osten wie im Westen hat der literarische Diskurs bei der Bestimmung der deutschen Identitäten eine zentrale Rolle gespielt.[9] Vor allem in der DDR, wo die Literatur der sogenannten Reformsozialisten "eine Ersatzöffentlichkeit anstelle einer nicht zugelassenen Presse- und Medienöffentlichkeit" schuf (Emmerich 1998: 5), trug sie zur Herausbildung einer kritischen kollektiven Identität bei, indem sie die Rolle einer ausgeprägten *moralischen Instanz* übernahm. Diese Rolle hatte die Literatur im Westen seit den 70er Jahren im Zuge einer Literatur der "neuen Innerlichkeit" weitgehend verloren. Das Thema der individuellen, nicht der kollektiven Identität, beherrschte zunehmend die literarischen Texte. Die politisch aufgeladene Konzeption der "Sprache als Hort der Freiheit", Leitidee der engagierten Literatur Heinrich Bölls,[10] überlebte nur in den Schreibvorstellungen weniger westdeutscher Autoren, die sich auch weiterhin mit dem Thema der deutsch-deutschen Identität beschäftigten.

Der unterschiedliche Verlauf der literarischen Entwicklung in den beiden deutschen Staaten hatte bereits in den 50er Jahren eingesetzt, als die DDR-Regierung versuchte, ein am sozialistischen Realismus orientiertes Modell einer *Nationalliteratur* zu entwickeln, deren erste Aufgabe darin bestand, bei der Konstruktion einer eigenständigen DDR-Identität mitzuwirken und zur Ausbildung des Individuums im und für den sozialistischen Staat beizutragen. Die Unterschiede zwischen Ost- und Westliteratur verfestigen sich in den 60er Jahren.

---

9   Über die bestimmende Rolle der Literatur bei der Konstruktion von nationalen Identitäten vgl. Anderson, Benedict: *Die Erfindung der Nation. Zur Karriere eines folgenreichen Konzepts*. Frankfurt a.M.: Campus 1996, und Thiesse, Anne-Marie: *La création des identités nationales. Europe XVIIIe-XXe siècle*. Paris: Seuil 2001.
10 Zum Vergleich der Schreibkonzepte von Heinrich Böll und Christa Wolf s. Krauss (2005: 271).

Uwe Johnson, der die DDR früh verlässt und mit dem Thema der geteilten Identität Deutschlands entscheidend zur Entwicklung der westdeutschen Literatur beitrug, konstatiert 1964 in folgender Weise die Herausbildung unterschiedlicher deutscher Denkweisen:

> Ich halte den Satz für zweifelhaft, daß wir alle in einer gemeinsamen Sprache schrieben oder uns ausdrückten. Zwischen den Schriftstellern der beiden Währungsgebiete in Deutschland herrscht durchaus eine Meinungsverschiedenheit über den einfachen deutschen Satz. Sie sind sich nicht einig, welcher Satz auf eine literarische Weise gut ist. Ein anderes Beispiel: die Wortwahl, die verschiedenen Parteiungen, die in den Worten enthalten sind. Ist das noch eine Sprache, wenn man über so gründliche Dinge nicht einer Meinung ist? [...] Die Literatur der DDR hat z. B. die Aufgabe, das Bewußtsein ihrer Leser von der Lage zu verändern. Eine ganz ausgesprochen sozialaktivistische Aufgabe. Eine solche Aufgabe hat die westdeutsche, die westlich deutsch sprechende Literatur nicht.[11]

Ausgehend vom Unterschied der sprachlichen Vorstellungen zwischen Ost und West reflektiert Johnson hier schon die wesentliche Differenz zwischen den beiden deutschen Gegenwartsliteraturen: Einen "sozialaktivistischen" Auftrag, der für die DDR-Literatur zentral ist, gibt es für die westdeutsche Literatur nicht. Nicht zuletzt aufgrund dieser erzieherisch-kommunikativen Bestimmung, die ihr offiziell und programmatisch zugewiesen wurde, galt die DDR-Literatur im Urteil der an einer modernistischen und postmodernistischen Ästhetik orientierten westdeutschen Literaturkritik als *eingeschränkt* und daher als zweitrangig. Man sprach von einer literarischen Vor-Moderne und von Provinzialismus, was jedoch nicht nur aus den vor-modernen Voraussetzungen des sozialistischen Realismus zu erklären ist, sondern auch mit der politischen und wirtschaftlichen Vorrangstellung des literarischen und kulturellen Systems der Bundesrepublik zu tun haben dürfte. Zwischen beiden Staaten bestand eine Beziehung kultureller Dominanz, die im Bereich der Literatur deutlich zu Tage trat.

---

11 Uwe Johnson in einem Gespräch mit Kollegen aus Ost und West, zit. n. Emmerich 1996: 519f.

Nur wenige DDR-Autoren haben im Westen ein breites Interesse gefunden: Zu nennen wären Georg Heym, Franz Fühmann, Christa Wolf, Volker Braun, Heiner Müller und, seit den 80er Jahren, Christoph Hein, Schriftsteller, die alle zu den "Reformsozialisten" zählten und dem Gesellschaftssystem der DDR kritisch gegenüberstanden. Besonders seit dem Bau der Mauer übte die "große" Literatur der Bundesrepublik deutlich diese kulturelle Dominanz aus. Als Beispiel sei der offene Brief angeführt, den Günter Grass am Tag nach dem Mauerbau an Anna Seghers, die Vorsitzende des Schriftstellerverbandes der DDR, schrieb und in dem er sie aufforderte ihre "Stimme [zu] beladen", um sie gegen die Panzer, die den Bau der Mauer bewachten, zu erheben und "gegen den gleichen, immer wieder in Deutschland hergestellten Stacheldraht an[zu]reden, der einst den Konzentrationslagern Stacheldrahtsicherheit gab" (Grass 1990: 123). Grass meldet sich hier als Vertreter der Gruppe 47, der literaturbestimmenden Bewegung der westdeutschen Nachkriegs- und Wirtschaftswundergesellschaft, zu Wort. Auch wenn Grass sich in seinem Brief an Seghers verpflichtet, im Gegenzug weiter den Antisemitismus im Westen zu bekämpfen, bedeutet seine Andeutung, dass die DDR mit dem Mauerbau die Tradution des deutschen Faschismus fortsetzt, eine implizite Verurteilung der systemkonformen und -tragenden ostdeutschen Literatur.

Die Literatur der DDR trägt deutliche Züge einer "kleinen Literatur" wie Deleuze und Guattari sie modelliert haben: Es ist die Literatur "einer Minderheit, die sich einer großen Sprache bedient", eine "deterritorialisierte" Literatur. Sie ist außerdem eminent politisch: "Ihr enger Raum bewirkt, daß sich jede individuelle Angelegenheit unmittelbar mit der Politik verknüpft". Und schließlich gewinnt in ihr "alles kollektiven Wert",[12] "die Literatur produziert aktive Solidarität"

---

12 "Gerade wegen ihres Mangels an großen Talenten fehlen ihr die Bedingungen für individuelle Aussagen, die ja stets Aussagen des einen oder anderen 'Meisters' wären und sich von der kollektiven Aussage trennen ließen. [...] Was der einzelne Schriftsteller schreibt, konstituiert bereits ein gemeinsames

(Deleuze / Guattari 1976: 24f.). Demgegenüber beruht die "große Literatur" auf der Identität der "großen Meister", auf individuellen Themen, sie ist autonom, autoreferentiell in dem Sinne, in dem Grass 1989 für die Literatur der Bundesrepublik feststellt, es sei "eine Literatur, die sich sehr stark mit sich selbst beschäftigt" (Grass 1990: 22).

Nur wenige Vertreter dieser großen Literatur haben sich also mit dem DDR-Thema und mit der Problematik der deutsch-deutschen Identität auseinandergesetzt. Zu ihnen gehört Günter Grass. "Bilden die Deutschen eine Nation? Sollen die Deutschen eine Nation bilden?", fragt er sich 1967 in einem Spiegel-Interview und kommt zu dem Schluss, dass "der Begriff der Nation an sich keinen Wert darstellt." Er fordert eine Politik, "die den Rückfall in die Nationalstaatlichkeit ausschließt, die den sinnentleerten Begriff 'Wiedervereinigung' vermeidet und dafür eine schrittweise Annäherung versucht, die sich die Konföderation zweier deutscher Länderbünde zum Ziel setzt" (Grass 1990: 103f.). Zwei Jahrzehnte später bezieht er sich in einer ähnlichen Argumentation auf den Herder'schen Begriff der "Kulturnation" (ebd. 15), die Idee einer kulturellen Identität der Völker, bei der nicht die staatliche oder politische Einheit im Vordergrund steht. Grass' Modell ist das einer "Politik der Anerkennung",[13] die darauf abzielt, die im Verlauf einer differenten und antagonistischen Entwicklung enstandenen deutschen Identitäten zu bewahren.

Eine ähnliche Antwort auf die Frage der deutsch-deutschen Identität gibt Peter Schneiders Erzählung *Der Mauerspringer* (1982), der Referenztext der westdeutschen Literatur in den 80er Jahren zu diesem

---

    Handeln, und was er sagt oder tut, ist bereits politisch, auch wenn die anderen ihm nicht zustimmen" (Deleuze / Guattari 1976: 25f.).
13 Die Forderung nach "Anerkennung" ist grundlegend für jede individuelle und kollektive Identitätsbildung und setzt also sowohl den Schutz der allgemeinen Menschenwürde der Individuen, als auch die Anerkennung ihrer partikulären Bedürfnissen als Mitglieder von besonderen kulturellen Gruppen voraus. Vgl. Taylor 1992: 37ff.

Thema. Der Ich-Erzähler, ein Schriftsteller, der Geschichten über die Mauer sammelt, geht häufig vom West- in den Ostteil Berlins, der "siamesischen Stadt" (Schneider 1984: 6). Er ist das Bindeglied für eine Serie von Dialogen, Episoden und Digressionen über die Bedeutung der Mauer, die "den Deutschen im Westen zum Spiegel [wurde], der ihnen Tag für Tag sagt, wer der Schönste im Land ist" (ebd. 12), und über die Verschiedenheit der beiden deutschen Gesellschaften. Die Protagonisten seiner tragikomischen Mauergeschichten – darunter Herr Kabe, der als eifriger Bergsteiger die Mauer immer wieder in der *falschen* Richtung, von West nach Ost, überwindet – und die Freunde des Erzählers im einen wie im anderen Deutschland sind Figuren zwischen zwei Welten, Menschen die "mißtrauisch geworden [sind] gegen die hastig ergriffene Identität, die [ihnen] die beiden Staaten anbieten" und die ihren Ort "nur noch auf der Grenze" (ebd. 21) finden.

Schneiders Text ist auch ein Kompendium der deutsch-deutschen Klischees, Gemeinplätze und Missverständnisse, die im Verlauf von vierzig Jahren entstanden sind. Der Ich-Erzähler bemüht sich, weder in die DDR- noch in die BRD-Perspektive zu geraten, beide Länder werden vielmehr verglichen und aus demselben Grund kritisiert: "Die Programmacher beider Staaten ähneln sich darin aufs Lächerlichste: aus dem eigenen Lager lassen sie nur die Meinung der Herrschenden, aus dem feindlichen Lager nur die der Unterdrückten zu Wort kommen" (ebd. 101). Er reflektiert das zwiespältige Bewußtsein der DDR-Intellektuellen, die die Seite wechseln aber ihre Ost-Identität im Westen weiter verteidigen, und ebenso die Widersprüche der linken West-Intellektuellen, die "jeden Hinweis auf gewisse Lebenseinschränkungen im Osten [...] durch Schreckensmeldungen aus dem Westen zu überbieten" versuchen (ebd. 58). Der Text handelt also von der berühmten "Mauer im Kopf", die niederzureißen "länger dauern [wird], als irgendein Abrißunternehmen für die sichtbare Mauer braucht" (ebd. 102).

Die Lösung, zu der Schneiders Erzählung sieben Jahre vor dem Fall der Mauer gelangt, nimmt merkwürdigerweise das Motto der Leipziger Demonstrationen, "Wir sind das Volk", vorweg und erinnert an den Vorschlag von Günter Grass und seinen Verweis auf den Begriff der Kulturnation. Der Ich-Erzähler entwirft ein Identitätsmuster, in dem er die Möglichkeit verwirft, sich mit irgendeinem "Wahnsinn" der beiden deutschen Staaten zu identifizieren. Er kommt zu dem Schluß:

> Falls mein Vaterland existiert, so ist es kein Staat, und der Staat, dessen Bürger ich bin, ist kein Vaterland. Wenn ich auf die Frage nach meiner Nationalität ohne Zögern antworte, ich bin Deutscher, so optiere ich damit offensichtlich nicht für einen Staat, sondern für meine Zugehörigkeit zu einem Volk, das keine staatliche Identität mehr besitzt. [...] Solange ich von einem Land namens Deutschland spreche, spreche ich weder von der DDR noch von der BRD, sondern von einem Land, das nur in meiner Erinnerung oder Vorstellung existiert (Schneider 1984: 108).

Dieses imaginierte Land wird mit der deutschen Geschichte und Sprache identifiziert, also mit einer utopischen deutschen Kulturnation, die politisch nirgendwo existiert. Somit stellt Schneiders Erzähler sich nicht auf den Standpunkt der Taylor'schen "Politik der Differenz", die die Anerkennung der besonderen Rechte einer *real existierenden* deutschen Nation fordern würde. Seine Reflexion wird weitergeführt, indem sie an die ursprüngliche Bedeutung des Wortes *deutsch* erinnert und damit die Grundbestimmung einer "Politik der allgemeinen Menschenwürde" übernimmt:

> Das Wort deutsch bezeichnete ja ursprünglich weder ein Volk noch einen Staat, sondern bedeutete 'Volk', 'volksmäßig', als Bezeichnung der gemeinsamen Sprache verschiedener Stämme, die die gesprochene Sprache gegen die lateinische Urkunden- und Kirchensprache durchzusetzen begannen (Schneider 1984: 108f.).

Mit diesem Bezug auf das "Volksmäßige", das sich gegen das "Kirchenlatein aus Ost und West" (Schneider 1984: 109) durchsetzen soll, identifiziert Schneider den Charakter des Deutschen mit dem des universalen Bürgers, der das "principle of equal respect" (Taylor 1992: 43) einfordert, die Anerkennung seiner universalen Rechte als Individuum. Dieselben Rechte eben, die die Bürger Ostdeutschlands zu Beginn ihrer friedlichen Revolution gegen den kommunistischautoritären DDR-Staat reklamierten. Ihre universale egalitäre Forderung wurde verkehrt, als sie mit der Frage der deutschen Identität verbunden wurde. Im Rahmen einer "Politik der allgemeinen Menschenwürde" kann keine partikuläre Identitätsforderung eindeutig beantwortet werden.

III Christa Wolf und die Leiden der "kleinen" DDR-Literatur nach der Wende

Die Vereinigung Deutschlands, und vor allem die beschleunigte Art und Weise, wie sie vollzogen wurde, brachte vor allem für die ostdeutsche Autoren eine abrupte Konfrontation mit der Frage der deutsch-deutschen Identität mit sich. Für viele bedeutete sie einen gravierenden Verlust an Integrität,[14] an kultureller und beruflicher Identität. Betroffen sind in erster Linie die Schriftsteller der "zweiten Generation" der "Reformsozialisten" (u.a Stephan Heym, Christa Wolf, Volker Braun, Christoph Hein), die ihr Werk in der DDR geschrieben und, mit mehr oder weniger starken Beschränkungen, auch veröffentlicht haben. Ihre kritische Position gegenüber dem DDR-Staat, deren *ultima ratio* auf eine vom inneren Widerstand ausgehende Veränderung des Systems gerichtet war, ist mit dem Verschwinden der DDR ins Leere gelaufen.

Im Jahre 1990, einige Monate nach dem Fall der Mauer, definiert Christa Wolf rückblickend die Aufgabe ihrer Literatur folgendermaßen:

---

14 In dem Sinne der persönlichen (physischen und psychischen) Unverletzlichkeit, in dem Axel Honneth den Begriff aktualisiert hat. Vgl. Honneth, Axel (2003): *Kampf um Anerkennung. Zur moralischen Grammatik sozialer Konflikte.* Frankfurt a.M.: Suhrkamp.

Seit Jahren hatte die bewußt in Opposition stehende Literatur sich bestimmte Aufgaben gestellt: Durch Benennen von Widersprüchen, die lange Zeit nirgendwo sonst artikuliert wurden, bei ihren Lesern ein kritisches Bewußtsein zu erzeugen oder zu stärken, sie zum Widerstand gegen Lüge, Heuchelei und Selbstaufgabe zu ermutigen, unsere Sprache und andere Traditionen aus der deutschen Literatur und Geschichte, die abgeschnitten werden sollten, lebendig zu halten und, nicht zuletzt, moralische Werte zu verteidigen, die der zynischen Demagogie der herrschenden Ideologie geopfert werden sollten (Wolf 1994: 19).

Dieses Selbstverständnis eines Volkserziehers, gepaart mit der "bewußten Opposition" zur herrschenden kommunistischen Ideologie der DDR konnte nach der Wende nicht aufrechterhalten werden. In ihrem Selbstverständnis als "moralische Instanzen" der Gesellschaft waren die kritischen DDR-Schriftsteller ihren Kollegen der Gruppe 47 vergleichbar, die für eine ausgeprägte politisch-moralische Funktion der Literatur plädiert hatte.[15] Aber während diese westdeutschen Autoren in dem Maße, wie die Rolle der Literatur in der öffentlichen Meinung der Bundesrepublik von anderen Medien besetzt wurde, nach und nach in den Hintergrund getreten waren, wurden die ostdeutschen Schriftsteller wie die gesamte Gesellschaft der DDR 1989 in wenigen Monaten mit einem totalen Integritätsverlust konfrontiert. Christa Wolf spricht vom Gefühl des "Unheimlich[en] vor dem Verschwinden der Realität" (Wolf 1994: 330), von einer "rasend fortschreitende[n] Desintegration fast aller bisherigen Bindungen", die der Gesellschaft keine Zeit lässt, um darauf zu reagieren, und die "erbitterte Verfechter ökonomischer und politischer Einzelinteressen auf den Plan" bringt (Wolf 1994: 19). Gleichzeitig stellt sie in diesem Zustand bereits das Einsetzen einer gewissen Ostalgie fest:

> Unter der Oberfläche herrscht ein geschäftiges, angstvolles skrupelloses Leben und Treiben, jeder verkauft, was er kann, auch sich selbst. Wie harmlos dagegen der sichtbare Ausverkauf von Devotionalien der alten DDR am Brandenburger Tor, Orden Ehrenzeichen, Uniformstücke, Fahnen, Medaillen, der Handel blüht (Wolf 1994: 47).

---

15 In diesen Zusammenhang bezieht sich Christa Wolf auf "Böll, Fried, Peter Weiss, Grass, Walter Jens" als „langjährige[] Verbündete[]"(Wolf 1994: 19).

Den Bürgern des Ostens blieb also im beschleunigten Tempo der Wende wenig Zeit zu reagieren, wie es auch in dem Manifest "Für unser Land" vom 26. November 1989 heißt, das von Christa Wolf und vielen anderen Intellektuellen unterzeichnet wurde, welche das Fortbestehen der DDR als einer anderen, solidarischen Gesellschaft neben der westdeutschen fordern und der "Liquidierung der materiellen und geistigen Werte" des Landes und seiner *Annektierung* durch die Bundesrepublik entgegentreten wollen.

Paradigmatisches Beispiel für den Integritätsverlust ist das berühmt gewordene Gedicht, das Volker Braun im Juli 1990 zunächst als *Nachruf* in der Tageszeitung "Neues Deutschland" und später unter dem Titel *Das Eigentum* veröffentlicht hat. Braun, wie Christa Wolf einer der auch im Westen anerkannten Autoren der DDR, artikuliert den Zorn einer Schriftsteller-Generation über ihr Land und über sich selbst: "Da bin ich noch: mein Land geht in den Westen. / [...] Ich selbst hab ihm den Tritt versetzt. / [...] Und unverständlich wird mein ganzer Text. / Was ich niemals besaß, wird mir entrissen. / Was ich nicht lebte, werd ich ewig missen" (Braun 1993: 51).

Das Gedicht ist kein bloßes Zeugnis von Ostalgie, sondern konstatiert die Situation eines existentiellen Scheiterns als Folge der Konfrontation mit einem autoritären Staat, der plötzlich aufgehört hat zu existieren. Der Grund für dieses individuelle und kollektive Scheitern liegt aber auch im ambivalenten Status der "kritischen Intelligenz" zwischen Regimekritik und Sozialismustreue, die den raschen "Umbruch" der DDR kaum vorausgesehen hat. Braun selbst hat seinem Staat metaphorisch "den Tritt" versetzt, weil er durch das Festhalten an der Utopie eines demokratischen Sozialismus nicht die Konsequenzen aus seinen kritischen Überzeugungen gezogen hat.[16]

Letzten Endes hat sich nicht vermeiden lassen, dass, wie Jürgen Habermas im November 1991 in einem Brief an Christa Wolf

---

16 Sommer (1996: 160) spricht von einem "'Prinzip Hoffnung' (Bloch), das den zugleich regimekritischen und staatstreuen DDR-Autoren zur 'Falle' wurde. Sie versuchten den Spagat zwischen einem realen Sozialismus, den sie kritisierten, und einem idealen, theoretischen Sozialismus, dem sie Treue hielten".

schreibt, "die Geschichte der DDR unter den Teppich einer westdeutschen Siegergeschichte gekehrt wird" (Wolf 1994: 148) und dass, wie Wolf es 1994 schreibt, "die Vereinigung [...] sich auf wirtschaftlicher Ebene wie ein Verteilungskampf entwickelt [hat], in dem die meisten Ostdeutschen keine Chance hatten", wie eine "Kolonisierung der ostdeutschen Gebiete durch westdeutsche Verwalter" (Wolf 1994: 335). Habermas und Wolf plädierten wie die große Mehrheit der Intellektuellen aus Ost und West eher für ein föderatives Modell, ähnlich wie Grass es vorgeschlagen hatte, und für einen Dialog der verschiedenen, ja entgegengesetzten Traditionen. "Wir haben unterschiedliche Geschichten", antwortet Christa Wolf auf Habermas, "darauf sollten wir bestehen, und wir sollten anfangen, uns diese Geschichten zu erzählen" (Wolf 1994: 154).

Davon, wie schwierig es ist, sich diese Geschichten zu erzählen, und davon, dass die "Kolonialisierungstendenz" nicht nur im wirtschaftlichen Bereich bestand, zeugen die – zum Teil sehr heftig geführten – literarischen Debatten, die die deutsche Literaturgeschichte während der 90er Jahre begleiten und in denen Christa Wolf das exemplarische Opfer für eine ganze Schrifsteller-Generation darstellt.

Wie die Politik erlebt auch der deutsche Literaturbetrieb aufgrund der Wiedervereinigung heftige Konvulsionen. Das Thema der deutsch-deutschen Identität, das trotz der Schriftsteller der DDR, die von diesseits und jenseits der Grenze im Westen publizierten, kein vordringliches Thema der westlichen Literatur gewesen war, drängt mit den ostdeutschen Autoren in den Vordergrund und provoziert eine Art Kampf ums Überleben und um die literarische Dominanz im vereinigten Deutschland.

Die erste Runde dieser langen Debatte wird 1990 aus Anlass der Veröffentlichung von Christa Wolfs Erzählung *Was bleibt* eingeläutet, eine Fortsetzung ihrer literarischen Versuche, die eigene Erfahrung mit der Historie und Posthistorie ihres Landes zu verbinden und dabei die Realgeschichte in dieser Suche nach der literarischen Wahrheit, nach der Identität, eben nach dem, "was bleibt", zu transzendieren. Die deutlich autobiographisch geprägte Erzählung spielt Ende der

70er Jahre und beschreibt einen Märztag im Leben einer DDR-Schriftstellerin, die über lange Zeit hinweg von der Staatsicherheit überwacht wird. Für die Ich-Erzählerin ist die Konfrontation mit der mechanischen Unterdrückung des Staates der erste Schritt zu einem Verlust der persönlichen Integrität – "seit dem vorigen Sommer [fühlte ich mich] in meiner eigenen Wohnung nicht mehr zu Hause", erzählt sie (Wolf 2001: 26) – und der Beginn einer virtuellen Existenz, einer Zeit des "Als ob": leben, als ob niemand sie beobachtete, als ob sie Briefe schreiben könnte, die nur von ihren Empfängern gelesen werden würden, als ob niemand, dem sie vertraute, Berichte über sie schreiben würde.

Dieser Verlust der persönlichen Integrität ihrer Protagonistin findet in der Nachwendezeit seine Entsprechung in demjenigen, den Christa Wolf selbst nach der Veröffentlichung ihrer Erzählung erleidet. Die tonangebende westliche Literaturkritik sieht in *Was bleibt* ein geeignetes Motiv, um jenen doppelten, kritischen aber zugleich auch staatstreuen Charakter der DDR-Literatur frontal anzugreifen. Wolf wird der Heuchelei beschuldigt, weil sie sich als Regime-Opfer dargestellt habe, während sie als ehemaliges Mitglied des Zentralkomitees der Partei (von 1963 bis 1967) in Wirklichkeit eine trotz ihrer kritischen Haltung vom System tolerierte "Staatsschriftstellerin" gewesen sei, der viele Freiheiten und Privilegien gewährt wurden, die den gewöhnlichen Bürgern versagt blieben.

Es ging in diesem ersten Kapitel der Literaturdebatte des vereinigten Deutschlands vor allem um die Vorrangsstellung im Literaturbetrieb und um den eher marginalen Platz, den die westdeutsche Literaturkritik der Literatur der ehemaligen DDR einzuräumen bereit war, und damit auch um die Aktualität des Modells einer politisch engagierten Literatur im vereinigten Deutschland. Es verwundert nicht, dass Christa Wolf in dieser Diskussion von Günter Grass und anderen Autoren verteidigt wurde, die am Konzept des Schriftstellers als gesellschaftlicher moralischer Instanz festhielten, im Gegensatz zu

Kritikern und Germanisten wie Karl-Heinz Bohrer, die das Ende dieses Modells in der Postmoderne proklamierten.[17] Tatsächlich hat Christa Wolf ihre Rolle als engagierte Schriftstellerin auch nach der Wende nicht aufgegeben: "die Person [...] unverstellt [...], ohne sich zu entblößen, der Blick betroffen, jedoch nicht vom Bodensatz ungeklärter Ressentiments getrübt, nicht kalt, anteilnehmend, so unsentimental wie möglich" (Wolf 1994: 9).[18] In ihrer Erzählung *Leibhaftig* (2002) stellt sie erneut ihre eigene Biographie zur Disposition, um metaphorisch die gesellschaftliche Dekadenz der DDR vorzuführen. Erzählt wird der Krankenhausaufenthalt einer Schriftstellerin, die (wie die Autorin selbst), durch eine Blinddarmoperation an den Rand des Todes gerät. Die Rekonvaleszenz wird im Verlauf des Textes nach und nach mit der tödlichen Erkrankung eines Staates in eins gesetzt, der wie nach einem physischen Zusammenbruch verschwinden wird. Die unerklärliche Verschlimmerung der Krankheit verweist auf die Bestürzung über die soziale Desintegration: "der Krankheitsverlauf begründe[t] nicht ausreichend den Zusammenbruch [der] Immunabwehr" (Wolf 2002: 125). Umgeben von Bildern des Schmerzes, des Todes, der Auflösung durchlebt oder träumt das Bewußtsein der Erzählerin Momente einer persönlichen Geschichte, die Bezüge zum kollektiven Scheitern der DDR aufweisen, wie zum Beispiel die Auseinandersetzung mit Urban, einem regimetreuen Freund, der sich während des Krankenhausaufenthaltes der Erzählerin das Leben nimmt. Urbans Treue zum DDR-Staat wird als eine Art geheimnisvolle Kollektivverschwörung dargestellt, für die die Erzählerin auch selbst anfällig ist:

> BIG BROTHER. Damit muß man leben, sagte Urban einmal zu mir. Überall auf der Welt müssen wir damit leben. Irgendwann hatte er angefangen, auf diese neue, beinahe verschwörerische Weise 'wir' zu sagen. Wir, sagte er geheimnis-

---

17 Bohrer plädiert in seinem vieldiskutierten Aufsatz "Kulturschutzgebiet DDR" (*Merkur*, Oktober 1990) für eine endlich von Ethik und Politik befreite Ästhetik und greift die „Gesinnungsästhetik" Wolfs an.

18 Über die literarische Entwicklung Christa Wolfs nach *Was bleibt* vgl. Krauss 2005: 272f.

voll, von den eigenen Leuten beargwöhnt im eigenen Land, einer größeren Bruderschaft zugehörig, die ihn tröstete und rechtfertigte und von der eine starke Verführung ausging. Auch auf mich? Ja. Auch auf mich. Eine Zeitlang wohnte *sie* in ihrer realen Stadt mit diesem Metallkästchen im Keller, in dem ihre Telefonleitung konspirativ verschwand, und zugleich in einer anderen Hoffnungs- und Menschheitsstadt, die ihre eigentliche Heimat war oder sein würde, die wir der Zukunft noch entreißen, die wir uns schaffen würden, 'wir', die auch Urban meinte. Seit wann fühlte sie sich nicht mehr angesprochen, wenn er 'wir' sagte [...] (Wolf 2002: 136, Herv. J.F.).

Mit der Veränderung der Erzählperspektive von der ersten zur dritten Person reflektiert die Erzählerin die ambivalente, doppelte Existenz als Trägerin und Opfer des Systems, die zwischen der Faszination einer Gemeinschaftsutopie und der Bedrohung durch eine offensichtliche Stasi-Bespitzelung schwankt. Die Rekonvaleszenz markiert dabei das Ende der Verführung, den Prozess der Trennung vom utopischen geliebten Land, das zusammenbricht, "weil es die besten Leute nicht mehr integrieren konnte, weil es Menschenopfer forderte" (Wolf 1994: 262). Sie überwindet schließlich ihre Krankheit, in dem Bewusstsein, "dass der Schmerz, den man bei einem Verlust empfinde, das Maß sei für die Hoffnung, die man vorher gehabt habe" (Wolf 2002: 183). Zum Schluß bleibt die Gewißheit, dass die Schriftstellerin und der Arzt "den gleichen Beruf" haben: den Schmerz aufspüren, der Arzt den Schmerz im Körper, die Schriftstellerin "anderswo" (Wolf 2002, 160), etwa in der Sprache oder der Seele des Menschen. "Die Einsicht," wie Hannes Krauss (2005: 272) feststellt, "dass der marxistische Geschichtsoptimismus eine Illusion war, erleichtert paradoxerweise das Weiterschreiben." Christa Wolf kann weiter das Private mit dem Öffentlichen verschmelzen, das eigene Leben in die Schrift einsetzen, nicht wie in DDR-Zeiten um kritisch die Entwicklung eines Landes zu begleiten, sondern vorerst um im vereinten Deutschland auf die eigene Erfahrung als Maßstab für ihr Engagement zu insistieren. Diese Haltung ermöglicht es ihr, der deutsch-deutschen Literaturdebatte der 90er Jahre standzuhalten, die vom Standpunkt einer moralischen Überlegenheit des demokratischen Kapitalismus gegenüber den "Bewohner[n] einer Quarantäne-Baracke, infiziert mit dem Stasi-Virus" (Wolf 1994, 294) weitergeführt wurde.[19]

IV *Provisorische* Identitäten: Wolgang Hilbig

Da wo Christa Wolf um ihre schriftstellerische und moralische Identität "mit vollem Körpereinsatz" (Krauss 2005: 273) kämpft, eröffnen uns die Romane von Wolfgang Hilbig eine andere, weniger eindeutige Perspektive. Hilbig ist hier Stellvertreter für die Generation von Ost-Schriftstellern, die noch vor den Fall der Mauer die DDR verlassen hatten und, wie die Figuren des *Mauerspringers,* sich eine Position 'an der Grenze' erarbeiteten, eine vorläufige, nicht in der Bundesrepublik bzw. im vereinten Deutschland "angekommene" Existenz.[20] Dies erhellt schon aus dem Titel des bis heute letzten Romans von Hilbig: *Das Provisorium* (2000) stellt die zerrissene Existenz des Schriftstellers C. dar, der wie Hilbig selbst einige Jahre vor dem Mauerfall zunächst *provisorisch* mit einem Visum in den Westen geht, aber nicht mehr in die DDR zurückkehrt.

19 Als 1993 Informationen über ihre sehr frühe IM-Tätigkeit auftauchen, da sie zwischen 1959 und 1962 Berichte für die Stasi verfaßt hatte, wird Christa Wolf erneut der Doppelmoral bezichtigt; auf dem Höhepunkt der Debatte, die sie selbst als Lynchjustiz an ihrer Literatur versteht, stellt man ihr gesamtes literarisches Werk in Frage. Dabei wird die Tatsache, dass sie und ihr Mann seit 1969 zwanzig Jahre lang Gegenstand der Stasi-Überwachung waren, über die 41 Bände Stasi-Unterlagen existieren, wenig beachtet. Obwohl die Berichte, die sie in ihrer Jugend geschrieben hatte, harmlos waren, sieht Wolf sich mit der Erfahrung konfrontiert, "daß es nicht immer möglich ist, gleichzeitig 'moralisch' und menschlich zu handeln. Als ich das merkte, war mir klar, daß ich in einer Klemme saß, aus der ich nicht unangefochten herauskommen würde" (Wolf 1994: 261).
20 "Der Westen, das war etwas für sein Volk da drüben, für diese Idiotenherde mit ihrem brachialen Appetit auf Langnese-Joghurt und auf Kondome mit Bananengeschmack; für ihn selber war dieser Westen nichts" (Hilbig 2001: 183).

Wie in den meisten seiner Texte (hier ist seine Schreibweise mit Christa Wolfs Gleichsetzung von Leben und Literatur vergleichbar) zehrt Hilbig für die Konstruktion seiner Schriftsteller-Figuren von der eigenen Biographie. C. wird vorgestellt als "ein typisches Produkt der DDR, physisch und psychisch [...] ein Ergebnis des Provisoriums, das sich DDR nannte ... [...] Er gehörte zu den menschlichen Vorläufigkeiten, aus denen sich die DDR zusammensetzte" (Hilbig 2001: 269). Die DDR-Zugehörigkeit bedingt also schon eine prinzipielle Identitätskrise, die zunächst mit einem kollektiven und individuellen Autonomie-Defizit charakterisiert wird. DDR-Bürger "waren Leute, die unablässig auf ihre Eigenheit und ihr Selbst pochten, auf die gleiche Weise, wie die Regierung dieses Landes der Begriff 'Souveranität' als Dauer-Sprechblase aus dem Rüssel hing. In diesem Land war man nichts weniger als souverän" (ebd. 269).

Die Existenzkrise C.s ist dann auch von Anfang an eine Schreibkrise, die aus der "notwendigen Lüge" der Schriftstellers in der DDR erhellt: aus den "Vorspiegelungen", "Täuschungsmanövern" (ebd. 275), aus der nötigen "Verstellung" (ebd. 277) der "Verbarrikadierung" und "Verpanzerung", die er anstellen muss, um "ein[] winzige[s] Stück[] freier Zeit" zu gewinnen (ebd. 279). Bei C. handelt es sich nämlich nicht um einen Schriftsteller, der in die typiche dialektische Falle von Staatskritik und Staatstreue hineingeraten ist. Er ist, wie Wolfgang Hilbig selbst, ein Autor, der keine besondere Position innerhalb der DDR-Gesellschaft gehabt hat, der sich verstellt und versteckt hat, weil er als Arbeiter-Schriftsteller[21] nicht bereit war, sich mit den vorgeschriebenen Themen des Arbeiter-Alltags zu befassen. C. irrte "durch eine Vielzahl von Fabriken und Baustellen" (ebd. 274), ohne seine Berufung mit seinem Schicksal als "Industriearbeiter"

---

21 Der Arbeiter-Schriftsteller war, in Opposition zum intellektualisierten "Kopfarbeiter", ein Wunschtyp der offiziellen DDR-Literatur, da er als "Handarbeiter" am besten in der Lage sei, "einerseits die alltäglichen Kämpfe und Fortschritte im Produktionsbereich zu dokumentieren und sich andererseits durch die eigene Schreibtätigkeit, die literarische Produktivität zu den 'Höhen der Kultur' emporzuarbeiten." (Emmerich 1996: 129).

(ebd.) in Einklang bringen zu können.[22] Sein autodidaktisch erarbeitetes schriftstellerisches Konzept hat dagegen klassisch-romantische Wurzeln: Der Leitidee künstlerischer Autonomie gemäß mussten Schriftsteller "frei sein (mochte dies bedeuten, was es wollte), unabhängig, um in Freiheit ihrer Inspiration nachjagen zu können. Immerfort waren sie dieser Inspiration auf der Spur, Dauerreisende oder Wanderer, zumindest waren sie Spaziergänger, einsame Spaziergänger" (ebd. 280).

Dieses Außenseitertum wird im Westen fortgesetzt, wenn nicht gar verstärkt. C.s durch ein Visum geduldete Ausreise aus der DDR ändert nichts an seiner "depressive[n] Handlungsunlust" (ebd. 20). In der Bundesrepublik versteht er seine neue Rolle einer "öffentliche[n] Figur"[23] als eine "Maske" (ebd. 132), weiterhin als "eine Fälschung von vorn bis hinten" (ebd. 130). Seine Schreibkrise wird im Literatursystem des Westens vertieft. Hier betrachtet C. seine Schriftsteller-Kollegen als "Angestellte[] des Literaturbetriebs" (ebd. 242), als "wandernde[] Komödianten" (ebd. 118), in deren extrem selbstbezogenen Texten es meistens bloß "um die Existenzbedingungen von Schriftstellern", "um die Darstellung der Schicksale, durch welche die Personen zu schreibenden Personen geworden waren" (ebd. 118f.) geht. Auf seinen ununterbrochenen Lesereisen ist er zugleich auf der Flucht vor diesem Literaturbetrieb.

Mit der Hilfe massiven Alkoholkonsums entwickelt C. Aussteiger- und Todesphantasien,[24] erkundet Topoi des Provisorischen,[25] ver-

---

22 "Es war der Irrweg eines Vereinzelten durch die brüllende, verschworene, triebhaft arbeitende Masse, zu der er vergeblich Kontakt herzustellen suchte" (Hilbig 2001: 274).
23 "Jene[] Öffentlichkeit, vor der er sich verkroch und die er gleichzeitig anbetete" (Hilbig 2001: 133).
24 "Er hatte das Geld genommen, Stipendien und Literaturpreise, und dann war er erstarrt und hatte nicht mehr weiter geschrieben. Manchmal, wenn er betrunken genug war, hoffte er, daß er schon tot war ... nur als Toter konnte man aussteigen aus dem finanziellen Handel und Wandel der Gesellschaft" (ebd. 30).

sucht Strategien, um sich in der Öffentlichkeit unsichtbar zu machen,[26] gerät dabei jedoch immer tiefer in die Zwickmühle des Provisoriums: Zum einen reflektiert er seine Situation als "Bewußtseinslosigkeit" (ebd. 18), "Halbschlaf" (ebd. 214), sich selbst als "Gespenst" (ebd. 36, 193), zum anderen will er aber auch nicht "zu einem Dasein erwachen [...], das ihm völlig unbekannt war, das er als bedrohlich empfand, als provisorisch, von jedem zufälligen Einfluß abhängig, ohne *Wahrheits-gehalt*" (ebd. 265, Herv. J.F.).

C. gerät in eine unauflösbare Identitätskrise zwischen Ost und West, er fühlt sich "überhaupt keiner Welt mehr zugehörig" (ebd. 24). Sein Integritätsverlust ist jedoch anderer Art als der der Figuren von Christa Wolf, da er nicht in dem Dilemma zwischen Staatskritik und – treue verhaftet ist. Im Westen findet er seinen "Wahrheitsgehalt" nicht, aber auch schon in der DDR hatte er jede Hoffnung auf einen demokratischen Sozialismus verloren. Daher verurteilt er auch das "neue[] Establishment" (ebd. 108) der DDR-Literatur; er hatte

> nicht die Fähigkeit, sich als ein kultureller Abgesandter seines Staats aufzuführen, als einer von jenen DDR-Schriftstellern, die an der DDR, besonders an ihrer Kulturpolitik, zwar viel zu kritisieren hatten, die diesen Staat aber als den ihren bezeichneten. Eine solche Haltung wurde vom westdeutschen Publikum gutgeheißen, sie wurde sogar sehr gut aufgenommen, und dagegen hatte er keine Chance. Er hatte an der DDR, so wie er sie kannte, nichts zu kritisieren, er hielt das für zwecklos (ebd. 127).

C.s Erfahrungen und Überlegungen nagen heftig am tradierten Bild des Schriftstellers als bedeutende öffentliche Figur in der DDR, er betrachtet das Land im Gegenteil als "eine abseitige und zurück-gebliebene Enklave [...], wo die Literatur nicht wirklich etwas bedeu-tete, der Rummel um die Literatur in den Ostblock-Ländern war ein aufgesetztes Schauspiel" (ebd. 70). Dass dieses Schauspiel im Westen

---

25 Vor allem der Bahnhof als "Fluchtburg" (ebd. 121), das Hotel als "die proto-typische Behausung für ein Dasein in der Vorläufigkeit" (ebd. 133), aber auch die Liebe (vgl. ebd. 120).
26 C. "begriff, daß er sich am besten zum Verschwinden brachte, wenn er das vortrug, was er seinen Text nannte" (ebd. 156).

Erfolg hat, verstärkt seine Identitätskrise. Er verleugnet seine Rolle als kritischer DDR-Autor, der "in die schönsten europäischen Städte" (ebd. 126) eingeladen wurde:

> die Zustimmung, die er geerntet hatte, für seine Anwürfe gegen das System und die Zustände da drüben, sie fand er ebenso ekelhaft. Er gehörte nicht in diese Literaturgesellschaft, in der es um nichts anderes ging als um Zustimmung ... *die kritische Phase der Literatur war vorbei, wie eine Modeerscheinung war sie vorbeigegangen*, rasant und eloquent bis in den Bartwuchs" (ebd. 71, Herv. J. F.).

Der Niedergang der Literatur im Westen besteht für C. darin, dass sie als bloße Unterhaltung, als "Zerstreuung" geduldet wird.[27] In einem "übersatten Markt" verlieren die Bücher jede Seinsrechtfertigung, die Schriftsteller werden "Produzent[en] für die Ramschkiste!" (ebd. 180). Gegen diesen prekären Zustand, wo der literarische Diskurs förmlich erlischt in einer literarischen Öffentlichkeit, in der C. nur noch "das Geschwätz über den 'Stellenwert', welcher der Literatur geblieben sei" (ebd. 181) wahrnehmen kann, setzt er weiterhin auf ihren tradierten "Wahrheitsgehalt". In seiner Absolutheit überwindet dieser Begriff die bloße Vorläufigkeit, die Inkonsistenz eines meinungsmachenden gesellschaftlichen "Stellenwerts", bei dem der Öffentlichkeitscharakter der Literatur schwindet.

"Der Wahrheitsgehalt", schreibt Adorno, "ist nicht außer der Geschichte sondern deren Kristallisation in den Werken".[28] So bezieht C. schließlich seine Kritik am Westen und an der Wende auf jene historischen Ereignisse zurück, die am Anfang der Identitätsbil-

---

27 "Die Literatur, die sich weigerte, der Zerstreuung zu dienen, wurde auf dem Markt mit Nichtbeachtung gestraft..." (ebd. 70). Nicht nur hier, sondern allgemein im Zusammenhang seiner Reflexionen über den "Wahrheitsgehalt" der Literatur, bezieht sich die Argumentation C.s auf Grundbegriffe, mit denen die Frankfurter Schule die Gesellschaft der Weimarer Republik analysiert hat. Zur "Zerstreuung" vgl. die Analysen von Siegfried Kracauer über *Die Angestellten* (1929) und über das Kino als "Zerstreuungskultur".
28 Vgl. Adorno, Theodor W. (1974): *Ästhetische Theorie* (Gesammelte Schriften 7). Frankfurt a.M.: Suhrkamp, 200.

dungen von DDR und Bundesrepublik standen, die ihre gemeinsame geschichtliche Grundlage bilden. C. konfrontiert die deutsche Gegenwart der Vereinigung mit den unaufgelösten Fragen der Nachkriegszeit.[29] C.s *Exilsituation* in der Bundesrepublik, seine anschließende "Staatenlosigkeit" (ebd. 241) im vereinten Deutschland wird mit dem Schicksal der Vertriebenen nach dem Krieg verglichen, "Menschen ohne Visum", die sich "Tag und Nacht, während des Wachzustandes im Schlaf und Traum" befanden. Sie sind ebenfalls vom "Provisorium" gezeichnet: "In ihrem Provisorium dämmerten sie dem nächsten Provisorium entgegen, irgendeinem Fürsorgeheim, einem Altersheim oder dem Friedhof ..." (ebd. 203f.).

Auch das Holocaust-Thema wird bei der Darstellung des Provisoriums aktualisiert. In den ersten Jahren seines West-Aufenthalts hatte C. eine große Sammlung von Büchern über "Holocaust & Gulag" angeschafft, die er in zwei entsprechend gekennzeichneten Kisten aufbewahrte.[30] Diese geschlossenen Kisten, "zum Bersten gefüllt mit dem unausdenkbaren Entsetzen der *Neuzeit*" (ebd. 154), bilden das Bindeglied zwischen individueller und kollektiver Identitätskrise. C. sieht sich im Halbschlaf

---

29 Schon einige Zeit nach seiner Ausreise aus der DDR waren die ostdeutschen Städte für C. "noch einmal ausgelöscht worden, und zwar, so schien es, wirksamer als durch Bombenteppiche. Wirksamer, weil diese Auslöschung ihn in einem Moment erwischt hatte, in dem er ohne jede Festigkeit war. Eine Staatsgrenze hatte dies vermocht [...], eine Mauer, ein Sperrgürtel bürokratischer Verordnungen" (Hilbig: 2001: 36f.). Auch Christa Wolf bezieht sich in ihrer Erzählung *Leibhaftig* (2002) in ihrer physischen und persönlicher Krise (die ein Sinnbil der kollektiven ist) nicht nur auf die Geschichte der DDR, sondern auch auf die Nazizeit: auf die Judenverfolgung (Wolf 2002: 74f.), auf die Kriegszeit (ebd. 114ff.), auf die Zeit der Vertriebenen (ebd. 101).

30 "Diese Bücher, sagte er sich, waren das unabdingbare Wissen dieses Jahrhunderts, sie enthielten das einzige *wirklich notwendige Wissen des 20. Jahrhunderts*. Und er sammelte diese Bücher manisch, mit einer fast unbezähmbaren Gier, er umstellte sich mit ihnen, er schüttete sich mit ihnen zu, er mauerte sich mit ihren Reihen ein" (Hilbig 2001: 153).

zwischen seinen beiden Bücherkisten [stehen], die zerschrammt und an den Kanten eingerissen waren, so daß die Bücher fast hervorquollen; rings um ihn wallte das von der Nachmittagssonne beschienene Leben, die unaufhörliche gottgefällige Feier von *Shopping & Fun*. Schon lange stand er so, er sah ziemlich abgekämpft aus, unrasiert, ungewaschen und etwas schmierig ... worauf wartete er: er wartete auf den Abtransport. – Aber niemand achtete auf ihn; und links und rechts von ihm gerierte sich die Konsumrevolution, der absolute Zeitgeist stelzte durch den Sonnenbrei. – Der würde, so sagte sich C., drüben in der DDR in tausend Jahren noch nicht ankommen ... [...] Denn die Welt ist dort, wo sich Käufer und Verkäufer mit leuchtenden Gesichtern am Eingang zum Elysium begegnen ...

Shopping macht frei, so steht es in attraktiven Lettern über all diesen Eingängen zu lesen ..." (ebd. 262f.).

Die Bücherkisten versinnbildlichen das Unaufgearbeitete der beiden deutschen "Nachkriegsersatzidentitäten": die Lüge der "antifaschistischen" Identität des Ostens, die Vertreibung und Gulag ignorierte; die Lüge der westlichen "Wirtschaftswunderidentität", die letztlich die "Schuldfrage" überlagerte und neutralisierte.[31] Mit seiner grellen, radi-kalen Verbindung von "Holocaust & Gulag" mit "Shopping & Fun" treibt C. seine West- und damit seine Wende-Kritik zum Äußersten. Was offenbart wird ist die anhaltende Verstrickung der deutschen Gegenwart der Vereinigung mit der Vergangenheit von Holocaust und Gulag, die in den beiden deutschen "Ersatzidentitäten" falsch aufge-arbeitet wurde. Es kann deshalb jetzt in der Wende- oder Nachwende-zeit nicht darum gehen, eine neue "Wunderidentität" zu konstruieren, die die deutsch-deutsche Geschichte ignoriert.

Welche Rolle hat dabei ein Schriftsteller zu spielen, der weiterhin am "Wahrheitsgehalt" der Literatur festhält, der davon weiß, dass es "mit der Unschuld des Erzählens vollkommen vorbei [war], seit es

---

31 Das (deutsche) 20. Jahrhundert wird von C. charakterisiert als "das Jahrhundert der Lüge": "Das ganze Jahrhundert sei ein einziger Zug von Lügen gewesen [...], in Form einer Lüge und beladen mit Lügen sei dieser Zug vorwärtsgefahren, durchgefahren, vorübergefahren, mit einer Lokomotive als Führungssymbol... und die restlichen Jahre des Jahrhunderts würde er noch so weiterfahren" (ebd. 255).

Berichte aus dem Gulag gab ..." (ebd. 257), und der trotzdem das Ziel hat, zu dem "fernen kindischen Zustand zurück[zu]kehren [...]: für Gott zu schreiben oder für sich selbst, was auf einer ganz banalen Ebene dasselbe war ..." (ebd. 242)?

Nach seinem identitätsauflösenden Weg durch die zwei deutschen Staaten bleibt ihm in der gesamtdeutschen Zeit nur eine Außenseiterrolle am Rande der *Betriebsgesellschaft*, eine Art des Schreibens als verdeckte und subversive Tätigkeit aus der Identitätskrise heraus: "Die einzige Möglichkeit war, zusammenzubrechen und überhaupt nichts mehr zu schreiben. Den Debilen markieren ... und dann vielleicht klammheimlich schreiben, das Sozialamt durfte davon keinen Wind bekommen ..." (ebd. 243). Somit ist C. wieder am Anfang seiner schriftstellerischen Laufbahn angekommen, seinem heimlichen und unverstandenen Schreiben als Industriearbeiter in der DDR: "Die Arbeiter waren genau solche ökonomischen Auslaufmodelle wie die Schriftsteller, wenigstens das hatten sie gemein" (ebd. 183). Am Ende seines Herumirrens durch den Osten, den Westen und das vereinte Deutschland schließt sich der Kreis seiner Existenz- und Schreibkrise zu einem dauerhaften Provisorium, das auch den kollektiven Zustand der Berliner Republik kennzeichnet.

Die literarischen Figuren von Hilbig und Wolf ziehen sich an einer imaginären Grenze zurück, aus der sie kritische Entwürfe einer individuellen wie kollektiven Identität erstellen, die die Ersatzidentitäten der beiden ehemaligen deutschen Staaten aufheben sollen. Jenseits der Utopie vom demokratischen Sozialismus, wie auch der vom allgemeinen Wohlstand und Freiheit, kann es nur um eine hybride Identität gehen, die der Geschichte von DDR und BRD Rechnung trägt. Dies kann keine endgültige Identität sein, sondern nur eine, die sich im Provisorium einrichtet, um nicht wieder in die Sackgasse einer Ersatzidentifikation zu geraten – eine provisorische, ständig im Wandel begriffene Identität, die sich aus vielfältigen Loyalitäten gegenüber den verschiedenen geschichtlichen Traditionen Deutschlands zusammensetzt.

Zitierte Literatur

Arnold, Heinz Ludwig, Hg. (1994): *Wolfgang Hilbig*. Ed. text + kritik (Heft 123), München.

Arnold, Heinz Ludwig, Hg. (2000): *DDR-Literatur der neunziger Jahre*. Sonderband text + kritik, München.

Arns, Inke (2001): "Vorspiel, Zwischenspiel, Nachspiel. Schlaglichter auf deutsche Debatten. Vom 'kausalen Nexus' des Historikerstreits (1986) zur 'deutschen Leitkultur' (2000)". *Vulgata. Kunst der 1990er Jahre in Slowenien*. Berlin. http://www.projects.v2.nl/~arns/Texts/leitkultur.html

Braun, Volker (1993): "Das Eigentum". *Von einem Land und vom andern. Gedichte zur deutschen Wende*. Hg. Conrady, Karl Otto. Frankfurt a.M.: Suhrkamp, 51.

Deiritz, Karl und Krauss, Hannes, Hgg. (1991): *Der deutsch-deutsche Literaturstreit oder "Freunde, es spricht sich schlecht mit gebundener Zunge". Analysen und Materialien*. Hamburg: Luchterhand.

Deleuze, Gilles / Guattari, Félix (1976): *Kafka. Für eine kleine Literatur*. Frankfurt a.M.: Suhrkamp.

Emmerich, Wolfgang (1996): *Kleine Literaturgeschichte der DDR*. Erweiterte Neuauflage. Kiepenheuer: Leipzig.

Emmerich, Wolfgang (1998): "Versungen und vertan? Rückblicke auf 40 Jahre DDR-Literatur und Geschichtsschreibung der DDR-Literatur." *Oxford German Studies* 27, 141–168.

Grass, Günter (1990): *Deutscher Lastenausgleich. Wieder das dumpfe Einheitsgebot. Reden und Gespräche*. Frankfurt a.M.: Luchterhand.

Hilbig, Wolfgang (2001): *Das Provisorium*. Fischer Taschenbuch: Frankfurt am Main.

Krauss, Hannes (2005): "Was ist geblieben? Rückblicke auf einen (Literatur-)Streit."
www.daad.ru/wort/wort2006/24_Krauss_Wolf.pdf, 263–274.

Ledanff, Susanne (1997): "Die Suche nach dem 'Wenderoman' – zu einigen Aspekten der literarischen Reaktionen auf Mauerfall und deutsche Einheit in den Jahren 1995 und 1996." *Glossen*, Heft 2.

Mühlberg, Dietrich (2002): "Vom langsamen Wandel der Erinnerung an die DDR". *Verletztes Gedächtnis. Erinnerungskultur und Zeitgeschichte im Konflikt.* Hgg. Jarausch, Konrad H., Sabrow, Martin. Frankfurt a.M.: Campus, 217–251.

Neuhaus, Stefan (2002): *Literatur und nationale Einheit in Deutschland.* Tübingen: Francke.

Rutschky, Michael (1995): "Wie erst jetzt die DDR entsteht. Vermischte Erzählungen." *Merkur* 49 (9/10), 851–864.

Schlesinger, Klaus (1998): *Von der Schwierigkeit, Westler zu werden.* Aufbau: Berlin.

Schneider, Peter (1984): *Der Mauerspringer.* Hamburg: Luchterhand.

Simanowski, Roberto (2000): "Die Wende der DDR als doppelter Kulturkonflikt." *Unerledigte Geschichten: der literarische Umgang mit Nationalität und Internationalität.* Hgg. Essen, Gesa von / Turk, Horst. Göttingen: Wallstein, 201–227.

Skare, Roswitha (1999): "'Das wahre Leben im Falschen'. Erscheinungsformen ostdeutscher Identität in Nach-Wende-Texten." *Nordlit: arbeidstidsskrift i litteratur* 5, 1–25.

Soldat, Hans-Goerg (1997): "Die Wende in Deutschland im Spiegel der zeitgenössischen deutschen Literatur". *German Life and Letters* 50, 133–154.

Sommer, Rose (1996): "Volker Braun: 'Das Eigentum'". *Poesia tedesca contemporanea. Interpretatzioni.* Hgg. Chialroni, A. / Morello, R. Alessandria: Eddizioni dell'Orso, 159–165.

Taylor, Charles (1992): *Multiculturalism and "The Politics of Recognition"*. Princeton University Press.

Wolf, Christa (1994): *Auf dem Weg nach Tabou. Texte 1990–1994*. Köln.

Wolf, Christa (2001): *Was bleibt*. München: Luchterhand.

Wolf, Christa (2002): *Leibhaftig*. München: Luchterhand.

Antón Figueroa

Discourse on National Identity: Notes from Galicia

It seems easy, at first glance, to distinguish between the following two discourses: that which is involved in the formation of national identities and that which analyses this first one and its effects as a social practice. The former would normally be classified as political, the latter academic or scientific. However, if we agree with Anne Marie Thiesse (1999: 14), who claims that the existence of the nation and of national feelings presupposes a collective adhesion – which is itself the product of a particular pedagogy and proselytism whose function is to instil "national" collective knowledge – we can then conclude that both discourses are at times closely connected and interdependent to a greater or lesser degree depending on the historical moment and cultural space in which they are inscribed. In *Meditations Pascaliennes*, Pierre Bourdieu warns against the preconceptions that the academic world brings to the analysis of non-academic practices. I contend that both the academic world and academic discourse are conditioned by the national beliefs in which they are inscribed and from which, to a certain extent, they derive. These beliefs can modify the analyses of our own, or someone else's, identity. In a passage from his work mentioned above, Bourdieu refers not only to the constitution of the *homo academicus*, but also to what (paraphrasing him) one could call the *homo nationalis*:

> Le 'philosophe' étant à peu près toujours aujourd'hui un *homo academicus*, son 'esprit philosophique' est façonné par et pour un champ universitaire, et imprégné de la tradition philosophique particulière que celui-ci véhicule et inculque: auteurs et textes canoniques subtilement hiérarchisés qui fournissent à la pensée la plus 'pure' de ses repères et ses phares (en ce domaine comme

ailleurs, *les programmes nationaux, écrits ou non écrits, produisent des cerveaux nationalement 'programmés'*[1]); problèmes surgis de débats historiquement constitués et pérennisés par la reproduction scolaire [...] concepts qui, malgré leur apparente universalité, sont toujours *indissociables d'un champ sémantique situé et daté et, à travers lui, d'un champ de luttes souvent limité lui aussi aux frontières d'une langue et d'une nation;* théories plus ou moins mutilées et rigidifiées par la routine de la transmission scolaire (1997: 41).

Therefore, academic/scholarly discourse should not be understood as being immune to the influence of collective knowledge, belief, *doxa* or national "common sense", especially if one conceives of discourse as a social phenomenon and is thus interested in analysing it as an element of communication with different circumstances of reception.

I Identity and Academic Discourse

Cultural fields are almost always inscribed within the framework of national institutions. The nation, as Anne Marie Thiesse states, is the object of a pedagogy (1999: 14). I believe that this pedagogy leads to the establishment or restoration of a way of seeing reality and of establishing certain values; that is, of a "common sense" which, in Bourdieu's words, is "en grande partie national parce que la plupart des grands principes de division sont jusqu'ici inculqués ou renforcés par les institutions scolaires qui ont pour mission majeure de construire la nation comme population dotée des mêmes "catégories", donc du même sens commun" (Bourdieu 1997: 118).

---

1   Pierre Bourdieu is quoting C. Soulié (1995): "Anatomie du goût philosophique". *Actes de la recherche en sciences sociales*, 109, 3-28 and R. Rorty, J. B. Schneewind and Q. Skinner, eds. (1984): *Philosophy in History: Essays on the Historiography of Philosophy*. Cambridge : Cambridge University Press. Emphases added.

Transnational fields also exist; indeed, the academic world itself generates specialised transnational sectors. Yet, the making of a nation requires a national pedagogy of the present and past, as well as of art and literature. This also entails, at times, the institutionalisation of a language as the national tongue. For this reason, the various discourses that emanate from the Humanities – not only artistic discourses (carried out by writers, musicians, painters), but also theoretical and interpretive ones (coming from historians, philologists, teachers, and philosophers) – are often "tarnished" by nationalist ideology. This applies to those discourses involved in the projects of nation and identity-building as well as to those that strive to preserve the nation.

In the academic field the struggle between academic and heteronomous interests takes on (as in any other field) a particular form that is subtly expressed in learned discourses. Academic discourse, perhaps more than any other, claims to be autonomous, disinterested, "pure", independent, and universal; this claim is expressed through the use of a specific language, a jargon, which is somewhat self-defensive and usually cryptic. Notwithstanding, the academic field is also affected by the autonomy/heteronomy dichotomy characteristic of cultural fields. There are external forces of all types at work within the academic field: economic, political, and personal (for example, the search for public notoriety or the temptation to be on television or in the press). There are also those forces that originate from what can be called the national *field* (which, ultimately, is also political though it presents itself as arising naturally). These forces condition both discourse and its reception.

Even when the academia seems, in practice, to recommend maintaining some semblance of internationalism (hence, not exhibiting too much national *passion*), the academic discourse that analyses its own or another national identity can become, even if originating from a *savant* field, "impure", because scholars have not only an academic homeland but also a national homeland, which they obviously share with their fellow citizens. As eventual recipients, these citizens can "infect" an initially "pure" discourse with national or political heteronomy. Indeed, this is the case, to which I will later allude, of the historical discourse through which new groups or "national" projects are invented.

Academic discourse can be conditioned both by its belonging to the national field and by the historical moment in which it is produced and the history of the academic field itself. For example, the cultural sphere is more openly involved in the politics of national affirmation in the earlier phases of the birth and expansion of the national "common sense" than in the later stages when this national "common sense" is fully established, incorporated, and naturalised. In these stages it is very difficult for academic discourse to become aware of its own political contribution to the logic of identity it attempts to analyse. Scholars may be either immersed in the process of national affirmation or quite detached from or completely outside of this process. In any way, they will always be conditioned by the logic that their own national condition imposes on them.

Furthermore, if we consider the discourse that analyses national identity as part of a communicative situation, it is evident that scholars – though they control the discourses they produce – may not control the results of their own discourses when received by others. The amount of coherence, value and *sym-pathy* ascribed to the identitary practice that is being analysed will be determined by the historical processes in which the given discourse is inscribed and on the objective, but always asymmetric, distance which separates the world of the observer from the world of the observed. In other words, it depends on the distance separating the communicative context of the addresser and the addressee as well as their respective ideologies. This means that analytical discourse may produce a refraction and distortion of the analysed practice due to the historical evolution of the established "common senses". Thus, for instance, the attempts to establish new borders in the twenty-first century can become more unpredictable and heterodox as we move away from the nineteenth century, which today seems to have been a *reasonably suitable* period for the "invention" of nations. An identical refraction occurs when the process is observed from either a different point in time or space.

The observing discourse may refract and distort an observed practice not only because of its national logic but also because of its own academic logic. The scholar is therefore conditioned by the *habitus of objectivity* which could eventually make the national logic impervious and prevent an historical analysis of the interests which can mediate his or her "discoveries". The notion of field entails a web of relations as well as the establishment of ways to see reality and to appreciate and constitute values:

> Chaque champ est l'institutionnalisation d'un point de vue dans les choses et dans les habitus. L'habitus spécifique, qui s'impose aux nouveaux entrants comme un droit d'entrée, n'est autre chose qu'un mode de pensée spécifique (un *eidos),* principe d'une construction spécifique de la réalité, fondé dans une croyance préréflexive dans la valeur indiscutée des instruments de construction et des objets ainsi construits (un *ethos*) (Bourdieu, 1997: 120).

The "croyance préréflexive" of the academic field is the faith in reason, which eventually limits self-analysis and the scholar's capacity for observing how his or her discourse is created. Scholars believe in their own objectivity, which is precisely what restricts them from gauging the effects of that other (national) belief. This is particularly the case when the national belief itself is the object of study. For this reason, the purity and objectivity of academic discourse and practices are affected inasmuch as this discourse theorises the practices (and also the theories) of national construction. Academic discourse may find it difficult to do without its own beliefs and habitus for objectively analysing how these very beliefs are established, or it may simply be incapable of such an analysis. It is easy to find cases of scholars who transform their beliefs into a dogma and organise their discourses according to pre-rational premises. The national question comprises, therefore, a source of heteronomy which manifests itself differently from the economic heteronomy of the academic field.

In this sense, national logic is quite mystifying because the discourse and its object are part of the same logic. Even if this were not the case (i.e., if discourse and object belonged to different national fields), national logic would intervene all the same. From Galicia we see, for example, how foreign countries are sympathetic towards autonomist movements within Spain while opposing similar movements or attempts in their own territory. If it is difficult for scholars to reflect on the making of their own premises, it is even more so for those carrying out identity-oriented analyses. (This inevitably makes our discourses quite "national", as is readily apparent at international conferences).

"Nationalising" discourse is a problem and a temptation for scholars whenever there is a conflict of identities involved. Some of them cannot resist making themselves known in the media where, paradoxically, they address public opinion by creating scientific discourses that inevitably become political. In Spain, for instance, when scholars are confronted with territorial conflicts ("regional" or "national", both of these being conflictive terms), they frequently produce discourses which, though based on scientific premises, are in reality political. A case in point is the Real Academia de la Historia and its complaint about the "deviation" found in textbooks in Autonomous Communities. Obviously, where communities struggle to build their national identity, textbooks and manuals comprise a crucial tool for national pedagogy, as they do everywhere. In any case, they are a clear indicator of how difficult it is to bring together political discourse and academic discourse. Therefore, in those instances where representing the past plays a major role, academic discourse cannot help being political. Historians, for example, may not control the effects of their own discourse and thus be caught unawares by the public's enthusiasm or hostility.

The complexity of the situation is also due to the fact that these processes dubbed "national" are really also "international". For its existence, a nation needs internal as well as external recognition. In the context of international relations (be they explicit and intentional or the result of the national doxas inscribed in academic discourses) the autonomy/heteronomy dialectic at work inside cultural fields (academic, literary, etc.) tends to be modified. This happens because the national character of a particular culture along with the subsequent national interests constitute important factors in international relations.

So, what was truly autonomous in relation to the power within the national cultural field seems less autonomous when related to "foreign" fields. In the latter case, we could state (hypothetically, at least) that the dialectics between the sub-field of large-scale production and the sub-field of restricted production and between the political or economic fields and the artistic or intellectual fields become somewhat diluted under the national perspective. As a result, the mutual objectives of these fields tend to vanish as well, so the elements that make up their relationship (like the reasons to import or export cultural products) are mixed or transformed. Furthermore, the relationship may also be affected by political motivations. Likewise, "pure art" and everything related to the artistic sphere becomes less "pure" in the context of international literary or artistic relations precisely because of the incorporation of national "common sense" and beliefs. The transmission of national cultural products leads to the emergence of international cultural *politics* that defend national interests.

The presence of specific national beliefs in intercultural relations depends, at least partially, on the international status of the nation to which these beliefs belong. The weaker the nation's international recognition, the greater the degree of politisation. In those cases in which national status constitutes a project still in progress, the academic world and literature itself play a special and extra-literary role whose effects inside and outside the literary field are especially interesting. These projects in progress take place not only outside those spaces that are legitimised and naturalised as "common sense" but also, and to a certain extent, outside the period that is nowadays considered legitimate for the formation of nations (*grosso modo* the eighteenth and, particularly, the nineteenth century). This legitimation which is already established as a national belief makes all attempts at establishing a new national belief seem anachronic.

Generally speaking, when people come into contact with another cultural field and borrow some of the field's elements (model, form, manifesto, etc.), they do it from the perspective, set of beliefs and aspirations of their own cultural field. It is therefore obvious that national fields play a part in international academic relations. International domination, which is so crude and often also violent in political and economic fields, is not so evident in the cultural field, where interests claim to be disinterested. Cultural domination (from academic discourse itself to pop music sung with an English accent in one's own tongue) is exerted through more unconscious and much more subtle means.

All of this implies that, whatever its national background, scholarly discourse and, particularly, discourse engaged with identity-oriented issues always contain some element that is originally or explicitly political, or *ends up being political* given the particular "common sense" incorporated by its addressers and addressees. This makes the scholar a political agent. For instance, writing in a particular language or organising a conference or a seminar makes him a political agent regardless of his explicit personal stance. In any academic discourse there is a variable political ingredient that makes the discourse one that speaks "on behalf of".[2] This delegated function, which is very overt in the early stages of the cultural projects of so-called minority tongues, minority cultures, or minority literatures, is also at work in different, yet powerful, ways in discourses coming from "major" cultures or those that have established themselves on great literary traditions.

The possible misapprehensions in the reception of this type of discourse do not seem to derive specifically from lexicological misconceptions but from problems caused by social factors at work when the discourse is produced and received in its own context of national beliefs as well as in those with different beliefs. Furthermore, misunderstandings of this type do in fact increase when this very same discourse originates in a space in which the national project goes through a spirited stage and *is heard* in spaces dominated by logics that are different from that in which it is formulated.

---

2   See Bourdieu 2000: 56–57. See also: Bourdieu 1984: 49–55.

II Academic Discourse and Identitary Discourse: The Galician Case

If national passion and belief are part of the discourses produced in nations internationally recognised as nations, it is perhaps more reasonable and logical to expect a similar passion in discourses on the national question in cases like Galicia, where this issue in itself is the object of a struggle for the recognition of an identity-based "common sense", which is reclaimed (partially, at least) against a consolidated "common sense" of identity. It is not a totally successful struggle, of course, or else the fight would not go on. This confrontation between lived and incorporated "common senses" is the cause of great confusion, which is inevitable to a certain extent, but not at all new.[3]

The academic field is often called upon to intervene in the pedagogy of the national "common sense" both in its establishment and in its preservation or eventual restoration. This entails political action which, as such, is heteronomous yet persistent and, to a certain degree, hidden due to its obvious, naturalised and incorporated character. In similar situations, the academic, critical, and historical discourses engaged in analysing the social situation almost always have a public and external impact as a result of their articulation. Political reasons can therefore appear when interpreting these discourses; moreover, these discourses can be "contested" not with the same logic that structures it but with a different logic that is political in nature. There is a pragmatic axiom according to which speakers, in

---

3   On a similar line of thought, M. Gondar argued that "except for a scarce number of recent authors, the great majority of analysts of identity – and Galician analysts are not an exception – have adhered to an *essentialist* and, even, Romantic conception. [...] The reason for this attitude lies in the wrong perspective adopted. The great limitation of almost all the theoreticians of collective identity (in the past as well as at present) is to admit the spontaneous perception of the problem as experienced by social actors themselves" (Gondar 1995: 28).

order to understand each other, must already share some discursive universe which is the base for their presumed "honest cooperation". If in a hypothetical act of communication various discursive universes overlap, honest cooperation would be very difficult, not to say impossible. This is exactly what happens when the academic, or any other, universe and the political universe become involved in the same act.

It may be the case that academic discourses end up being contradictory not for academic reasons, but rather for heteronomous reasons; that is, for politico-national reasons that "are taken for granted". At times the discourses produced to justify or explain the present belief systems (the process has not concluded) of the different European nations come into conflict:[4] they not only contradict each other but some feel attacked by the others' social imaginary. This is particularly so when in the so-called peripheries there are attempts to build cultural spaces that are really autonomous or national. In the case of Galicia, where certain discursive acts of an academic nature (critical, literary, and so on) have a political impact, this type of misunderstanding is quite frequent. The "central" discourse uses two standards: on the one hand, it justifies its own legitimacy; on the other hand, it denies the legitimacy of the other national project through a mystifying operation that is not always equally conscious of its own functioning as it condemns as illegitimate those very same means it has had recourse to in order to "invent" its own nation. The concept of "democracy" is hardly problematic in the first case, while it is very problematic in the second. This is true, for example, when minority rights are demanded only in the peripheries or when a national tongue seems "natural" in the centre, whereas in the periphery, it is considered "boorish" and artificial. The representation of space, regarded as obvious and even sacred in the first case, is deemed provincial and essentialist in the second. Likewise, artistic and literary monuments

---

4   Similarly, the discourse that is being manufactured to build the future European nation may become conflictive, as it is at present when confronted with non-European projects.

that are "universal" and numerous in one case are provincial and insignificant in number in the other; or national history is viewed as obvious and reasonable in one place, but perceived as invented in the other.

Therefore, both sides run the risk of causing a scandal in the name of their respective rationales deriving from their respective "common senses". The simple fact of pointing out the existence of this asymmetry of domination can be interpreted by the dominator as provocation. Domination is a social practice which institutes certain representative discourses, which derive from the same social practice that institutes and sanctifies these discourses as essential and true, and rationalises them into a "common sense". Dominant discourse employs the rational character of historical analysis in order to (dis)qualify and explain the heterodoxies that arise, but it never uses this discourse on itself to explain how its own orthodoxy originated. On the other hand, from the point of view of the dominated and of those agents that attempt to build new fields of identity, the type of abstraction we have just mentioned (theoretical abstraction included) may be seen as a superfluous game in the face of an urgent call to action, or even considered treason. A "rational consent" regarding the historical (not essential) character of a dominated identity-based movement can be viewed as an action in the opposite direction, as a concession to the dominator, insofar as the historical (not essential) constitution of domination remains unexplained.

Logically, the greater the capacity of self-reflection and methodical suspension of one's *doxa* (in both producer and recipient), the weaker these national determinants are. Political determinants are more powerful in discourses that are produced and received in contexts or projects that are still in their foundational stages (as is the case with Galicia). They are different depending on whether they are part of the process or whether they are observed by those who oppose the process, or are outside of it (which does not necessarily imply a greater degree of objectivity). After just writing the word "projects", I avoided adding the modifier, "national". Depending on whether I had written "national" or "*national*" (in italics), my discourse could be taken as orthodox, heterodox, or "curious" and exotic. This would depend on the reader's nationality as well as his or her national and academic stance because national beliefs condition academic discourse when this discourse deals with identity.

Some of the identity-based processes initiated in the nineteenth century (like in Galicia, and definitely in Catalonia and the Basque Country) did not achieve public political recognition at all, or only partially through the Statutes of Autonomy granted to the three during the Second Spanish Republic and in the post-Francoist regime. They did, however, establish some sort of cultural dividing line based mainly on their different languages and constituted literary and artistic fields insofar as, after an initial stage (quite epic and communal), competing positions and position-takings were gradually established. As in many other cases of cultural birth, rebirth, or regeneration – such as, to a certain extent, the Spain of 1898 – not only arts like literature or music but even academia was urged to carry out national tasks which were political tasks, and, therefore, heteronomous. We may consider, for instance, the Galician national discourse of Vicente Risco, Alfonso D. Rodríguez Castelao or Ramón Otero Pedrayo. A political-academic discourse emerged that was conditioned by a national belief, by a certain essentialist ideology of *the land* and *the people*, which instituted a particular worldview and imposed norms on the artists as well as on academic discourse. If we examine some excerpts from Castelao's *Diario*, during the period he was in Paris and observed Avant-Guard production, it is evident that his judgements of what he sees comprise a product of his previous set of beliefs. His discourse reflects these beliefs and attributes certain values to works of art according to the ideal of *pobo* (people) and *terra* (land):

> The new colour is absolutely predominant in the scenography, and not because it has what they call new, but *because it has what is popular*. The use of pure colours, always with courage and in that spirit of synthesis that is characteristic of the so-called bad taste of the people, which for many is exquisite. We painters must go to the people as musicians do (Castelao 1922: 3. Italics added).

> Here is my opinion of the exhibition of Russian art, in general. It does not have one single character, but many. It is individualism, nationalism and futurism (true futurism). It is the Russian land with all the variety of flowers that can grow in her. No philosophies, no recipes, no leaders. There are artists who, *consciously or unconsciously guiding themselves by the Land's mandates, met the genius* (Castelao 1922: 8. Italics added).

Moreover, a certain degree of anti-intellectualism can also be detected in this passage. This feature is still present nowadays in nationalist discourse for a very simple reason: any firm belief or any established "common sense" refuses to explore the reasons and the processes of its own institution precisely because it really works as a belief and "common sense". (We should not think, of course, that anti-intellectualism is exclusive to this type of situations: it also surfaces in the academic field inasmuch as the latter is incapable of reflecting on the processes that condition its own premises).

This belief in *a terra, o pobo*, and in the "soul" of the *pobo*, produces a discursive habitus that interprets its own artistic reality as well as foreign works. Otero Pedrayo's article "Occitania e Atlántida", a very revealing title indeed, is an exercise of comparative literature based on these premises. Otero Pedrayo contends that Europe has two different souls: the first is a classical, Mediterranean, Germanic soul that believes in fate and is the soul of Occitan lyricists (*félibres*). The second soul is Atlantic, Celtic, and Romantic; it is the soul of the bards, who believe in *saudade* (a melancholy due to homesickness) and free will.[5] "The Celts are *saudosos*. A Protestant Celt is for me inconceivable. *Saudade* makes one embrace *libero arbitrio*". (Otero Pedrayo 1934: 130) He then writes: "Paul Valery, the epitome of super-Cartesianism, mathematician, stylist of classicism and modernity who aims at pure ideas, could not hide his national origin. He has no faith in the landscape, nor in history. [...] Paul Valery is a *félibre*. I hope this does not sound odd. Also, Leconte de Lisle was a bard" (Otero Pedrayo 1934: 127).

---

5   *Saudade*: Word-emblem of the Galician identitary feeling.

Although Otero Pedrayo, Castelao and Risco were very different intellectually, their works are testimony to the involvement of all the cultural field – not just the literary field – in the process of affirmation and theoretical justification of Galician identity. In this sense, the cultural field fulfils an important political function which grants writers, historians, musicologists, and so on a particular social status. It also creates a highly politicised discourse and introduces repertoires of interpretation and reading that tend to outlive the discourses that gave life to them.

Particularly important within academic discourse is the problem of historical discourse. In theory it is easy to distinguish objective history as a series of events from the historical (historiographic) discourse that describes them. In a context of national construction, one tends to forget that historiographic discourse produces objective history and even often becomes the object of historical discourse. The history of Galician nationalism is to a large extent the history of its discourses and of its power to build identity; that is, to produce history. This power of historical discourse to produce object-history is an element that some researchers seem not to take heed of when they judge nationalist historical discourse outside its context, as if it were a dialogue between colleagues who jump around historical periods and spaces. They attribute, deny, or criticise values without understanding the effects that this discourse has; that is, the *doxa* and the "common sense" that it establishes. A mere analysis of its formal content is not enough to understand this historiographic discourse as historical object: its situation, its motives, and its effects must also be analysed. I have stated elsewhere (Figueroa 2001: 73) when quoting Bourdieu that when a discourse which is supposedly rational, logical and founded on empirical science tries to analyse these social struggles to establish a "common sense", it usually forgets that practical and political discourses contribute to objectively producing an unquestionable social reality, despite the fact that these discourses are often "scientifically" questionable if only "objectivist" criteria are applied. Independently of their foundation *in re*, because the *re* is inscribed in the discourse itself, these discourses or the practical criteria they employ (for example, language, history, geography, or economy) are mental representations. Thus, I quoted the following passage from Bourdieu (1982: 136):

> On ne peut comprendre cette forme particulière de lutte des classements qu'est la lutte pour la définition de l'identité "régionale" ou "ethnique" qu'à condition de dépasser l'opposition que la science doit d'abord opérer, pour rompre avec les prénotions de la sociologie spontanée, entre la représentation et la réalité, et à condition d'inclure dans le réel la représentation du réel, ou plus exactement la lutte des représentations, au sens d'images mentales, mais aussi de manifestations sociales destinées à manipuler les images mentales (et même au sens de délégations chargées d'organiser les manifestations propres à modifier les représentations mentales).

Historical science, probably because of its academic habit, finds it difficult to understand its own and inevitable power to construct and produce history. What we call the political character of historical discourse – which we perceive today as a very frequent element in the epic stages of national processes – is still present in some fashion either in the academic discourses produced from consolidated national logics, or even more so from those produced from processes that are still in an initial stage. Robert Lafont's famous statement, "les études de diglossie appartiennent au projet de destruction de la diglossie"' (1984: 5), is relevant to show that academic discourses produced in a situation of national construction belong to the process of national construction itself (they belong to or *end up being* part of this process). In Galicia these discourses were mainly historical at the beginning (particularly in the period before the Civil War), which is the reason why Galician historiography, in tune with the times, started out being closely connected to the differential or national claims. At present, discourses have come to adopt "a perspective that is even distant (and often scarcely patriotic) in relation with the past" (Villares 2004: 16).

Contrary to the logic of Bourdieu's argument, which claims that economic heteronomy is produced when the literary field is consolidated and the writer occupies an important position and enjoys wide public recognition, here in Galicia political heteronomy appears at the birth of the field. This heteronomy conditions the field of restricted production in an original way. It does not threaten the field's artistic autonomy in the same way or for the same reasons as it does in consolidated cultural fields; moreover, it does not evolve in a similar fashion or produce the same effects. While in a consolidated field political heteronomy tends to grow and impose its own rules, in a successful minority field this heteronomy usually disappears, though some of the characteristics and misunderstandings I have brought to light remain.

It is evident that in the last quarter of the twentieth century in Galicia, history as well as science and art in general have become more autonomous in relation to the political obligation of contributing to the consolidation of the national belief. Notwithstanding, this belief system created by only a few spread throughout society to such an extent that the scientist's increasingly detached and demystifying gaze is in no way an obstacle for the past to grow in importance.

The difficulties for academic discourse derive from the fact that these processes are ones of struggle in which beliefs sometimes come into conflict with one another because one's beliefs impede acknowledging the other's legitimacy. Beliefs cause one to reject self-analysis and to recognise their own constructed nature. But, these same beliefs accuse opposing beliefs of being constructed. Behind all this we find the usual distinction between what is essential (one's own belief) vs. what is constructed (the other's belief). In the confrontation between an established logic and one that struggles to establish itself, if someone claims that these are historical processes, this claim may go against the "common sense" and be considered heterodox. In these cases, the scholar's rational displacement of the object of science from the established and "naturalised" *doxa* to the process of social action produces heterodoxy. To consider the effects of identity-based discourses as an object of study without admitting the existence of any previous orthodoxy except for that which is really at work constitutes a provocative attitude. The institutionalised power always tries to protect itself through rational evidence and refuses to recognise itself as an institution established by those that fabricated it and preserve it.

Cultural situations like the one in Galicia manifest a permanent characteristic: a high degree of consciousness and politisation that tends to transform cultural products into a tool for building cultural and political identity, though political identity may not yet be clearly defined and delineated. This militant character has effects on the act of reading and writing, on the workings of the field as a whole, on its relations with other systems, and on critical reflection. If this militancy can destroy the necessary degree of social spontaneity in the artistic sphere, in academic discourse it can also compromise the autonomy of the academic realm (consciously in some cases, but in many others *malgré lui*). For this reason, it is indispensable for scholars to reflect on their own discourses in order to maintain their autonomous character and control its reception. The naturalising effects of the very discourse that analyses naturalisation constitutes a major difficulty, which the academic must confront. Depending on the historical period and the social space in which a *text* is both produced and read, scholars must bear in mind that their discourses on identity may, to different degrees, turn into a discourse of identity.

WORKS CITED

Bourdieu, Pierre (2000): *Propos sur le champ politique*. Presses Universitaires de Lyon: Lyon.

Bourdieu, Pierre (1984): "La délégation et le fétichisme politique". *Actes de la Recherche en Sciencers sociales*, n° 52–53, 49–55.

Bourdieu, Pierre (1997): *Méditations Pascaliennes*. París: Seuil.

Bourdieu, Pierre (1982): *Ce que parler veut dire*. Paris: Fayard.

Figueroa, Antón (2001): *Nación, Literatura, Identidade*. Vigo: Xerais.

Gondar Portasany, Marcial (1995): *Crítica da razón galega.* Vigo: A Nosa Terra, 2nd ed.

Lafont, Robert (1984): "Pour retrousser la diglossie". *Lengas.* 15, 5–35.

Otero Pedrayo, Ramón (1934): "Occitania e Atlántida". *Nós* 128/129, 128–131.

Rodríguez Castelao, Alfonso Daniel (1922): "Do meu diario". *Nós* 10, 2–9.

Thiesse, Anne-Marie (1999): *La création des identités nationales.* Paris: Seuil.

Villares Paz, Ramón (2004): *Historia de Galicia.* Vigo: Galaxia.

DOLORES VILAVEDRA

The Galician Reader: A Future Project?

The aim of this essay is not to establish a thesis but to give rise to a series of questions about a phenomenon which, more and more, strikes me as paradoxical: the apparent irrelevance of the reader within the Galician literary system. Complaints about its small number are reproduced daily in the media. But what is of interest to me is not the sheer numbers of Galician readers, which are undoubtedly surprisingly low, but what those numbers represent in terms of the qualitative definition of the *Galician reader*.[1]

As a starting point I will take for granted two obvious premises: that there is no literature without a reader and that literature is the discourse through which the symbolic codification of the Galician identity is traditionally articulated. That the latter premise does nowadays seem natural to the Galician population (though it need not be so) is basically explained by the fact that Galician culture expresses itself in a language of its own. Thus, there is a natural transfer between language and identity that affects almost all aspects of public life.

The process of "philologisation" of cultures that have a minority language has already been delineated by Antón Figueroa (1988). Here I would just like to highlight the *defensive* dimension that that process has in Galicia, which, apparently, results naturally in reification of all the verbal discourses in general and of literary discourse in particular. Although I will examine this point in more detail later on, for now suffice it to say that such reification exerts a kind of tacit

---

1 Whenever we talk about the *Galician reader*, we will be referring to those people who read texts in Galician. Likewise *Galician literature* will refer to literature written in Galician.

protectionism on the different manifestations of that common heritage that is language, which, because it is collective by nature, is overburdened with an identitary function. Consequently, it plays a leading role in the different processes of structuration of the community itself insomuch as it allows us to establish a clear limit between identity and alterity. Historically, literary discourse as the privileged means of the symbolic codification of the community (my second premise) has been questioned only occasionally and in an anecdotal fashion. It has always been implicitly accepted that Galician literature is literature written in Galician and that it plays a leading role in terms of identity, even in today's youngest generations. As late as 2004, a young journalist wrote the following: "The Galician publishing industry [...] has been the agent of the *heroic resistance* of Galician culture from the mid-twentieth century onwards. The political and historical transformation have made the sector [...] *the flagship of the defence and advancement of a ridiculed country*" (Castro Moreira 2004: 64. My italics). Here is a perfect example of the "defensive dimension" that language has at least in terms of identity.

But we need to be ready to change this defensive mentality insofar as the situation itself is changing within the new framework of the Europeanist civic paradigm and the much commented process of globalisation. For this framework may offer alternative identity models in which the identitary value of language is diminished while its commercial and economic value are emphasised. Where have those militant readers who used to shield their identity behind the protective covers of the Galician book gone? At what point did they exit the road whose cultural goal is to have the publishing sector be declared a strategic one for the Galician economy? Today, a literature without readers has no reason to exist at all, and much less so when the defence of Galician culture and language starts to be based more and more on pragmatic arguments. So, we must have readers in order to survive. But, where are they?

Let us first refer to the number of speakers of a language: Are they comparable to the number of readers? Are we to look for readers within the community of speakers alone? Even though at first it is not unreasonable to say that both instances overlap to some degree, a simple contrastive study does nevertheless reveal that the equivalence of speakers to readers is not a given. Thus, trying to find readers among Galician-speaking people seems to have not proved a very successful strategy. The sociolinguistic data available make us raise the following questions concerning the Galician reader: if 31.4% of Galicians speak exclusively or primarily in Spanish and 68.6% speak exclusively or primarily in Galician, how can we explain that a mere 0.5% read only in Galician whereas approximately 50% do so exclusively or regularly in Spanish?[2] Leaving aside very influential factors such as linguistic competence or the smaller degree of availability of and accessibility to all kinds of reading material in Galician, what about that 20% of Galician speakers who do not read in their own language at all but rather in Spanish?

That Galicia is a linguistically hybrid society is further suggested by the following facts: (1) 50% of the population speak and read in both languages (20.1% mainly in Spanish and 29.9% in Galician), (2) 40% believe that "both" Galician and Spanish are the language for the Galician people[3], and (3) 50% consider themselves both Galician and Spanish.[4]

As there is no available research in the field of literary reception, we cannot formulate sustainable hypotheses about the identity of the reader. Yet, some authors have defended a broader conception of Galician identity, one in which language is not the only determining factor[5] (only 31% believe that to be Galician one has necessarily to

[2] Data taken from Seminario de Sociolingüística (1995: 94).
[3] Information taken from Seminario de Sociolingüística (1996: 216).
[4] Information taken from Siguán 1999: 73–76.
[5] See, for instance, H. Monteagudo's proposal for a possible future of the language: "Galicians as a group will be bilingually productive both in Galician and Spanish, a large majority will also be fluent in English, and disparate sectors of the population will also be in different degrees capable of reading, understanding, speaking and writing in French or German. Galician will get closer to Portuguese and the relations with Portuguese-speaking countries will become more intense to the point that the linguistic competence of native

speak in Galician) and one that would help circumvent the possible risk of social fracture,[6] with the desirable secondary effect of freeing the Galician language from its current state of identitary hypertrophy. And, if society as a whole views that *speaking Galician* is not necessarily synonymous with *being Galician*, why, then, could this not be extended to *Galician readers* as well? Be that as it may, the following points are clear:

1. Language choice, implicitly at least, does not necessarily entail a particular audience, as normally thought.
2. The percentage of Galician speakers who also read in their own language is insignificant.
3. Some Spanish speakers (10–20%) *could become* readers of Galician.

The awareness of the diffuse entity (and identity) of that polymorphic concept called *reader* is perhaps the reason why there are no studies that deal with the issue of literary reception from any methodological perspective whatsoever. Studies based on reception theory, which was introduced in Galicia by Darío Villanueva and timidly followed by Anxo Tarrío and myself, quickly came to a dead end because of a total lack of sociologically inspired approaches to literary reception, including even those of a merely statistical nature, like the ones produced regularly in France or, in our closer and less rich neighbour,

---

speakers will allow them (supplemented with a little learning effort) to keep a fluent intercommunication with the speakers of the second language. This future would entail the consolidation of the Galician language as a domestic language that reaches and maintains a pre-eminent position in a series of fields, allowing the simultaneity with Spanish in some of them and, in others, the preference for the latter and/or English [...] so that a sociolinguistic configuration of the country can obtain which is compatible with the sustainability of the Galician language [with no] exclusive [field] for the latter, but with a series of fields in which it will surely maintain a clearly pre-eminent position" (Monteagudo 2000: 133).

6   As, in my opinion, is the case with the Basque Country.

Portugal.[7] Potential researchers are to some degree reluctant to tackle this issue for fear of having to come face to face with scientific evidence that would force us into questioning the integrity of the whole apparatus of the Galician literary system that was so laborious to build. It is better not to know, safer to keep on producing literature (and literary research) without really knowing for whom we are doing it. For, if we take the only information available to us seriously, then we would come to conclusions that are, to say the least, alarming. This is certainly true if we take a look at the defining members of the Galician market: of the 2,500,000 inhabitants, only 25% read in Galician, of which 400,000 are schoolchildren.[8]

Thus, we may conclude that the potential amount of "natural" readers of Galician books is around a quarter of a million. If we compare this figure with the fact that in 2003 only 13% of the books sold in Galicia were written in Galician (including text books and mandatory reading at schools) we then reach a conclusion that goes beyond mere numerical figures; namely, not only are Galician readers a minority group, but also they come dangerously close to occupying a marginal position, a very risky situation in a society ruled by capitalist logic. This is further confirmed by the publishing and sales figures: of the books published in Galician, 33.4% are textbooks, 26.6% are works of creative writing, 17% are studies in humanities and social sciences and 15.4% are children's and juvenile literature; 75% of the total amount of books sold are included in mandatory reading lists and 19% are textbooks, which leaves a ridiculous 6% of free sales within a highly regulated context. In conclusion, the Galician reader is a captive reader who does not read much and, when he does read, he is

---

[7] E.g. Freitas, Eduardo de, José Luís Casanova e Nuno de Almeida (1997): *Hábitos de leitura. Um inquérito á populaçao portuguesa*. Lisboa: Dom Quixote, or Guy, Jean-Michel and Lucien Mironer (1997): *Les publics du théâtre*. Paris: Ministère de la Culture et de la Communication/DEP/La documentation française.

[8] The empirical data offered on publishing and sales figures are taken from Cabrera and Freixanes 2003.

highly conditioned by the great degree of institutionalisation of the Galician book.

If we consider the 17,677 entries in the ISBN index, "the basic corpus of our present publishing production" (Cabrera and Freixanes 2003: 136), the situation does not seem to be so serious. However, things look different when we take into account that "between 1975 and 2003 there were more books published in Galician than in the whole previous history of our language" (ibid.). But, if, as Horta Nunes argues, "the subject constitutes himself as a reader within a social reading memory", what is that memory? (Horta Nunes 2003: 25). What has become of the concept of tradition? Where is the social reading memory in the Galician language? Where is the poor reader? In our case, we would be talking about a neophyte reader, with little historical conscience, brought up in an alien field of meaning and almost dispossessed of any native referent with which to establish a dialogue. In this sense, reading (and writing too) in Galician is not only a political practice, but also a subversive one because of its lack of role models. We do not know how the Galician subject-reader was historically formed. We know very little or almost nothing about his subjective experience, and we lack reliable descriptive accounts of a practice that was only made objective as an *event*. Naturally, this exceptional character of the Galician reader was a hindrance in the conceptualisation of the literary event which was reified by that anomalous process of historical constitution of the Galician audience. Such reification (which prevents discourse from having the dynamism that guarantees its permanent renovation and causes its stagnation) had a serious side effect: the social division of reading (Orlandi 2003: 22), the socio-historical distribution of its practice. The space in which the Galician subject-reader traditionally carried out his practice remained thus neatly fenced off, marked by the metaphorical effect that the transfer of the valence of *militancy* had on it due to the intrinsically subversive nature that, as we have already pointed out, writing and reading in Galician have always had.

The solution may lie in reusing the concept of *addressee*. I do not intend to create a new category for an instance that has been a victim of typological excesses like that of the reader (implicit, real, virtual, desired, ideal, and so on), but to emphasise the functionality of the addressee as a "productive literary force" which, as a pre-literary element, materialises its functionality when "the intention manifested in the choice of addressee results in aesthetic structural elements" (Zimmermann 1987: 48). In this way, I believe that it is only by increasing the social base of its addressee that Galician literature can liberate itself from its reifying straitjacket and function as a real discourse of social communication. Quite another question would be whether, as a consequence of this expansion, an amplification of the *interdiscourse*[9] that writers and readers share should take place. We should have to wait and see if all of us are willing to favour such an amplification. And I say "all of us" because it is not just authors and potential readers who must make the effort, but also the group of actual readers whose reading practice is determined by the way we view one another inside a field of meaning which we have up to now shared with relative easiness. Undoubtedly, the event of such an expansion of the social base of the reader of Galician literature would force the diverse agents to relocate themselves. Furthermore, it is perhaps pertinent to ask ourselves whether certain sectors would be reluctant to accept an expansion which they consider a distortion because it would mean the loss of their systemic positions. But this is another story.

We must not forget that "authors who write for a traditional audience [...] do so with an inspiration which is not exclusively literary, but historical and social as well to give evidence of the group's predecessors and contemporaries; and the latter can naturally lead to the continuity of the referential modes and to the refusal of postmodern experiments and stagings" (Dimic 1999: 216). Here is the crux of the matter: do Galician authors have to go on writing for that "traditional audience"? I believe that doing so would be economic and aesthetic suicide. Do they continue to do it anyway? If this is indeed

---

9   Defined by Orlandi as "the cluster, historically and linguistically defined, of what can be said" (Orlandi 2003: 12).

the case, which everything seems to indicate is true, then it will have a paralysing effect on the evolution of literary models.

Fortunately, there has been a recent attempt in the field of Galician literature to broaden the frontiers of interdiscourse by breaking down the codes shared by traditional producers and recipients in a search (represented, above all, by the postmodern novel) for a new way of reading which is not just "a mere *discovery* or an *unveiling* of meaning", but, rather, a more active and, above all, different one whose sole objective is no longer the creation of meaning. (Leenhardt 1980: 205) But this attempt has not brought about a similar expansion in the case of readers. What has gone wrong? Maybe, the intention of recent literary experiments has not been to expand the potential readership, although we thought that the former would attract the latter. The crux of the matter does not seem to lie in the ability of Galician literature to create new models, a front on which, to be fair, it has been active of late.

Paradoxically, the conscience of literature's identitary value which Dimic spoke of in the passage quoted above favours the social division of reading I mentioned. For, used as we are to considering that the main function of art is to establish consensus through the creation and confirmation of the identitary norm, or to express the group's vision of the world, it will always be *the others* who exclude themselves. Galician literary discourse presents itself as a project of integration and structuration with no counterforce in Spanish literature (apart from metaliterary discourse), freed from that identitary burden that we accept as natural. The moral: No one joins that project of integration unwillingly. But is it really a project of integration?

Of course, throughout its history the Galician literary system has developed different strategies to attract new readers. In the mid-1980s Ediciòns Xerais vindicated "the power of readers"[10] to give them more prominence in tune with critics and theorists who were concerned with the category of reader (at a time when reception

---

10 This is the motto of the house's narrative prize created in 1984 and whose jury is made up of non-professional readers (such as critics and writers).

theories were being introduced and circulated in Galicia). This was taking place at the same time that a process of revaluation of narrative forms and models was trying to do away with the traditional pre-eminence of lyrical poetry. But, something else was at stake in the process; namely, the willingness to move away from a conception of literature focused on the writer to a reader-oriented one, to use Walter Mignolo's termino-logical distinction (Mignolo 1978: 278ff.). According to Mignolo (who draws on Uspenski's semiotic approach to culture) writer-oriented cultures fall into the esoteric type and give priority to poetry, whereas reader-oriented cultures give priority to prose. This means that in the latter the writer respects the reader's rules, while in the former the reader must abide by the writer's rules. Therefore, in hindsight, it becomes clear that it was not a coincidence that both the vindication of "the power of readers" and the great development of the novel occurred simultaneously.

To keep certain social sectors which could contribute to holding together the Galician literary system from agreeing that Galician literature is in crisis and that the solution is to abandon the language, the only alternative is to search for new readers among non-Galician speakers. This means that language choice should not entail a choice of audience, the consequences of which are assumed at all levels like interdiscourse, where traditional authors and readers should engage in creating a new frame of reference and a new field of meaning.

It is imperative that we stop praising new works just because they reproduce canonical models, as often happens in Galician literary reviews. Public recognition solely in terms of continuity with the past may find the approval of some sectors, but it definitely discourages readers unfamiliar with the work of canonical authors from joining the ranks of the Galician readership. They feel inhibited to do so because they fear they are incapable of valuing new work adequately as they lack the necessary interpretive tools. Be it unconsciously, or with the best of intentions, endogamy as a mode of reading is still promoted.

The future is, of course, uncertain. In view of this, two solutions are at hand: either to keep on supporting a culture of heroic resistance (as the young journalist I quoted at the beginning defended), or to try to provide literary discourse with new identitary valences, functionally more integrative in terms of language, addressed specially to attract those potential readers who, without a doubt, exist within that section of the population who consider themselves both Galician and Spanish. Seemingly, a third way exists according to some social agents who call for a type of social recognition for the language which is "not a mere liturgy, as is usually the case, but as an added value, an identity value [...] of what we could call a *Galician product* (the value of difference) in a uniform, globalised society". (Freixanes 2003: 5). Prestige based on economic profitability sounds attractive, but until it is clear how to obtain it, and where readers are concerned, I would prefer to come up with more realistic alternatives.

Perhaps the normalisation of Galician readers entails their invisibility. Will the readers' transparency, *their non-being*, be the solution? Or, on the contrary, would the solution be to develop Schmidt's proposal of "a conscious separation of the reader in a real I and a ficticious I" (Schmidt 1987: 204) and suggest to potential readers a fictitionalisation capable of seducing them? Have Galician writers ever intended to do this in a systematic manner? Obviously, underlining the fictitious role of the reader can be a coherent and effective strategy in a society like Galicia that seems to be condemned to a certain degree of schizophrenia.

Somehow, readers are always a future project for texts. Paradoxically, so is Galician literature – still!

WORKS CITED

Cabrera, Mª Dolores and Víctor F. Freixanes (2003): "Algunhas reflexións arredor do libro galego". *Grial* 160, 136–143.

Castro Moreira, Nuria (2004): "Crise na industria editorial. O Parnaso galego, cuestionado". *Tempos novos* 88, 66–69.

Dimic, Milan V. (1999): "Las literaturas canadienses de menor difusión: observaciones desde un punto de vista sistémico". *Teoría de los polisistemas*. Montserrat Iglesias ed. Madrid: Arco, 207–222.

Figueroa, Antón (1988). *Diglosia e texto*. Vigo: Xerais.

Freixanes, Víctor F. (2003): "O galego é útil (e necesario)". *La Voz de Galicia*, 12–7–2003, 5.

Horta Nunes, José (2003): "Aspectos da forma histórica do leitor brasileiro na atualidade". *A leitura e os leitores*. Orlandi, Eni Puccinelli ed. Campinas: Pontes, 25–46.

Leenhardt, Jacques (1980): "Toward a Sociology of Reading". *The Reader the Text*. Suleiman, S. and I. Crosman eds. Princeton University Press, 205–224.

Mignolo, Walter (1978): *Elementos para una teoría del texto literario*. Barcelona: Crítica.

Monteagudo Romero, Henrique (2000): "Lingua e cultura". *Galicia 2010*. VV. AA. Asociación Proxecto Galicia 2010, 93–142.

Orlandi, Eni P. (2003): "A leitura proposta e os leitores possíveis". *A leitura e os leitores*. Orlandi, Eni Puccinelli ed. Campinas: Pontes, 7–24.

Schmidt, Siegfried (1987): "La comunicación literaria". *Pragmática de la comunicación literaria*. Mayoral, J. A. ed. Madrid: Arco, 1987: 195–212.

Seminario de Sociolingüística (1995): *Usos lingüísticos en Galicia*. A Coruña: Real Academia Galega.

Seminario de Sociolingüística (1996): *Actitudes lingüísticas en Galicia*. A Coruña: Real Academia Galega.

Siguán, Miquel (1999): *Conocimiento y uso de las lenguas*. Madrid: CIS.

Zimmermann, Bernhard (1987): "El lector como productor". *Estética de la recepción*. Mayoral, J. A., ed. Madrid: Arco, 39–58.

JON KORTAZAR

Diglossia and Basque Literature

> Lan hau Galiziako lagun guztiei eskainia dago:
> Kikeri eta Loliri, Marilar eta Ramoni, Rafisari,
> Arturori eta Irisi, Inmari, Manueli, eta
> Helenari haiekin ikasitako guztiarengatik.

Following Dolores Vilavedra's recommendation, I first read Antón Figueroa's *Diglosia e texto* in 1999, a book which deeply impressed me. *Diglosia e texto* discusses the ways in which diglossia affects literatures written in minority languages, in this case Galician, and also takes further evidence from the situation of Provençal following the studies of P. Gardy and R. Lafont.

In my first reading of the book I soon realised that some of its basic premises could be easily applied to literature written in Basque. The theoretical and methodological framework proposed by Figueroa, which was in line with reception theories and their focus on the reader's relevance for the reception and rewriting of texts, constituted a useful means to account for the current situation of the Basque literary system.

The aim of this essay is, therefore, to apply the model drawn from *Diglosia e texto* to the analysis of the Basque literary system and to examine its operational validity. The differences between the Galician and Basque literary systems may help us to reflect on the model itself.

One of the most frequent questions that Basque writers have to endure in any journalistic interview is "Why do you write in Euskera, the Basque language?" That this question is becoming less and less frequent may be regarded as a symptom of linguistic normalisation. The answers given go from ironic to serious. Yet the question is certainly serious; therefore, it is necessary to bear in mind that the decision to write in a particular language depends on various factors that cannot conceal the evidence that literature is a social system. Whenever an author decides to write in a minority language he is integrating himself within a literary system that partakes of the symbolic order of a given society and that is placed within a system (literary) of systems (political, ideological and social).

The above question can be formulated from a different perspective: does the choice of a particular language and, consequently, the integration within a literary and symbolic system have implications for the writer's work? Lately, authors writing in Basque have argued that language choice has no implications for the final artistic product. Such a consideration can, therefore, be included among those analyses that insist on the social dimension of literature.

The notion of system emerges out of the conscious need to renew literary studies and of a will to discover a new epistemological paradigm that was presumably functional and empirical *versus* the historical and hermeneutical character of the paradigm within which literary theories were traditionally engendered. Inspired by various approaches from disciplines such as cultural semiotics (Yuri Lotman), literary sociology (Pierre Bourdieu) and polysystemic theory (Even-Zohar), the systemic criterion presupposes a view of literature as a net of interdependent elements defined in opposition to one another. And, regarding literature as a sign system that is socially organised, it is placed within more complex systems, namely, culture (Vilavedra 1999: 16–17).

Similarly, I also believe that literary processes should be regarded as historical processes insofar as the more normalised a literature becomes in the course of time, the more restricted the effects of diglossia will be within its system. It may prove convenient to place Figueroa's reflection within the historical evolution of the society sustaining the literary system and, above all, within the evolution of its educational institutions. I suspect that one of the main differences between the Basque case and the Galician case lies in the different role of primary and secondary school in both systems and, perhaps, more subtle but equally important, in the relevance given to language itself; that is, whether or not speakers are conscious and proud of possessing a language of their own, an attitude to be presumed in speakers and readers within a literary system.

I The Lack of Distinction between Text and Literary Text

When applying Figueroa's theoretical framework to the Basque literary system, it must be pointed out that the distinction announced in the title of this section has to do more with the perception and definition of literature put forth by literary historians (who carry out the function of canonisers) than with actual literary practice.

What Figueroa actually emphasises regarding literatures of minority languages is the absence of a 'social matrix' that would clearly establish the precise boundaries separating an informative text from a symbolic one, a primary text from a secondary one.

From early on in the historical study of Basque literature, the definition of what should be considered as "literary" has never been clear. In fact, to legitimise its existence, this literature has defined itself by using an accumulation of various heterogeneous texts. Such a strategy brought about the construction of an encyclopaedia-like conscience in which every single text written *in* or *on* Basque was given the status of 'Basque Literature'. A good example is one of the first histories of Basque literature written by Father Luis Villasante (*Historia de la literatura vasca*, 1961). This work included not only the name of authors who wrote in Basque but also the name of philologists who studied theirs texts, no matter if their work (which, of course, was not literary) was written in languages other than Basque. Thus, German and Czech philologists writing on Basque literature in their respective languages were included in this book.

Such an example evidences the lack of a typological distinction between text and literary text. From a historical point of view, the definition of Basque literature has always been problematic due to the evolution of the concept of literature itself. What was classified as literature in the seventeenth century (a work of spiritual ascesis, for instance) is not regarded as literature nowadays, and, thus, while major literary genres such as prose, poetry and essay remain homogeneous categories, doubts arise concerning the subgenres. In fact, there is an ongoing debate as to which of the proposed corpuses of "Basque Classical Literature" (sixteenth and seventeenth centuries) does actually deserve the name "literary". The two opposing views of this debate are as follows: a more general view, which labels all texts written in Basque, even translations of catechisms and religious works, "literature"; and a more restrictive view, which labels as such only those texts belonging to the three major genres. No matter which position we take, distinguishing literary texts from other text types is by no means an easy task. From the perspective of polysystems theory, the study of religious translations into Basque is a useful way to reveal the permanent presence of what historians such as Ibon Sarasola and, later on, Jon Juaristi call a "traditionalist" ideology and its transmission through Basque Literature from the eighteenth century onwards.

II The text in the histories of Basque Literature

Let us begin this section with an account of why minority literatures tend to "'preserve' texts which in a normalised situation would probably not be appreciated. This brings about a sort of real 'Prometheism' which can be explained in a logical way: a text is seen as a factor of resistance against language A, and this is why all texts tend to be 'preserved'" (Figueroa 1988: 23).

The unification of the Basque language in 1968 was marked by a tendency towards the fetishisation of a linguistic model believed to be exemplary in the creation of a unified linguistic standard. Classics from the seventeenth century (basically Axular and his work *Gero)* were republished and, above all, imitated in the new literary creations. Thus, authors with little symbolic value served as linguistic models for the literature produced during those years.

The debate over what a classic literary work really is and which works should be included in the Basque literary canon has been a sporadic one. As already advanced, there is a wish to preserve all types of texts which coexists with a preference for excluding some non-literary texts (such as devotionaries or catechisms) from the canon, but not a firm or clear determination to accept only literary works.

III The Discontinuity between Spatial and Temporal Models

The first novel written in Basque appeared quite late, and it was also late when schooling in Basque was established. Probably the only exception is the Enlightenment period, when Basque literature was influenced by that produced in France and when the political and economic achievements of the country's petty noblemen were indeed revolutionary for those times.

It has already been pointed out how the historians of Basque literature Sarasola and Juaristi emphasised the relevance of religion and traditionalism on the evolution of Basque literature, both functioning as constraints to liberalism. This counter-liberal position dominated Basque literature all throughout the nineteenth century and consequently motivated the late emergence of literary texts modelled on modern bourgeoisie aesthetics. A few liberal works were published in those years (in the French Basque Country), yet their marginal character reveals the great difficulties that Basque literary works had in being admitted as "normal" texts within the system. Traditionalists and fundamentalists clearly enjoyed a hegemonic position within the Basque literary system and the exceptions of poets like Indalecio

Bizcarrondo, "Billintx" (1831–1876), and the members of the School of San Sebastian (late nineteenth century) evidence the practical problems that Basque liberals had to face. In this sense, while the first novel written in Basque is included within the historical genre, the next two novels by the same author, Domingo Agirre (1846–1920), published in 1906 and 1912, respectively, are costumbrist works. The late emergence of the Basque novel together with its costumbrist character are the two most frequent examples given to prove the late incorporation of modern aesthetics to the Basque literary system. These ideological principles constitute the premises on which a given work is considered literary or not.

Nevertheless, the arguments offered in this essay may have their weaknesses and thus may be subjected to criticism. So far we have primarily been referring to the situation of Basque literature up to the nineteenth century and the early years of the twentieth century. But, the social situation of the Basque literary system has greatly improved, both in terms of quantity and quality. The inclusion of Basque within school curricula and as a language in which to teach, the development of editorial houses, the professionalisation of a few authors, the increase in readership (though the majority of readers is found at schools), the increase in the number of Basque books translated into other languages, and the instauration of Basque Philology as an academic discipline – all these positive elements enable Basque literature to enjoy an unprecedented status. Even some of its present-day authors have marked aesthetic tendencies in other literary systems. Therefore, is it possible to hold the view that if there is a *delayed* presence in Basque literature, it is because it remains attached to *old* aesthetic premises?

In this respect, two aspects must be emphasised. The first is the presence of historical avant-garde movements in poetry. When the dominant literary model is a kind of poetry characterised by a clarity of form, the Basque avant-garde has played an important role in the configuration of aesthetic worlds.

The second aspect is the creation of an aesthetic universe, above all in poetry, closely attached to a literature of national compromise highly concerned with the idea of the Basque nation and Basque identity. Koldo Mitxelena has called this tendency the *nigar haria*, "the thread of lament", a lamentation caused by the lack of political independence of the Basque Country. This reference may also exist within the creative universe of other literatures.

These two constants clearly remain as basic features of the creative world of Basque literature. Of course, we may ask whether the conception of Basque literature is directly influenced by the presence of a presumable political conflict and its materialisation in a political system and in the creation of symbolic bases that preserve the lament for what could have been, but never was; whether the influence of politics may be considered stagnant or old; and whether this tendency of political resistance may also be found in other literary systems such as the Galician one. Indeed, the survival of the historical avant-garde does not necessarily imply a withdrawal from present real-life conditions. The constant and prevailing presence of the avant-garde in the Basque system is significant and, moreover, even reveals some of its weaknesses. It is evident, however, that presently what is contemporary is more readily accepted because its communication has been facilitated and the rigid aesthetic positions within the system have been abandoned.

IV The Importance Given to Folkloric, Ethnological and Mythological Elements

The importance of oral elements in Basque literature has already been described by most historians of Basque literature. What we will emphasise here is the relevance assigned to elements that play a role in the aesthetic and epistemological configuration of literatures in a situation of diglossia.

Folklore, ethnology and mythology certainly contribute to the historical development of Basque literature. Again we must refer to

Domingo de Agirre, the father of the Basque novel and, therefore, the founder of a particular view of the Basque country – at least in literature. The elements of costumbrism (frozen, circular or natural time vs. historical time; paradise vs. town, idyll, cyclical rituals, customs: in short, folklore) were already present in Agirre's writings.

The imprint of the rural world on Basque prose has been operative for a long time. Basque texts situated in rural settings contribute two basic components to the creation of a particular social myth. First, they perpetuate the image created by historical and traditional nationalism that Basque identity is rooted in the countryside. Second, it must nevertheless be borne in mind that the presence of Basque was mainly restricted to rural areas, as it was hardly spoken in cities. The same holds true for the quality of the language, which was only preserved in rural areas. Hence, styles (rather than aesthetic trends, properly speaking) using a large amount of rhetorical figures found their themes mainly in rural settings. Nevertheless, we agree with Figueroa in that there is a general tendency , in what concerns contemporary narrative practices, to consider "valences" the folkloric, ethnographic and mythical elements which replace the authentic aesthetic work (Figueroa 1988: 23).

V The Tendency towards Philologisation

For an appropriate understanding of this section it is necessary to clarify beforehand that the unification of the Basque language occurred late, so that it is only after 1968 that we may speak of a unified standard of the language. This brought about a very intense debate on the language and not only between the supporters of the *euskara batua* (progressive and secular sectors of society in favour of a renewed nationalism) and those against its use (clergymen and the most traditional sectors, the supporters of a conservative nationalism). Such a confrontation involved the institution of new models of language, the recreation of the literary canon, a great concern for the value of grammar, and an eager search for philological peculiarities. At that time the philologisation of literature was already taking place. The real debate which soon emerged, however, focused on the representation of diverse linguistic registers and social styles in literature as well as on the realistic representation of social registers not existing in Basque and (more recently) on the relationship between the Basque standard and Basque dialects. In other words, what is really spoken are the dialects, not the linguistic standard, which is just a grammar (and, often, an incomplete grammar that is mainly concerned with orthography and nominal and verbal morphology) with no dictionary or words of its own since words are *of* and *in* dialects. This is the reason for the particular relevance of new linguistic tendencies: anything labelled "*batua*" (unified) would first be readily used, though later on it would be seen as ungrammatical, so a return to the beginning would be considered to be imperative. This changing situation offers plenty of room for philologisation, for the extreme relevance that the word itself has in Basque literature, that philology has, that is.

VI The Lack of Horizon of Expectations

The instability of the linguistic situation is a major source of problems in the relationship between the writer and his readers. What Figueroa points out in relation to the Galician case may be relevant in this connection as it bears some basic resemblances with the situation in the Basque Country. A situation like that of Galician, where it is not uncommon to find a vast number of Spanish borrowings in spoken use of the language (which in literary communication may or may not be interpreted as such by authors and readers, with its subsequent consequences in reading and writing), where there is a great number of dialectical varieties, where there is an extensive use of absurd hyper-traditionalist terms (yet admitted by most speakers as part of the norm), and where even sometimes we hear individual claims of the right to invent words and language rules is a situation that has a direct and serious influence on literary communication. Both authors and readers will frequently feel at a loss. Authors will not even control their readers' most minimal expected response (Figueroa 1988: 28).

Bernardo Atxaga, undoubtedly one of the better-known Basque writers, has confessed that he envisions his readers as if they were an audience to whom he reads his works in a public theatre. Such an image of his reading public together with the feeling of seeing himself as the "other" helps him to produce his own literary style. Atxaga's case is an example of the author's need to ascribe a stable horizon of expectations to his readers.

VII   An Author's Writing Career

When a literary system is weak, authors may find it difficult to first publish and later distribute their works. However, when literary systems are stronger – as is the case with the present-day Basque system – the difficulties authors come across publishing their works and starting and maintaining a writing career, that is, communicating with their reading public, are not only more bearable but quite *normal* in fact. Nonetheless, I am not optimistic as regards these systems because the stronger they become, the more they force writers into overproduction. Hence they pump out the ever so profitable "novel a year", oiling the wheels of the publishing industry to which they are indebted, among other things, for giving them an opening to publish.

The present-day Basque literary system makes it possible for fairly successful authors to make a career; that is, it guarantees the publication of their works. Nevertheless, not long ago there was a considerable number of one-work authors (poetry in the early 1980s being a good case in point). The existence of this type of authors (with all due respect for them) is often a symptom of a weakness in minority systems. Although one-work authors can still be found today, they are not very common in Basque literature.

Continuity in Basque literature, at least among canonised authors, means that not being published for some time is not necessarily a synonym of having fallen into oblivion. In fact, authors who began to publish their works in the late 70s (Ramón Saizarbitoria) or early 80s (Koldo Izaguirre) and resumed their literary careers in the early 90s after more than a decade of silence have been praised for managing to maintain their literary dignity in an often unrelenting industry and for remaining silent for the sake of their work.

Added to this optimistic view is the fact that today the number of occasional writers is significantly lower than in the 1980s. By occasional writers we mean those authors with no established writing careers whatsoever: those writers who win a prize and afterwards vanish from the literary scene and those whose initial or only motive for writing has more to do with preserving the language than with developing their own literary style (as was common practice in the early twentieth century). Although there are still some occasional writers of Basque literature, the fact that their numbers have significantly decreased is certainly a reason for celebration, especially in such a complex situation as the Basque literary system.

VIII   Ludic Sense and Epic Sense

The opposition ludic/epic is possibly one of the outstanding features of the Basque literary system, because of the impact of political history on the configuration of the Basque identity, or the survival of terrorism, or the great amount of suffering by a part of the population and the dominant discourse on it. In this context, the way facts are represented is more important than the objective account of those facts. Such a politicised context leaves little room for irony, which, in fact, may become a stylistic ground full of interpretive obstacles for readers.

For this reason, when the critic approaches the opposition between the ludic and the epic senses, he needs to question why the ludic sense is regarded as more "aesthetic" than the epic and why irony is presumed to be more modern (which it truly is) than epic style. Such questions may suggest that we are taking for granted that Basque literature exhibits a temporal disruption of typological forms, in other words, that the Basque literary system still retains forms (such as the epic) already obsolete in other literary systems.

Therefore, this question must be clarified somehow. In Antón Figueroa's opinion, every literary work is to a certain extent a committed product of its time as it cannot be isolated from the historical conditions in which it is produced. There is even another sense in which literary works are historically committed products: they attempt to renew the aesthetic conditions fixed by society. Yet, in a highly divided society such as in the Basque Country, in which the main tendency is to follow parallel tracks, it is very difficult to set the boundaries between the "official" and the "innovating", the new and the established, especially when the revolutionary and the reactionary can change their masks. Such confusion and disorientation may be the cause for the inclusion within the Basque literary system of cartographic books like *Galderen geografia* (*A Geography of Questions*, 1997) by Felipe Juaristi o *Kartografia* (*Cartography*, 1998) by Rikardo Arregi Díaz de Heredia.

In a society in which the epic sense is so deeply interwoven with the literary conscience, it is possible to reflect on the ludic sense as a creative possibility linked to the theory of the possible worlds. In this sense, the text may be seen as a product not so much of imposed conventions but of the laws of the imagination. "Ludic sense" would, therefore, mean the possibility of creating new worlds, and, in this way, the ludic would prove aesthetically superior to the epic.

IX A Final Reflection by Way of Conclusion

We have delineated the complex situation of Basque literature by attending to its opposing and disparate elements. Two main conclusions can be reached in view of the description given above.

Firstly, the methodological framework provided by Antón Figueroa in *Diglosia e texto* has proved to be useful to describe the Basque literary system, yet there are some areas where it does not apply. Why? I believe that Figueroa's proposal (unconsciously, at times) is restricted to minority literatures that exhibit cultural factors present in the romantic period. It is undeniable that romanticism had a great influence on the development of minority literatures (at least in Spain their revival took place in the nineteenth century under the influence of the German romantics, a development that also accounts for the beginning of Spanish romanticism). Therefore, some of the aspects discussed above, for instance, the survival of folklore and ethnography, appear as obsolete or at least marginal in the Basque system. I believe that the more romantic the literary system is, the more operative Figueroa's framework will be, or the more accurate since its operativity lies also in the elements under discussion here: that is to say, its operativity is also at work in the debate itself.

Secondly, every literary system is a historical process, mutable and in permanent evolution. I am not saying that Figueroa thinks otherwise, quite the contrary. What I do mean to say is that, no matter the situation of the literary system (for instance that of Basque with its lack of readers, the short shelf life of works in libraries, its excess of propaganda), in any process of literary normalisation, the more normalised and consistent social conscience is towards the language and its literature, the less likely it is for the framework to be operative. More attention has been paid here to those features in which the Basque and the Galician systems differ (even though they have obvious similarities). In the historical process of literature's normalisation (carried out especially through the educational system) the lesser the situation is affected by diglossia, the more complex the analytical framework will be. This is in fact what we have been attempting to offer here: a comprehensive description of the situation of the system of the literature written in Basque.

Translated by Ana Losada Pérez

WORKS CITED

Figueroa Antón (1988): *Diglosia e texto*. Vigo: Xerais.

Vilavedra, Dolores (1999): *Historia da literatura galega*. Vigo: Galaxia.

JAUME SUBIRANA

National Poets and Universal Catalans. Writers and Literature in Contemporary Catalan Identity

I   An Approach and a Warning

As in other highly "linguistic" national communities, in Catalonia the creation and management of national identity has been – and continues to be – associated with language, Catalan, and, from a very early date, with literature. A brief historical survey from medieval chronicles to a recent Nobel Prize candidature promoted by the Catalan Parliament will illustrate this point. The close relationship between literature and identity explains the importance and thriving presence in Catalonia of the figure of the "national poet", to which, in the 1960s, Catalan culture added another and more specific icon of identity construction through literature: "universal Catalans", artists (the professionals) who triumph in their respective disciplines beyond the borders of the country without renouncing their roots.

Now a word of warning: my "literary nation" is essentially a linguistic one and it does not correspond to state or strictly administrative borders. It is not Spain, but neither is it Catalonia. The Catalan linguistic map and the Catalan political map do not coincide. Both have undergone changes, and there is no doubt that they will continue to change over time. This duplication of maps, and hence the coexistence of borders, of identities, is symptomatic of underlying complexities and tensions. Rather than being seen as a source of enrichment and as a factor that links us to one of today's great international debates, these tensions are frequently experienced – in fact, I would go as far as to say that now they have even been internalised, not only by Catalan men and women, but also by the few "others" who see us as having a different existence – as a problem.

II Language, in Other Words Culture, in Other Words Nation

Between the thirteenth and fourteenth centuries, Ramon Muntaner (1265–1336) – who was born in Peralada, lived in Valencia, and died in Eivissa – served several Catalan-Aragonese kings and wrote his life story in *Crònica* (*Chronicle*), a document which he considered "royal" and which we view today as both "royal" and "literary". In *Crònica*, Muntaner had no need, in order to demonstrate that control of the Mediterranean world was now in the hands of the Catalans, to invoke the old *traslatio imperii* (which involved writing the history of successive incarnations of divine power in the different ruling nations before evoking one's own people). It was sufficient for him to go back to the great King Jaume I and the legend of his wondrous birth in Montpelier (a story that comparative scholars can find with slight variations in Boccaccio's *Decameron* and Shakespeare's *All's Well that Ends Well*) as a revelation that divine will had elected the Catalan dynasty. Muntaner also records the lives of subsequent kings, from the birth of Jaume I in 1208 up to the coronation of Alfons III in 1328.

In 1833 the publication of the *"Oda a la patria"* (*Ode to the Fatherland*), a nostalgic poem by Bonaventura Carles Aribau (Barcelona, 1798–1862), marked the beginning of the so-called *Renaixença* (*Rebirth*) of Catalan literature:

> Plau-me encara parlar la llengua d'aquells savis
> que ompliren l'univers de llurs costums e lleis,
> la llengua d'aquells forts que acataren los reis,
> defengueren llurs drets, venjaren llurs agravis.
> Muira, muira l'ingrat que, al sonar en sos llavis

per estranya regió l'accent natiu, no plora,
que al pensar en sos llars no es consum ni s'enyora
ni cull del mur sagrat les lires dels seus avis.

En llemosí sonà lo meu primer vagit
quan del mugró matern la dolça llet bevia;
en llemosí al Senyor pregava cada dia
e càntics llemosins somiava cada nit.
Si, quan me trobe sol, parlo amb mon esperit,
en llemosí li parlo que llengua altra no sent,
e ma boca llavors, no sap mentir ni ment,
puix surten mes raons del centre de mon pit.

It delights me still to speak the tongue of those wise men
who filled the universe with their customs and their law,
the language of the strong who were loyal to kings of yore
who fought for their rights and when offended took revenge.
Death, death to the ingrate who, hearing on his lips again
on foreign soil his own land's accent, does not cry,
who thinking of his hearth and home does not pine or sigh
or take down from the sacred wall the lyres of ancient kin.

In Limousin my newborn wail first came to light
as suckling sweet milk at my mother's nipple I lay;
in Limousin I prayed to the Lord every day
and Limousin songs were in my dreams at night.
If I speak to my spirit alone, when no one is in sight,
in Limousin I speak, for no other tongue will it hear,
and then no lie ever can or will my mouth besmear
for my words in the centre of my breast abide.

History and glory were thus recovered, as were sentiment, intimacy and sincerity. Aribau, who wrote mostly in Spanish and was generally considered a bad poet, went down in the annals of Catalonian history as "the father of the *Renaixença*" and, as such, as one of the fathers of

Catalonia. His few discrete romantic verses were given a collective overdose of appreciation and were read as a symbolic starting point. Later he had a street named after him in the capital and occupied a privileged place in all the anthologies.

Aribau and his "*Oda a la pàtria*", however, are not alone in the *Renaixença*. Other literary texts that express the links between language, literature and collective identities also appear. In 1854, Antoni de Bofarull – one of the promoters of the *Jocs Florals*, a literary competition going back to medieval times – argued in a text written in Spanish that Catalans (who he claimed invented medieval poetry) had preserved their precious language within family walls, but the time had come to pay homage to it, with all due respect for "the official language, which is now indispensable for the unity of the nation" (meaning the Spanish nation). He wrote:

> Poetry – and I do not speak of feudal poetry or that of earliest times fathered by Catalans, as great writers recognise, but the poetry produced within the realm of science, and by this I mean that of the consistory, which made the wandering troubadours disappear, and attracted scholar poets – also had its school in the enlightened Barcelona [...] and in this school the strength and sweetness of our Catalan or Limousin tongue became known. This language, so varied now, was extolled in other times as the language of general usage, the language in which our rivals wrote, however remote their home lands were, and which we still use in family circles, preserving it and not abandoning it, whatever respect we have for the official language, which is now indispensable for the unity of the nation" (Molas, Jorba and Tayadella 1984: 115).

Five years later, in his speech as "President-Maintainer" of the recently restored festival of the *Jocs Florals*, Víctor Balaguer (Barcelona 1824 – Madrid 1901) linkened the question of the people's right to use their own language to the image (associated with the *Renaixença* as a whole) of a dawning, a renewal, a resurrection that comes about through literary, and especially poetic, practice:

> No, this is not only a literary tournament we have just attended. This is not the death of the Catalan language, which has brought together such an honourable and distinguished audience in this classic hall of our history, whose sleeping echoes still safeguard the memory of the voices of ancient and venerable

ministers, incorruptible guardians of the rights of the city and the impregnable walls of the country's freedoms. No, indeed not. We have not come as witnesses to the death of the language, but to welcome the dawning song of Catalan poetry" (Molas, Jorba and Tayadella 1984: 216).

On the first Sunday of May 1859 – five centuries after they were established in Toulouse and a bit later in Barcelona (1393) – the *Jocs Florals*, somewhat extemporaneously, began anew in the Gothic *Saló de Cent* (*Hall of the Hundred*) in the Town Hall of the Catalan capital. Thereafter, the motif of the festival was *Patria, fides, amor*.

The streets of the *Eixample* district of Barcelona also speak of the mental "map" of the nineteenth-century *Renaixença*. From the jocfloralesque fourteenth century to the beginning of the nineteenth century, the form of the city had not changed substantially (except for the 1714 Bourbon "intervention" in the Ribera neighbourhood). Between 1840 and 1860 liberals and progressives supported demolishing the city walls (Michonneau 2001: 19–26). In 1860 the writer and historian, Víctor Balaguer (let us note here how earlier-cited names keep reappearing), published *Las calles de Barcelona* (*The Streets of Barcelona*), which was commissioned by the *Ajuntament* (City Council). This book explains his proposal for building the streets of the new city (eventually the *Eixample*) as a life-size history of the city. The project's engineer, Idelfons Cerdà, had only provided words and figures for this project. Balaguer acted, in fact, more as a myth maker or myth organiser than as a historian, strictly speaking. Of the fourteen horizontal streets, three bear the names of the principal institutions of the Crown of Aragon (*Consell de Cent, Diputació* and *Les Corts* [Council of the Hundred, Provincial Council and the Parliament, respectively]), and six are named after historic territories of the Crown (*Aragó, València, Mallorca, Provença, Rosselló,* and *Còrsega*, along with *Nàpols, Sicília, Sardenya* and *Calàbria*, which are vertical streets). Of the thirty-two vertical streets, twelve carry the names of famous men (among them Roger de Llúria and Rafael Casanova), three of which are writers (Balmes, Aribau and Muntaner, the latter being the only one who regularly wrote in Catalan), while nine bear the names of battles linked to a diffuse, though quite evident, idea of Spain and Spanishness. In 1863 the Barcelona City Council approved Balaguer's proposals and made very few changes to them. For this reason, the map of the *Eixample*, where Barcelona residents stroll along with the millions of visitors who come to the city each year, clearly conveys the idea of a *Renaixença* that is conservative, historicist and nationalist (i.e., in favour of a Catalan nation), yet pro-Spanish as well (Michonneau 2001: 398).

Along with the *Jocs Florals*, and also linked with them, there is another archetypical icon of the *Renaixença* who unites language, culture, and territory: Jacint Verdaguer (See Fig. 1, p. 263), donning his distinctive Catalan cap with a peasant air the day he came from the rural heartland of Catalonia (nowadays called "Catalan Catalonia", a delicious tautology) to the capital to receive the prize he had won for his poetry in the *Jocs Florals*. Later, in 1894, the politician Enric Prat de la Riba, who became the first president of the *Mancomunitat* in 1914,[1] answered the question "What is the fatherland?" in his *Compendi de doctrina catalanista* (*Compendium of Catalanist Doctrine*): "A community of people who speak the same language, have a common history, and live together in a harmony of spirit that invests all the manifestations of their lives with something original and characteristic" (Prat de la Riba 1998: 218).

After the Civil War, the most successful attempts at defining the "Catalan being" originated from somewhat eccentric authors; for example, the philosopher Josep Ferrater Mora, who, in his *Les formes de vida catalana* (*The Forms of Catalan Life*, 1944), sums up a possible national identity in four mottos: continuity, good sense, moderation, and irony. Josep Trueta, a surgeon of international prestige and also an exile, published *L'esperit de Catalunya* (*The Spirit of Catalonia*, 1946) in Oxford. Historian Jaume Vicens Vives offered a very interesting reflection on the historical relationship between Catalans and power in his essay "Els Catalans i el Mino-

---

1 The *Mancomunitat* was an institution through which Catalonia recovered, for the first time since 1714, a certain degree of autonomous political power, and which was associated with the cultural movement *Noucentisme*.

taure" ("Catalans and the Minotaur"), which was published in *Notícia de Catalunya* in 1954. Years later, at the gates of the new democratic period, new poets acquired great popularity. One such example is Salvador Espriu with his sacerdotal, almost oracular (but in first person plural) tone: "Because we have lived to save your words for you / to return to you the name of each and every thing". Or Miquel Martí i Pol, who composed the following verses: "We shall be what we want to be. In vain / we flee the fire if the fire justifies us"; and "Now is tomorrow. Yesterday's fire gives no heat / and nor does the fire of today, so we shall have to make the fire anew".

This prominent role of books, authors, and literature in the creation and re-elaboration of national identity remains today. In the three brief episodes of self-government that Catalonia has undergone through over the last century (the *Mancomunitat*, the Republic and the present democratic period), the list of writers after which schools, libraries, parks, streets and squares have been named, and continue to be so, is exhaustive. The nationalist government in power between 1980 and 2003 under the presidency of Jordi Pujol frequently pointed out literary facts and figures from the book industry (for example, the sustained growth rate of books published in Catalan – which was almost 8,000 titles per year –, the hundreds of literary awards offered annually, the list of over 1,000 living authors) to prove that linguistic and literary "normalisation" was taking place, along with a presumed state of cultural well-being.

This brings us up to the present: in 2000, the Parliament of Catalonia approved (to the astonishment of the critics and with a remarkable degree of media and popular fanfare) a motion proposing the phantasmagorical candidature of Miquel Martí i Pol for the Nobel Prize for Literature. Since the initiative came from politicians, it made no sense and ran the risk of being counterproductive. On 26 May 2005, the same Parliament approved, by a large majority, a motion indicating who should represent the Catalan culture at the Frankfurt Book Fair in October 2007, when Catalonia will be the guest of honour. It would seem quite clear that in Catalonia writers have formed, and continue to do so, part of the cultural *kit* of Catalan identity and that they play a key role in what Itamar Even-Zohar would call the "system" of our essence as a community.

III National Poets

The concept and figure of the "national poet" is not a Catalonian invention nor is it limited to our case alone. We find national poets throughout the western world and within a fairly specific time frame. Scotland has Robert Burns (1759–1796); Finland, Johan Ludvig Runeberg (1804–1877); Hungary, Sándor Petöfi (1823–1849); Galicia, Rosalía de Castro (1837–1885); Romania, Mihai Eminescu (1850–1889); Nicaragua, Rubén Darío (1867–1916); Israel, Hayyim Nahman Bialik (1873–1934); and so on. In some other cases this figure appeared later; for example, Cuba's Nicolás Guillén, born in 1902, or the Dominican Republic's Pedro Mir, born in 1923. Today the figure of the "national poet" has still not lost its appeal; just as recently as 2005 Gwyneth Lewis was named the first "National Poet" of Wales. Irrespective of the time or place, these are figures seen as bards who represent the identity and principles of their community. They are the people who, as described in the psalms of David, can play the lyre and sing in the name of the people. The writer is thus linked with a territory or human group and gives this group an identity, which legitimates it as a nation. It is a nation to which the poet will have frequently "given a voice" at a time of rebirth.

In Catalonia some poets have had a powerful symbolic role at a specific time (Aribau, for example), or have been very popular (like Josep Maria de Sagarra). In my view there are only three poets who fulfil both of these conditions: Jacint Verdaguer, Salvador Espriu, and Miquel Martí i Pol, the most recent one of the three. Furthermore, these poets share a third characteristic: they are clearly identified by the community as its collective spokesperson.

Jacint Verdaguer (Folgueroles, 1845 – Barcelona, 1902), born and raised in a humble rural family, combines the idealised land with spiritual and popular dimensions: he was born in the centre of the country, in Osona, lived and wrote in Barcelona, and turned the Pyrenees into a mythical landscape in his work *Canigó*; he was a priest; and he wrote hymns and songs that are still passed down from parents to children. Tradition has it that his burial was the most massively attended public event in Barcelona until Durruti's burial in 1936, and the demonstration of 1977, in which one million people demanded freedom, amnesty and a Statute of autonomy. Moreover, his Catholic militancy and the considerable international resonance of his "pan-Hispanic" work *L'Atlàntida* (*Atlantis*) made him a viable "Spanish" product towards the end of Franco's dictatorship. Hence, he is pictured on the 500-*peseta* bill issued by the *Banco de España* in 1970–71 with an image of a Pyrenees village on the reverse side (See Figs. 2 and 3, p. 263). In a similar scenario, Galician poet Rosalía de Castro (who was bilingual and rather conservative) is pictured on a stamp (See Fig. 4, p. 265) issued by the State in 1968 in the "Spanish Personalities" series, and then again in 1979 on a 500-*peseta* bill that replaced the one picturing Verdaguer. Two national poets, one Catalan and one Galician, are thus easily assimilated into the project of another hegemonic nationality. However, as Pascale Casanova notes (1999), the context in which one reads always conditions the reading. Perhaps outside of Catalonia or Galicia in a post-Franco society it is difficult to see the tremendous latent aggression many of us experience with this image of Verdaguer in his Catalan cap portrayed beside the iconography of the Franco dictatorship and the word "*España*"...

Salvador Espriu (Santa Coloma de Farners, 1913 – Barcelona, 1985) wanted to write fiction, but eventually opted for poetry because of the situation following the Civil War. A cryptic and refined poet, he nonetheless became extraordinarily popular, particularly because of his civic attitude combined with the 1960 collection entitled *La pell de brau*[2], two theatrical renditions of his work, and a number of reasonably "comprehensible" poems enthusiastically popularised by one of the best proponents of the *Nova Cançó* movement:[3] the Valencian singer Raimon. Finally, Miquel Martí i Pol (Roda de Ter, 1929–2003) was, in the beginning, a marginal figure due to his humble origins (he was born and spent his whole life in an industrial town far from Barcelona), his working class status, his leftist political affiliations, and his personal situation (a long degenerative illness left him immobilised and progressively mute). However, his use of a simple and "sincere" voice originated a poetic discourse during the period of opposition and transition (starting in the 1970s), which was both secular and moralising in tone. Among his supporters were well-known personalities like the singer Lluís Llach and the soccer player Pep Guardiola. Eventually Miquel Martí i Pol became the centre of popular references and preferences in literary festivals and all kinds of family and collective ceremonies, and his collections of poems regularly topped best-seller lists, selling as many as 20,000 copies.

If we take a closer look at Verdaguer, Espriu and Martí i Pol – Josep Carner was regarded as "prince of poets", but never as a "national poet"; Ausiàs March belonged to a time that preceded the initial Romantic use of the term – and we compare these three national poets, we shall see that they have nothing in common from an aesthetic or ideological point of view. What they do share is their extraordinary popularity, which was clearly associated with their literary, and more specifically, poetic work. Ironically, this popularity and recognition – which went far beyond the limits of what is expected by poets and writers in general – led to their being looked down on by certain intellectual elites. Moreover, the three were collectively recognised as spokespeople for their culture and country. As noted above, these phenomena are not exclusive to Catalonia.

---

2   Translated as *The Bull-hide* by Burton Raffel (Redbird Series, Calcutta: Writers' Workshop, 1977) and in a subsequent edition by The Marlboro Press, 1987.
3   Literally "New Song", sung in Catalan.

What is peculiar to Catalan culture, though, is the much more recent label of "universal Catalans".

IV Universal Catalans

While the concept of "national poet" is quite widespread around the world, the notion of "universal Catalans" is evidently exclusive to us. The latter concept came into being during the 1960s and gained popularity to the point of eventually becoming a journalistic commonplace. In 1977 it was used as the title of Antoni Ribas's film *Catalans universals*, which won the 1979 City of Barcelona award, consisting of interview-reports that focus on thirteen characters: namely, Ignasi Barraquer (opthalmologist), Josep Trueta (surgeon), Francesc Duran i Reynals (cancer researcher), Montserrat Caballé (soprano), Pau/Pablo Casals (cellist), Josep Lluís Sert (architect), Joan Miró (painter, see Fig. 5, p. 265), Charlie Rivel (clown), Carles Buïgas (engineer), Antoni Tàpies (painter), Joan Oró (biochemist), Antoni Puigvert (urologist) and Salvador Espriu (writer). The term appeared again shortly afterwards in Enric Ripoll's book of the same title (1980), which includes the aforementioned film director.

However, the list of "universal Catalans" (like the concept) has never been unique, official or academic. It is more like a brand-name or general reference, the use of which is spreading in an increasingly natural way. Today it is a label associated with people born in Catalonia who have achieved outstanding professional recognition beyond our borders – as Avel·lí Artís Gener says in the Prologue to *Catalans universals*, they are "outstanding Catalans who, in addition to being ours, belong to civilisation" – and have also become well known as popular figures. Their recognition and popularity shields them from "exotisation" (Figueroa 2001: 160), which frequently occurs when little-known or unknown cultures are exported. Undoubtedly, the idea of "universal Catalans" springs from the obsession of "giving something to the world", for when "universal" is used, it is understood loosely to mean "of the world". An anonymous website on Salvador Dalí claims, "As a good 'universal Catalan', he disseminated his ideas around much of the world, while maintaining a deep attachment to his native land". Seen from another angle, behind the concept of "universal Catalans" there throbs the dual concern of the nation to transcend its limits geographically and to be deemed a community like any other through the success of some of the individuals who form part of the collective. Here we might highlight the presumed blend of individual and collective success: "We should not forget that their pre-eminence has been the result of a sustained personal effort while at once being a legacy of the essence, the idiosyncrasy and the collective base of a whole people, a country, a nation, which the passing of the centuries has shaped in permanent reaffirmation" (Ripoll 1980: 9).

To the names selected by Ribas and Ripoll, we might add several others which are often cited as icon-slogans in advertising the great tourist destinations that Catalonia and Barcelona have become: the architect Antoni Gaudí; the painter Salvador Dalí; the musician and showman Xavier Cugat; the tenor Josep Carreras (known around the world as José); the architect Ricard Bofill; the former Director-General of UNESCO, Federico Mayor-Zaragoza; and, more recently, the NBA player Pau Gasol and the chef Ferran Adrià. Some might even wish to include the former fascist leader and eventual president of the IOC, Juan Antonio Samaranch, who Manuel Vázquez Montalbán referred to as "the first Francoist who rose to the category of "universal Catalan"; or Floquet de Neu (Snowflake), the albino gorilla and emblem of the Barcelona Zoo, along with some intangible entities like the Barcelona Soccer Club, *catalan cava*, and *Chupa-Chups*. There is no problem in including individuals who are clearly lacking in what used to be called "national commitment". The photos of Samaranch dressed as a fascist leader may not be published in the newspapers, but many of us still remember them very well; Caballé has her residence registered in Andorra for taxation purposes and speaks to her daughter in Spanish; Dalí ended up being an apologist for Franco and left his best works in Madrid. Likewise, mute characters like Charlie Rivel, Floquet de Neu, and others with minimal capacity for linguistic expression such as Gasol and Adrià can be added to the list. Curiously, however, rarely do any writers make the list. It seems, then, that world-wide fame is sufficient to be a "universal Catalan". What has happened, in our present new conquest of the world, to our national poets and writers?

This brings to mind the character of Cacofonix, the Gallic bard of the Asterix books. He is described in these terms in the book series: "Cacofonix, the bard. Opinion is divided as to his musical gifts. Cacofonix thinks he's a genius. Everyone else thinks he's unspeakable. *But so long as he doesn't speak, let alone sing, everybody likes him*" (My italics)." Cacofonix belongs to the community (which, in one story, goes on a desperate search for him), but he is a pest when he exercises his art. One can compare this character with Catalan writers today who, like Cacofonix, are inseparable from their voices, from the Catalan language itself.

V Confirmation and a Question (rather than Conclusion)

The close relationship between language, literature, and identity that lies at the base of Catalan culture explains the significance and the effectiveness in our country of the figure of the so-called national poet. An analysis of the clearest cases (Verdaguer, Espriu and Martí i Pol) reveals that though they are aesthetically and ideologically different, they are similar in that they are extraordinarily popular, much more so than most writers, and they are also viewed as "the voice of the people". And if the figure of the "national poet" has clear foreign parallels (which can be linked with the Romantic Movement in the loose sense of the word), our culture adds another more idiosyncratic icon appearing only a few decades ago: the "universal Catalans". These are iconic figures whose names represent their triumph in their own disciplines elsewhere in the world without (presumably) renouncing a certain Catalan identity. However, in this new category, which might be seen as an extension or complement to that of the "national poet", Catalan writers themselves surprisingly do not make the list. In other words, when Catalan identity achieves international status, language, that key historical element, becomes a hindrance, a problem. Catalan writers who write in Catalan (welcome to the land of reiteration!) have, like the bard Cacofonix, an increasingly symbolic but hardly operative role. For many people would simply prefer them to keep their mouths shut.

And I wonder to what extent we could claim that the use of the concept and the excellence of "universal Catalans" constitute a sort of "revenge" (a relaxing) by a society, an identity, that is tired of always lugging around the burden of the language in its backpack. It would not be an anti-linguistic move of Catalans *against* Catalan, but it would clearly be an "a-linguistic" option, of Catalans *without* Catalan. This a-linguistic option, moreover, underscored by the undisputed inclusion on the list of "universal Catalans" of people who are mute, who stutter or have minimal linguistic skills. Honestly, I am not sure whether the different roles played by the language (and the different attitudes of the citizens) in the cases of national poets and universal Catalans is a question of evolution (diachronic because the language today has a less "central" role in defining the Catalan identity than it has had historically), or a question of adopting a more pragmatic, utilitarian attitude within a specific domain (deciding that the same language is essential within the country but relative outside it). I do not know, to put it nicely, whether the current absence of an identifiable Catalan national poet (along with the success and widespread fame of a list of universal Catalans that does not include writers) is due to post-linguistic or a-linguistic factors. Yet I do have a clear sensation that the role of writers and of other outstanding citizens in the construction of the Catalan identity is changing.

WORKS CITED

Casanova, Pascale (2001): *La República mundial de las Letras*. Barcelona: Anagrama (Original edition: 1999).

Figueroa, Antón (2001): *Nación, literatura, identidade. Comunicación literaria e campos sociais en Galicia*. Vigo: Xerais.

Michonneau, Stéphane (2001): *Barcelona: memòria i identitat. Monuments, commemoracions i mites*. Vic: EUMO.

Prat de la Riba, Enric (1998): *Obra completa. 1887–1898. Volum 1*. Barcelona: Proa/IEC.

Molas, Joaquim, Manuel Jorba, Antònia Tayadella eds. (1984): *La Renaixença. Fonts per al seu estudi*. Barcelona : Departament de Literatura Catalana de la UB, Departament de Filologia Hispànica de la UAB.

Ripoll, Enric (1980): *Catalans universals. De la història i l'anècdota a la perspectuva d'Antoni Ribas*. Barcelona: Hmb SA.

Thiesse, Anne-Marie (1999): *La création des identités nationales. Europe XVIIIe-XXe siècle*. París: Éditions du Seuil.

Fig. 1

Fig. 2

Fig. 3

Fig. 4

Fig. 5

Notes on Contributors

ALBRECHT, Andrea (University of Freiburg, Germany): Research Fellow at the German Department. Ph.D. in German Literature from the University of Goettingen (*Kosmopolitismus. Weltbürgerdiskurse in Literatur, Philosophie und Publizistik um 1800*. 2005). She worked at the Academy of Science in Goettingen on literature and science around 1900 and spent two years at UC Berkeley.

ANDRONIKASHVILI, Zaal (Chavchavadze State University, Tbilisi, Georgia): An Associate Professor of German, he is also a Research Fellow at the Center for Literature and Cultural Studies in Berlin. Ph.D. from the University of Goettingen in 2005 (*Generation of Drama-Text. The Narrative, Drama and Discourse Components of Plot Construction*). He worked at Javakhishvili State University of Tbilisi (2005–2006).

BARBEITO, J. Manuel (University of Santiago de Compostela, Spain): Professor of English. He has edited, among others, *Paradise Lost: The Word, the World, the Words* (1991), *Modernism, Modernity, Postmodernity* (2000), and *Feminism, Aesthetics and Subjectivity* (2001). He has published *El individuo y el mundo moderno* (2004) and *Las Brontë y su mundo* (2006), and is currently editing the book *The Order of Ghosts*.

BAUMBACH, Kora (University of Goettingen, Germany): A Rosa Luxemburg Fellow at the German Department. Master Degree in 2003 with a thesis on Uwe Timm and the student movement of 1968, she is currently working on her Ph.D. thesis on imperialism and colonialism in mid to late 20th-century German and Spanish Literature.

BEILEIN, Matthias (University of Goettingen, Germany): Course Coordinator of the Research Training Group "Wertung und Kanon" (Literary Evaluation and Canons). Lecturer of German as a Foreign Language and tutor for German Literature at the Californian Study Center of the University of Goettingen (2000–2006). He finished his Ph.D. thesis on contemporary Austrian Literature in 2006.

EAGLETON, Terry (Manchester University, England): Professor of Cultural Theory and renowned literary theorist and critic. Among his many works are *The Ideology of the Aesthetic* (1990), *The Illusions of Postmodernism* (1996), *The Idea of Culture* (2000), *Sweet Violence: The Idea of the Tragic* (2002) and *Holy Terror* (2005).

EPPS, Brad (Harvard University, USA): Professor of Studies of Women, Gender, and Sexuality and Professor of Romance Languages and Literatures. He has published widely on modern literature, film, art, architecture, and immigration from Spain, Latin America, Catalonia, and France. Among other works, he is the author of *Significant Violence: Oppression and Resistance in the Narratives of Juan Goytisolo* (1996) and co-author of *Spain Beyond Spain* (2005), *Passing Lines* (2005) and *All About Almodóvar* (forthcoming).

FEIJÓO, Jaime (University of Santiago de Compostela, Spain): Lecturer of German. He has published essays on literary theory and on different authors of the German and Austrian literary canon.

FIGUEROA, Antón (University of Santiago de Compostela, Spain): Professor of French. His research focuses on the sociology of French and Galician literature. *Lecturas alleas* (1996), *Communication littéraire et culture en Galice* (1997), *Nación, literatura, identidade* (2001) are among his most recent works.

KORTAZAR, Jon (University of the Basque Country, Spain): Professor of Basque Literature. His recent research focuses on contemporary Basque poetry. He is the author of *Literatura Vasca del siglo XX* (1993), *Baskische Literatur* (2005) and *Bernardo Atxaga: Basque Literature from the End of the Franco Era to the Present* (2006).

SACIDO, Jorge (University of Santiago de Compostela, Spain): Lecturer of English. His main research field is Joseph Conrad and the modernist writers of the British canon, and has also published works on literary theory.

SUBIRANA, Jaume (UOC, *Open University of Catalonia*, Spain): Associate professor of Catalan Literature, and writer. He is an expert in the field of contemporary Catalan literature. *Dotze sentits. Poesia catalana d'avui* (1996), *Literatura catalana contemporània* (1999), *Poesia catalana actual* (2002), *Willkommen in Katalonien. Eine literarische Entdeckungsreise* (2007).

TURK, Horst (University of Goettingen, Germany): Professor em. of German Literature, and Supervisor of the Drama Section and Project Coordinator of two Collaborative Research Centers (SFB): "Literary Translation" and "Internationality of National Literatures". Honorary doctorate from the universities of Tiflis and Szeged. Among many other works, he is the author of *Klassiker der Literaturtheorie* (1979), *Theater und Drama* (1992) and *Philologische Grenzgänge* (2003).

VILAVEDRA, Dolores (University of Santiago de Compostela, Spain): Professor of Galician Literature. She is the author of a large number of translations, editions and books on contemporary Galician literature. The latter include *Historia da literatura galega* (1999), *Sobre literatura galega contemporánea* (2000) and *Diccionario da literatura galega* (1995–2004).